T0295926

PRAISE FOR *ADJACENT LEARNING*

David Hayden and Steve George have produced a stimulating and inspiring read about how we can all learn from and transform our work through the other things we do for fun and the people we interact with. So many of the stories resonated with me, from my own experience of starting to draw and sketchnote for myself, and then finding it taking over my life. Read this at your peril, who knows what you might discover!

Rachel Burnham, Consultant and Director at Burnham L&D Ltd, former Chair of CIPD Manchester and illustrator of *HR for Hybrid Working*

Continuous learning is vital to the improvement of both the individual and businesses. As business environments evolve, learning from other experiences enables individuals and businesses to gain better improvements and results. The premise of this book is to understand and utilize those learning environments between learnt experience, knowledge of one profession and business and how they can be translated into a benefit for other organizations. The authors have been able to capture learnt experiences and how they are used. This book is vital to understanding that journey and those benefits and will be a valuable resource to individuals and organizations who want to have continuous development and improvement.

Ian Pegg, Development Manager, HMRC

David Hayden and Steve George have managed to hit the nail on the head by explaining and landing the concept of adjacent learning. They share insights from their own experiences and the experiences of some of the most amazing people I know in this field about leveraging interconnected communities, multiples sides of our identities and bringing great concepts and frameworks from the world of work into learning. Pick up this book, take a deep breath and get ready to go on a four-act journey to explore the power of transferable and non-traditional learning experiences in the context of development. Expect to be challenged on your current thinking and leverage new contexts in your practice.

Ciprian Arhire, FCIPD, EMBA, Global Head of People Experience and HR Service Transformation at Entain Group, speaker, HR leader and podcast host of *Leading HR into the Future*

This is a highly accessible read that would work well for experienced learning practitioners as well as people managers with a keen interest for improving performance through learning. It has a natural rhythm, almost poetic in places, with some well thought out points for reflection and application. By using the adjacent concept and framing learning to a performance in well-known theatre and cinema productions, the authors are able to lift our expectations and aspirations for learning, plus bring in a whole set of tips, techniques and practical, everyday examples. Using drama and theatre as adjacent disciplines to learn from – in particular the focus on the audience (what we want them to feel, how we want them to react, what we want them to remember) – is a particularly useful anchor. In these ways, this book differs markedly from an academic treatise which can often be conceptual, requiring a fair bit of work to translate into everyday practice. I found the section that focused on you (the reader) and your role in learning to drive your performance and that of your organization particularly valuable, including the focus on personal (as well as professional) development by encouraging curiosity, self-questioning and reflection. Additionally, the point on bringing purpose to learning was revelatory for me. For example, even compliance training can have a higher relatable purpose that gives it meaning and impact to the learner. The variety of valuable points, techniques and examples will enable you to improve the learning experience of your learners as well as their ability to translate that into the world of work.

Tony Osude, Commercial and Marketing Director at CIPD

I read *Adjacent Learning* with a couple of hats on! Firstly, as a manager of a large team across multiple functions, but also as an organizer of learning events on various scales. Finally, from the perspective of my own learning. What becomes abundantly clear is that we either don't recognize, or choose to ignore, the skillsets that we have acquired through life, outside of what would be termed 'work'. The authors' style and process offered the opportunity to explore and reflect on a personal basis, but has also sparked conversations with colleagues about their own experiences of learning outside of work, and how these can be applied in our business.

Ross Banford, Business Director at a media company

Adjacent Learning

Using insights from outside the organization to develop workplace performance

David Hayden and Steve George

First published in Great Britain and the United States in 2023 by Kogan Page Limited

2nd Floor, 45 Gee Street
London
EC1V 3RS
United Kingdom

8 W 38th Street, Suite 902
New York, NY 10018
USA

4737/23 Ansari Road
Daryaganj
New Delhi 110002
India

www.koganpage.com

ISBNs

Hardback 978 1 3986 0825 2
Paperback 978 1 3986 0823 8
Ebook 978 1 3986 0824 5

British Library Cataloguing-in-Publication Data

A CIP record for this book is available from the British Library.

Library of Congress Cataloging-in-Publication Data
Names: Hayden, David, author. | George, Steve (Learning Content Lead at CIPD), author.
Title: Adjacent learning: using insights from outside the organization to develop workplace performance / David Hayden and Steve George.
Description: 1st Edition. | New York, NY: Kogan Page Inc, 2023. | Includes bibliographical references and index.
Identifiers: LCCN 2022054149 (print) | LCCN 2022054150 (ebook) | ISBN 9781398608238 (paperback) | ISBN 9781398608252 (hardback) | ISBN 9781398608245 (ebook)
Subjects: LCSH: Organizational learning. | Employees–Training of. | Interpersonal relations. | Organizational effectiveness.
Classification: LCC HD58.82 .H39 2023 (print) | LCC HD58.82 (ebook) | DDC 658.3/124–dc23/eng/20221114
LC record available at https://lccn.loc.gov/2022054149
LC ebook record available at https://lccn.loc.gov/2022054150

Typeset by Integra Software Services, Pondicherry
Print production managed by Jellyfish
Printed and bound by CPI Group (UK) Ltd, Croydon, CR0 4YY

David

To Daisie: Every day is a learning day. Sometimes it is hard work, sometimes a joy; never miss a chance to step back and see just how far you have come.

Steve

To Sophie: Your curiosity, resilience, humour, empathy and compassion are a constant inspiration to me and so many others. You're awesome!

CONTENTS

LIST OF FIGURES AND TABLES

FIGURES

TABLES

ABOUT THE AUTHORS

David Hayden

At the time of writing the book David is a Learning Content Manager for the Chartered Institute of Personnel and Development (CIPD). He has been an employee there since 2014 and before that worked for CIPD as a volunteer for 13 years. After nearly turning down the opportunity to look after three youth trainees in 1988, within months he found himself on a European exchange visit and before long heading up a corporate learning function. Working in a variety of sectors and roles, including as a recruitment and development manager and as a lean engineer, as well as in a range of learning & development (L&D) roles, he has racked up more than 40 years of work experience.

He wants to start a movement to ban the words 'mandatory', 'I hope you learn something in this session' and 'managers should' from L&D's vocabulary.

David has been a contributor to CIPD podcasts (181/172/139) and the *GoodPractice/Mind Tools* podcasts (210/131/124). He is also the co-author of the 4th edition of *Learning and Development Practice in the Workplace* with Kathy Beevers and Andrew Rea, and writes the CIPD L&D factsheets.

Steve George

Steve is Learning Content Lead at CIPD at the time of writing. He found himself in learning almost by accident after working in IT support to fund backpacking trips, where he realized the best way to reduce call volume and have more time researching his next adventure was to train people how to fix things themselves.

Now with more than 20 years in the learning profession he is on a mission to spread the message that learning throughout a career, done well, changes lives. His path to CIPD has seen him working in learning for big multinationals and a bespoke digital agency, and for a while away from the profession working as a photographer too.

Having studied psychology at university he's continued his way through qualifications in counselling, mental health and more, and is passionate about wellbeing at work and out of it. An amateur historian and contributor of words and images to several travel guidebooks and magazines in his youth, his ambition is to spend a couple of years travelling the length of the Ganges and rekindling that documentary spirit.

LIST OF CONTRIBUTORS

Act 1

Eleni Anastasova
Cris Henriques
Mariano Gutierrez Alarcon
Jo Bteddini
Ian Shawcroft
Niall Gavin

Act 2

Fiona McBride
Jenny Gowans
Babs Burton
Julie Drybrough
Michelle Battista
Michelle Parry-Slater
Steve Burton
Wendy Soh
Linda Ashdown
Guy Gumbrell
Sarah Hayden
Nigel Hayden
Ian Pegg
Chris Baldwin
Claire Hayden
Chris Schiller
Richard Davies
Charlie Wesson
Hannah Pell
Aaron Hearn
Neil Cosgrove
Lior Locher
Krystyna Gadd
Rita Isaac de Matos
Meg Peppin

Act 3

Naomi Stanford
Andy Lancaster
Hilary Karpinski
Steve George
David Hayden
Nathaniel Redcliffe
Jake March Jones
Matt Mahoney
Georgia Gamba Quilliam
Jilly Julien
Sharon Fernandes

Act 4

Will Brimson
Sue Murkin
Mark Hudson
Phil Wilcox
Epilogue
Federico Gaggero

ACKNOWLEDGEMENTS

David

A huge thank you to my family Karen, Nigel, Sarah and Daisie, Claire, my parents and Elaine for their inspiration and seeing learning through their eyes and having the faith in me to deliver.

Steve, you were able to bring my idea to life in a way I never ever imagined, and for that I will be forever in your debt.

To Nigel, Ian and Tracey, who were there right at the start of the journey, quickly followed by Graeme, Kiernan and Emma, you all provided a wonderful source of learning for me and allowed me to go to some amazing places – a huge thank you for being you and being that amazing springboard for me.

A very special MASSIVE shout-out to everyone at the Chartered Institute of Personnel and Development (past and present) who has supported me, starting with Caroline Henbury who was my first manager there and really set the tone. Far too many people to mention (you know who you are, some of you are in the stories!). It is crazy to think just how much you have allowed me to grow and develop in my 50s!

To all the team at Kogan Page, especially Lucy and Zexna, thank you for your support, guidance and patience.

And a huge thank you to every single person who has been with me on this amazing rollercoaster of a ride to get to this point. The highs, the lows, the exhilaration, the stomach-churning moments all helped shape me, this book and what comes next.

Steve

Firstly I need to thank my family. My daughter Sophie and my wife Christine for their support, and my parents, who role-modelled lifelong learning for fun and an unconstrained breadth of interests across the arts, science and humanities.

All at CIPD too who have supported me in many different ways, a lot of whom have become friends as well as colleagues, particularly Andy Lancaster and Warren Howlett, two great bosses I've been privileged to learn from.

I must also thank Andrea Day and Carole Bower: incredible people and learning professionals who set me on my journey. I can't thank them enough for their influence on me personally and professionally, and it was them who first introduced me to exploring professions outside learning to broaden our work.

Lastly, of course I must thank David for the opportunity to be part of his vision in creating this book. It's genuinely an honour to have been invited to help bring it to life and I've learned so much from working on it with him, I'll always be grateful. Don't tell anyone else this David, but you're my favourite northerner.

David and Steve

We would like to thank everyone who contributed a story to us to demonstrate the value of learning from one arena and how that helps them develop and build their impact and enjoyment not just as an employee/worker but out of work too. We had a hunch their stories would help validate and refine our framework, but little did we realize the rich depth in the responses. We are truly honoured and humbled by what people shared with us. This book would not be the book it is without the insights you brought and for that we really appreciate your examples of adjacent learning.

All stories are used with kind permission.

We would also like to call out to the fabulous Federico Gaggero for creating icons and images for us. Fede is a joy to work with and has a wonderful talent for nailing an image from a sometimes vague brief. He can be contacted at federicogaggero.com.

HOW THIS BOOK WORKS

Overture

This is our introduction to the book – it sets out what inspired us to share our learning with you.

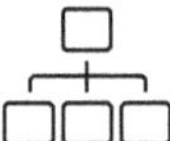

Act 1: The Framework

We give the detail of the framework in Act 1 – we offer insights into each action and the behaviour needed for that.

Pause

The pause sections are there for you to take a break from reading, to absorb the information you have taken on, and to work through how you have reacted and internalized the detail.

Action

The action section offers you a chance to transfer your learning from the book into your context. We give some prompts that are intended to show how you can apply the messages of this book, benefiting you and the people you are interacting with.

Reflect

The reflect sections of the framework are there for you to pause again and think through the detail. This is the first step of reflection. We mention in a number of places a 'what, so what and now what' approach to reflection. We actively encourage you to decide what you are going to act on as a result of your reading.

The ideas you have need action to bring them to life.

Consider this

Occasionally within the book we offer you a chance to take a moment or two to give some consideration to a particular point or issue. The aim is to give you an opportunity to think a little more deeply on an issue or give an angle that may not have been considered before. Sometimes we may be provocative, sometimes we may offer you a challenge and sometimes we share an insight that made us think a little more deeply about learning.

Stories

We have collected a range of insights from within our networks. We asked, 'Tell us something about what you do outside of work, be it a pastime, hobby, interest or event, and what impact that has had on your "day job" to develop and build your impact and enjoyment as a better worker/employee'.

It was deliberately rather vague. Some people wanted more information on top of the context we'd given (we'd mentioned the premise of the book), but we kept the information light. What we got in return was a wonderful mix that absolutely tied into a variety of elements of our framework.

Act 2: The Thinking About

Act 2 is where we actually started writing this book. The first draft of our storyboard had an 'A–Z' approach using the framework to identify and pull together insights which we structured on alphabetical lines for ease. We realized very quickly that this would not work, but we recognized the themes in these had some common threads. The themes fell into how we can develop ourselves, consider our audience and work better with them as well as the processes we follow. We added to this deeper thinking on topics.

We broke down this Act into four sections:

- Act 2.1 Thinking about yourself
- Act 2.2 Thinking about your audience
- Act 2.3 Thinking about the process you follow
- Act 2.4 Taking your thinking deeper

We have added to this Act stories from our network that connect our research and insights and validate further the connections we are making.

Act 3: The Thinking Beyond

In Act 3 we present an approach (similar to how to write a play or novel) to get the most from our framework, bringing it to life for your context. We offer a series of questions that you can use in your journal, blog or with a critical friend. We also go deeper with some of our network and the stories they share as well as giving an example from both of us against the framework. We break these down as follows:

- Act 3.1 Journal responses
- Act 3.2 Critical friend responses
- Act 3.3 Blog responses

to give ideas of what a set of responses could look like.

Act 4: The Adjacent Connections

In this section we pull together the threads of our narrative and share with you some of the giants whose shoulders we are standing upon. We also offer some food for thought on bias and on ethics related to what we have shared.

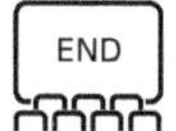

Epilogue

Any good book has a final piece. In *Harry Potter and the Deathly Hallows* JK Rowling provides not only an ending for the fans who have been through all seven books but the start of the stage play, *Harry Potter and the Cursed Child*. Those who bought the book in 2007 when it came out would not be aware of that connection; it is only when you see the play that you make the connections. Our epilogue is our ending for this but also hints at the foundations for what comes next.

FOREWORD

I was delighted when David and Steve approached me to write a foreword. They could not have picked a better time to share such insightful and practical advice on how organizations tap into all of the experiences that individuals carry with them.

The essence of their message resonates so much with my own experience. I was born in Uganda, raised and educated in the US and have been based in the UK for over 20 years. I have had the pleasure to work internationally across a diverse range of industries from construction to luxury retail, with courageous leaders at pivotal moments of change. As I progressed in my career, I found that it was applying a blend of my personal and work experience that added unique value to business challenges.

I have been collaborating with David and Steve for many years to shape and evolve the CIPD Organization Design course. I have been inspired by their enthusiasm for the learner and their passion to explore a variety of creative methods to help organizations drive individual and team performance. I remember working closely with Steve just as the pandemic was taking hold and face-to-face learning had essentially come to a halt. Steve was instrumental in guiding me to take the often complex concepts of a two-day face-to-face course and converting that quickly into a relevant online offering.

After many months of virtual conversations in different time zones, David and I finally met at a filming studio in Hackney. By this time virtual meetings, remote working and virtual learning had been normalized. David was focused on transitioning the learning experience to the next 'new normal'. We were meeting to record a series of self-serve modules. I remember David's guidance to authentically express my knowledge and weave in whatever natural experiences came to mind. It was the most creative and effective process I had come across to convey my own learning.

In organization design we anchor on the fundamental concept of focusing on the whole organization and appreciating the organization as a continuously developing system. Working with David and Steve, I came to appreciate the parallel to learning and development – that is the importance of harnessing the whole person, tapping into the rich experiences in all areas of their life.

The last few years have of course tested resilience and resolve at every level – individual, team and organization. Never before have we had to continuously navigate through multiple, concurrent challenges – health, economic, geopolitical, climate and so on. Individuals, teams and organizations have gone through more than anyone imagined. The workplace has changed and our relationship to work has changed. So then must our approach.

Taking the essence of David and Steve's message, individuals carry an incredibly rich source of learning from outside the business setting that can be applied in the flow of work if only practitioners understood how to do this. In every people discipline from HR to OD to leadership and talent, now is the time to go beyond traditional approaches so organizations are ever ready to solve whatever challenges arise. What an exciting time for practitioners passionate about learning and development to drive this collaboration.

In *Adjacent Learning* you will find a wealth of insight to spark new thought and even inspire new strategies. David and Steve have achieved a captivating balance of new thinking with practical advice. I know you will enjoy and keep coming back to this book as a source of inspiration.

Jaimini Lakhani

Overture

Welcome to our book

At its core this book is about learning.

Learning begins in the womb and is innately human, yet within workplace contexts it can be extracted and abstracted from the day to day: it's an intervention, something outside the business of 'getting the job done', and if we're honest about the way learning and training are seen by many, it's often also a burden. In one recent message we've even seen organizational learning described as a 'sanction' to address employee behaviour via 60 minutes of learning-by-numbers to tick a compliance box.

If, like us, that makes you shudder, then we believe you'll enjoy this book.

So, what is your role? And how are you seen in your organization?

In organizations, learning is often seen as the sole preserve of a formal learning and development function or a dedicated resource. It may or may not be wrapped into HR too. Is your role formal in a learning function like we both have? Or is it elsewhere in an organization but you have taken accountability for how your role encompasses supporting others in their development?

Wherever you 'sit', this book will guide you through learning from other professions, communities and networks to bring those developmental experiences to life in your context, be that at work or elsewhere. If you work in any form of industry that requires interaction with others, but especially in learning and development, we will give you some ideas for ways in which you can interact and how you create and deliver enhanced value through those interactions.

Adjacent communities

Other professions and networks play a big part in the way we both approach learning. You'll be able to find out a bit more about our stories in a moment, but we can both say that we've been intentional about the way we've chosen to bring in a broad spectrum of professions and experiences to our work.

The reasons why are many: a fear of being too narrow, natural love of learning from others, imposter syndrome creating its own momentum for validation and evidence... but at its heart there's a danger for us all that as we develop in our careers, whether as specialists or with a broad remit, our focus can necessarily narrow on what we need to do to get the job done fast. We rightly look to the experts in our field and seek to replicate their example, to learn from their experience and to hear how they would approach the challenges we face ourselves.

That's as it should be. Our caution is to ensure that environment, experience or expedience don't curtail our curiosity to discover for ourselves too. Curiosity and the behaviours that drive it should be seen as essential to our work. An idea attributed to Einstein, that curiosity is more important than knowledge, resonates with us both. For us, the two are inextricably linked, but the precedence of curiosity comes from the behaviours it both represents and supports. Knowledge is, of course, also important: the knowledge gained through curiosity may not be explicit or immediately 'useful' in the sense of having a practical application (though it often will be), but that doesn't mean it is redundant.

As professionals, as *learning* professionals, it is incumbent upon us to maintain our own development, to keep getting better at what we do. Learning is our USP, and whatever your role we believe it's yours too.

Take a moment to let that sink in: learning is our, your, USP.

Learning ourselves and working out how others learn is *what we do*. And we have a choice over what we do with that learning.

We know too that seeking to learn from adjacent communities is not unique to us: Andy Lancaster in his book *Driving Performance Through*

Learning offers a model where he talks about 'adjacent communities', and regular listeners to Owen Ferguson on the *GoodPractice/Mind Tools* podcast series will often hear him discuss the need to work with other professions to see what L&D can learn from them. For us this book represents an insight into the world of the arts, to explore what lessons we can transfer and apply to our own practice, and most importantly we show you the framework we use to do that effectively.

Not just for L&D

It may be bad practice to say what we won't do, especially in an introduction, but we're not going to share *how* to learn: that's outside the scope of this book and there are many books from great people that can do that. We have already said we start to learn from when we are in the womb, so you can also take credit for knowing *how* to learn! Nor will we take you through the learning cycle, how memory works or embracing the latest digital approaches and so on. (Should you wish that to be your starting point we have signposted some of our learning on this in Act 4.)

What we *will* do is show you how to gain wider horizons and depths to what you choose to learn, and we'll take you through our framework for applying this.

This book can be read by someone experienced in the inner workings of the systematic learning cycle as well as anyone who has a passing interest in finding out more about what it means to work with learning. It is also appropriate for anyone who has to deliver or present any sort of message, be it in corporate life or not. For those in L&D and outside it, it is intended to be both a resource and a reference.

The focus is for you to take time for yourself, to look beyond the boundaries of training, facilitating, L&D and HR in general to see what insights can be explored and what the people profession can glean, translate, transfer and ultimately gain from.

At the book's heart we offer a series of ideas and ideals which offer the start of an exciting approach for debate. We are not theatre-trained individuals, but we have extensive experience of working in our own 'theatres' and delivering many 'performances'. We are not musicians, but have an empathy with rhythm. We are not trained in the classics, but have an appreciation of the beauty of language. We are not film critics, but we know what we like and admire as well as what we can take away from a cinematic experience.

We say all this to show you don't have to be an expert in a topic to gain benefit from those who are.

While we work in an arena where there is debate about the depth and quality of academic study and its impact on the practice of L&D, this is not intended to be an academic study. However, along with our experience, it has been informed by wider reading and insights, some of which are shared in this narrative to allow for further exploration. There may well be some theories or models to support some of what we are saying that we have not come across before – and if there are it would be good to hear from you about these. This book, however, is built on the foundations of work with thousands of L&D practitioners over the combined 60-year-plus period of our careers and some of the collective insights from those interactions for which we are forever in their debt.

Please don't think that the examples given in this book (essentially insights from a world that may be perceived as having escapism and make-believe at its heart) are suggesting 'L&D is about fantasy', or worse, about scripts. This book is about things that have made us think about lessons from these disciplines and our adjacent communities. It is NOT an opportunity to follow these things in order to learn lines and deliver 'rote training'. It is about how we can use these aspects to help ourselves in facilitation and with delivering messages with an audience and their workplace.

Application

Our aim is that this book is above all practical and that you will take the learning and use it in your own work. When you reach the framework, you'll see that it isn't prescriptive. You may find that there are some steps you do instinctively, or having gone through the first couple of steps of exploration you find you don't need to do the others, or you start in the middle but we present it end to end, in sequence order, because this is how we have used it ourselves.

By reading this book you will be able to confidently consider what learning you can bring into your practice from other professions and other communities. L&D often cites marketing as the 'go-to' community, but the options are much broader – we use examples predominantly from the arts, theatre, cinema and music in this book, while in our jobs we bring in and apply learning from fields such as archaeology, product design, physiotherapy, athletics, photography, trauma therapy, environmental science, pharmaceutical research… there's a whole world of professions developing thinking in parallel to L&D that we can tap into and bring into our work.

Excited? We are!

Now, in the words of Driscoll (2007) and Rolfe, Freshwater and Jasper (2001) and others who have expanded on the 'what, so what and then now what' reflection model, we share our stories. We believe they set the context for what's coming, and like all good learning professionals we know information without context can quickly become just noise!

How did we get to this point? While we work together, our backstories to presenting this book have very different starting points. While David had the idea for the book, it was Steve who offered the mirror and the wider depth to change it from idea to reality.

David's overture

The idea for this book was conceived in a converted church in the grounds of York St John University. I was there for an open day with my daughter who was looking to study a Drama and English degree in 2010. The speaker asked the audience a question: 'When does your experience with a theatre performance begin?' After a moment of pause and reflection he explored the options available to answer his own question: 'Is it when the curtain opens? Is it when you take your seats? Is it when you step into the theatre? Is it when you choose your outfit to wear? Is it when you buy your tickets? Is it when you think about going? Is it when you see the theatre listings?'

This got me thinking. It got me thinking about (and remember, this was 2010 and I didn't know some of the stuff I know now) training courses. I started to change the questions. When does our relationship with the learning on a training course begin? Is it when the course starts? Is it when you arrive in the room? At the venue? When you get the joining instructions? When you have the need identified? In 2010 the parallels were there for me. It got me thinking about how we greet people in the room, how we send out joining instructions, how we work with managers to identify needs. My head was buzzing. At the time of the presentation I was coming to the end of my own study. I was doing a dissertation in student relationships with continuous professional development for an MSc. This was a series of questions I wished I'd had a few months earlier in the study.

And then a few months later, the idea for this book took hold further. I remember having a particularly difficult day at work. At the time I had a full-time job, but once a week I had the honour and pleasure of working with a group of L&D practitioners studying their CIPD Certificate in Training Practice qualification (again it was 2010, titles have changed). I remember thinking, 'I cannot go into the room stressed out.' I was still playing back a particularly tough session in my head from earlier that day, brooding over what was and wasn't said, what I planned to do the next day. The CIPD group had paid for their course and deserved my full attention. This took me to thinking about 'the zone' that actors discuss and how I needed to get into that zone. Acting – the link back to St Johns. The idea had started to germinate. And then a sudden memory from a past employment... Ann Davis and Shirley Valentine!

Ann was my line manager for about five years in the early 1990s, in fact my first line manager in a training role. She was an inspiration – she was a great coach and she inspired and role-modelled self-development. I had gone to the theatre to see *Shirley Valentine*, I think it starred Paula Wilcox (I have seen a few versions of it since), and remember remarking to Ann, 'It was a one-woman show – and she kept the audience gripped for over two hours… amazing – I wonder how she does it?' Ann took a long look at me and then said, 'What do you think you do in the classroom all day every day?' The whole keeping people's attention element took us on to a great set of conversations.

Then came *A Big Boy Did It and Ran Away* by Christopher Brookmyre. A brilliant novel bought for me as a birthday present. I used to say the phrase captured by Brookmyre in the title to my kids as a default answer to any type of 'who did that, dad?' question they had when I had no idea of the answer. So when the book came out, for my wife it was a no-brainer to buy it for me.

There are a couple of paragraphs in it where Brookmyre's chief protagonist asks a series of 'why' questions about life, the state of life and work, and why we put up with stuff we don't want to do and generally whinge about the cards we are dealt. He called these out as chains that bind us. Brookmyre's protagonist then challenges us to accept that perhaps we actually *like* the comfort of those chains that bind us. On reading this wonderful sentence about 'the chains', I stopped reading, put the book down and did a deep-dive reflection that actually lasted a few days. I was in a job that was not giving me any joy, worth or enrichment. I was being micro-managed despite earning a good salary, I had little trust and I did whinge about it every night when I got home. The sentence in the novel was a very clear, highly polished and high-resolution mirror held up very close for me to look into, and to look into deep and long.

The strands of my idea for this book took a few years to gain momentum and collate. A thought here, a conversation there. A couple of learners on the CIPD Certificate in Learning and Development qualification with an acting background expanding the thought and conversation.

And then three resounding reverberations!

Reverberation number one. Linda Ashdown! Working with Linda in early 2017 and seeing her writing and drama experience. Could I verbalize my thoughts to her and see what happened?

And then reverberation number two. Again in 2017, working with Richard Davies, sharing my idea, then almost immediately he had introduced me to two publishers and that was four people who knew the detail of my idea. Four people who said, 'GO FOR IT.'

The third reverberation, being bombarded relentlessly by Steve George and Mark Wilson in a pub in Kensington one Thursday evening in April 2017 saying, if these people know about it – *do it*!

So I did it, and here it is.

Steve's overture

That there is strength in learning from a variety of perspectives was, for me, one of those lightbulb moments. I was lucky to have a teacher at school who encouraged us to read viewpoints we disagreed with to challenge our own views and to encourage empathy and understanding of others. I've carried this into my professional career too, looking for breadth of understanding of other areas of work for inspiration that I can bring into my own. This is where my interest in David's proposal for this work began, in a pub in London, after a conference where I'd just overheard a group of other attendees complaining at how they perceived the learning and development profession.

> 'There's nothing new, just old ideas repackaged.'
>
> 'I didn't see anything today that we weren't already doing for our customers five years ago.'

There's nothing wrong with old ideas of course; often things that have stood the test of time have done so for good reason, and more than that an old idea will still be new to those who hear it for the first time. But as someone who had spoken at that conference that morning, this forced me into valuable self-reflection – was what they were saying true?

And honestly, a lot of it was.

Reflecting further on my own experiences in learning and thinking of the inspirational moments, I realized several things:

- Many of those who have inspired me have come from – and sometimes are still working in – environments and roles far removed from conventional L&D, and they bring that with them into their work.
- When I look for inspiration for work, the *stories* that resonate with me are often not L&D case studies, they are the stories from elsewhere.
- Learning – and certainly my path through it – has been blessed by pulling in ideas and working with people from many different fields and yet this seems rarely discussed in L&D, particularly around arts. Yet the arts have for millennia been doing what L&D professionals now do: from the methods of learning required by actors to recall scripts through to changing people's behaviour, and influencing, encouraging, inspiring action.

This work isn't to suggest that being a learning professional requires a performative aspect (though sometimes perhaps it does), but that as an adjacent community the arts has much to offer and bring into our practice. Some of what you read will resonate because you do it already, and some of it will resonate with thoughts of how to apply it in your work. Some of it may also seem abstract and unrelated at the moment. However, I'd encourage everyone to keep an open mind for where inspiration can come from and how it may be used.

While this book uses the arts for examples, the principles of course apply much more broadly. I've often attended conferences and free exhibitions that on the face of it have little connection to my role, and I regularly apply transferable skills taken from these, ranging from psychology to archaeology to beekeeping, even though any Venn diagram of the conferences in question and my role might have limited obvious overlap.

I'll end my overture with an anecdote about one of the best learning sessions I've been on as a learner myself. At the company I was working with we had several stakeholder relationships that were challenging to manage for us all. Members of the team went on training courses, we tried role-play learning, but all without real success when it came to facing the difficult conversations that followed in 'real life'. In the end one of the management team decided we'd do 'real-play' instead of 'role-play' and hired a scriptwriter who created a series of generic characters with challenging behaviours. The scriptwriter briefed actors to play those characters, gave them a backstory, some of it known to us and some not, so there was depth, and we had a couple of days in the office with them never breaking character, challenging us, testing us, responding to us just like 'real' people would. Alongside this we were coached in responding, diffusing and finding the 'win-win', with an opportunity to practise with skilled actors who blurred the line between fact and fiction perfectly.

This revolutionized our approach, and developed and gave us strategies, experience and practice at managing situations – and our mental and physical responses to those situations in a safe way – that went far beyond anything any other learning intervention had been able to offer. So this was a learning experience, with the idea generated by a learning professional, but the work, the impact and the depth and value of the experience came from the arts.

Are you sitting comfortably?

So, there you are, our stories. We are projecting the depth of what learning the arts offers, to inspire your development and drive performance in the workplace.

You may have already flicked ahead or read the chapter titles, in which case you'll have seen this book is arranged like a play:

- Act 1 – we introduce our framework.
- Act 2 – we get you thinking about yourself, your audience, your processes and encourage you to think more deeply.

- Act 3 – we explore our framework, sharing examples of looking beyond.
- Act 4 – we discuss adjacent connections.
- And we close with our final thoughts in our Epilogue.

So now let's get into the first Act... take your seat, make yourself comfortable and we'll raise the curtain.

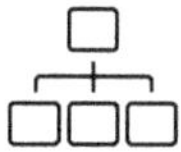

ACT 1

The framework

The framework positioned

The story starts here – or does it? It makes life easier if things have a focused beginning, middle and end. It is ordered, it makes sense, it flows. However, life is seldom so ordered. We have created a framework that is intended as a path to support getting the most out of learning from any adjacent community. However, as with any exploration, we may not have a clear beginning and the entry point can be messy and sometimes even only identifiable in hindsight. In exploring the framework you may well find your starting point is not as defined as we have suggested and may not end neatly at the finish point of the framework either. This is to be expected: it is a guide to support you, not a set of instructions to follow.

FIGURE 1.0 A framework to direct your development

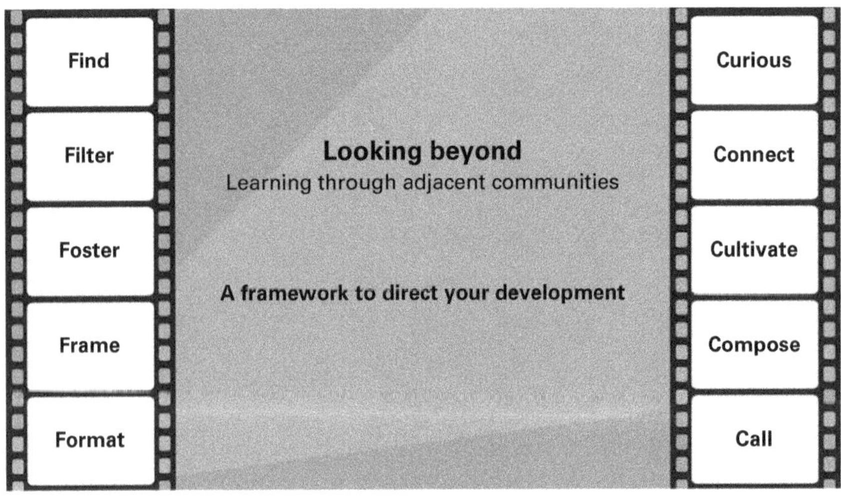

CONSIDER THIS

If you skim this section you may pick up some gems; however, you may also bypass some of the content. This would mean potentially missing the gem of an idea that could have been a pearl instead of a discarded piece of grit. Learning from adjacent communities is the same: what may at first appear irrelevant or not of interest can later be the missing piece of the puzzle.

Regardless of whether we begin knowing our end goal, the storyboard from the opening credits to the final scene in any drama, theatre performance, screenplay or novel is rarely linear or predictable. The important point is that the storyboard shows a journey, with each step building and flowing from the previous one: it is a progression with a direction, however unclear that may be, not an accumulation. We can reflect on the way this is presented in cinema.

Quentin Tarantino, for instance, will disrupt the flow of a story, starting with the end or the outcome and then playing backwards, or changing the flow of the story to show the same event from multiple perspectives – however, the journey is still there, the destination unchanged.

To aid with the flow of the story you build from adjacent communities we provide five stages in our framework, each with an action and a behaviour:

- The first stage of the framework covers: Find as the action and Curious as the behaviour.
- The second stage: Filter and Connect.
- The third stage: Foster and Cultivate.
- The fourth stage: Frame and Compose.
- The fifth and final stage: Format and Call.

At each stage, stories are shared for each action and behaviour. We also signpost moments to pause and consider what has resonated with you so that you can create a plan for making the most of your own adjacent community. In the pause section you will see we have a table that has prompts to help with your reflection and action.

We have also included some mini case studies of people from across our networks and how their learning from other professions and communities, and from their hobbies and interests, fits with the principles of the framework. We used these stories as a way of testing each of our stages.

ELENI ANASTASOVA, CLIENT SUPPORT MANAGER, UAE

Eleni explains how she recognizes the learning she transferred from tennis to work

Tennis is like chess at 150 kilometres an hour. Players must organize a game plan, programme how to begin a match and do the necessary adaptations during the game. In our personal and professional lives, often we have to deal with unforeseen circumstances, people we poorly judged or just a bad day.

I used to play tennis at a professional level in my youth and this has equipped me with qualities that I use in both my personal and professional lives. Some of those qualities are to anticipate future needs and complications, be agile and adapt, never let my emotions get the best of me and quickly snap out of a spiralling down situation.

It is often the case that you don't speak the same language with a colleague or a boss, be it on a project, in an email or just a casual meeting. When I was younger, I was like a box of matches next to a gas tank, always ready for a confrontation just to prove my point. When I was playing and let's say I was 6:3, 4:2 and 40:15 down the second set, I would either give in to my anger and lose or try to put myself together quickly and recover. It is the same with a co-worker or a boss who doesn't speak your language. The more you try to win with power, the more likely you are digging a deeper grave. In tennis you have 27 seconds between serves and 60 seconds every 2 games to recover and put yourself together – just as much time as you will have in an uncomfortable situation or conversation at work. You have to think smart, know your strengths, know who is in front of you and how you can best approach the issue.

1.1

Find and Curious

Our framework begins with Find and Curious. We encourage you to explore this section with what we are calling 'positive naivety'. What do we mean by that? To begin to answer that, let's first look at the actions that sit under Find.

Find

Sower et al (2008) describe Great Ormond Street Hospital exploring what Formula 1 racing teams did when changing wheels on the trackside. At first glance the links between Formula 1 and a children's hospital may not be obvious; however, the team at Great Ormond Street analysed the teamwork in a Formula 1 pitstop and explored how interconnected disciplines worked together, as this was an issue they wanted to resolve in the hospital. They had begun by defining the question they wanted to answer (broadly, how to make different disciplines work together more effectively) and from there sourced examples for insight and inspiration.

This story is encouragement to recognize that sources of learning are not always where, or what, we might recognize or expect them to be. We are encouraging you to widen your thinking about what learning is in a professional capacity and where that learning comes from. To explain further: you will find in Act 2 of this book that we have referred to podcasts, films, books and websites a number of times. At no point have we sat and said, 'Right, I am going to listen/read/watch this and learn something.' Each quote we have provided has been a moment where we have made a connection with our craft, a light-bulb moment where we have joined two or more dots. Those sources are all around us – the key is being open to letting those sources in.

To expand on this further, reflect on the interconnecting communities you are a part of – we are all part of interconnecting communities. Here are David's:

- husband, father, grandfather, uncle, brother, son, son-in-law, nephew;
- L&D professional;
- member of a running club;
- parkrun volunteer and tourist;
- member of neighbourhood WhatsApp group;
- occasional commuter;
- Eurovision fan;
- music collector;
- history enthusiast;
- crime fiction fan;
- podcast listener.

Each 'role' offers an interconnecting community and there are opportunities with each of these connections and touchpoints to access adjacent learning, a chance to be open to learning something from that group or setting.

Reflecting on the list, there is a depth of potential learning opportunities in each, offering different layers to explore, to impact and to transfer to another context. If we are up for learning from those different layers, what behaviours do we need to embrace?

Curious

Let's start off with sharing a Eurovision story from David.

CONSIDER THIS

Given everything we have written in 'Find', what is your immediate reaction to seeing the word 'Eurovision' in the opening sentence? For some it has a negative connotation, for some it is a thing to mock and ridicule. Eurovision will feature in a couple of stories in this book, and we will be sharing learning from this!

The 1976 Monaco entry to the Eurovision Song Contest was called '*Toi, la musique et moi*'.

It came third, and the English version got some airplay on Radio 2 in the UK. However, rather than enjoy the track, every time it came on David questioned the words he heard. His schoolboy understanding of French knew the title meant '*You, the music and me*' but the English version of the track playing on Radio 2 was called '*Thank you for rushing into my life*'. It really grated that rather than a direct translation, the lyricists for the English version took the opportunity to tell a different story. David was dismissive, not curious; he had no tolerance for the alternative English lyrics. He didn't want to explore why it was different.

To embrace the actions in Find, we need to think about our tolerance levels. To what degree are we open for discussing and exploring, to having our preconceptions challenged and to accepting that sometimes we are wrong? This is how we benefit from the insights of others outside of our 'known zone', and that positive naivety supports inquisitiveness. Do we have a range of exploratory questions that we actively use to build our insights? Do we start with 'tell me' or 'what do you mean when you say...?'? Or do we close down the opportunity for insights when we first hear something different? Are we open enough not to let previous negative experiences distract from new ones? Just because we tried something once and it didn't work, have we dismissed it? The key here for Curiosity is identifying that experiences need questions and that questions need responses, even if that response is 'I don't know and I want to find out more'.

Which then leads us to becoming more observant, taking stock and looking around, so rather than seeking out something specific we absorb what we see around us and pay attention to the detail without judgement. At first this may be challenging because it requires intention and effort and may be questioning your assumptions; however, we urge you to embrace this uncertainty with the recognition of the benefits that come from seeing things in different, sometimes surprising, ways.

So our call to you is to be intentionally curious and 'positively naive' without judgement or assumption about what you may find or where you may find it.

II

PAUSE

Take a few moments to engage with the detail of *Find* and *Curious* in Table 1.1 and explore the ways you are utilizing these skills and behaviours already, for example being confident in embracing uncertainty.

TABLE 1.1 Find and Curious: considerations for your story

Find	Curious
Define your development question/s that needs answers	Tolerance: discuss and explore the benefit from the expertise and insights of others with a willingness to be challenges
Establish where your adjacent communities are placed for your sources of learning	Inquisitiveness: build a range of exploratory questions (eg tell me, what do you mean. how do you...)
Describe the communities you are a part of or connected to	Openness: not allowing previous negative experiences to distract from new ones

(*continued*)

TABLE 1.1 (Continued)

Find	Curious
Observe and curate from these where practicable	Identifying: that experiences need questions and responses
Assess your motivations for being in different groups, the connections and touchpoints	Observing: seeing as well as seeking
Identify if you have areas of resistance to transfer learning	Attentiveness: paying full attention and exploring the detail you experience
Explore the depth and layers your adjacent community offers	Be secure: confidently embrace uncertainty in recognition of the benefits of surprise
	Intentionality: Make space to for intentional curiosity

CONSIDER THIS

How easy will it be for you to prevent previous experiences distracting you from new ones? (These experiences could have been either positive or negative – you may also wish to reflect on what made the perception positive or negative.) To what extent are you confident you can articulate your motivation and the benefits from learning from an adjacent community?

ACTION

Establish what elements are important for you and your context and devise your plan of action, ensuring you think about how you can apply it.

Now, take your outputs from *Find* and *Curious* and move on to the next stage.

CRIS HENRIQUES, INSTRUCTIONAL DESIGNER, UK

Cris describes how photography has helped her practise being observant and apply this in her role

I am an amateur photographer. I like photography because it's a solitary activity, it requires patience, you often must wait for the right moment, try to find the right angle, see things from different perspectives... and, occasionally, take the risk to ignore all this and be spontaneous to capture a unique moment. It requires observation.

I think photography is a hobby that fits well with my personality. I am an introvert; I will usually be the one just sitting quietly during a meeting, soaking in the information that's being presented. I will be observing more than interacting, waiting for the right moment to contribute. Just like when planning to take a picture, I will use my observant nature to read the room, people's reactions and the energy in the group.

In my work as a learning designer the aptitude of seeing things from different perspectives is key to be able to create meaningful learning for a diverse audience. It requires patience to understand the content and what is needed, find the right angle and approach to create the best learning experience, take risks to innovate and create appealing interactions.

When I go around taking pictures, whether on a trip to Italy or a simple trip to the supermarket, I am observing the world around me, spotting the subtleness in all things. Photography is the result of combining various techniques and discoveries, relating to seeing an image and capturing the image. I try to bring the patience, the curiosity and spontaneity of photography to my work, observing, exploring and capturing different points of view from colleagues and specialists to 'expose' the best solution.

1.2

Filter and Connect

In *Filter* and *Connect* we explore how we distil and bind together the insight and experience of adjacent communities. We'll begin by looking at the actions that sit under Filter.

Filter

One story told of how the Egyptologist Howard Carter found the tomb of Tutankhamun is full of circumstances that could be dismissed as luck or coincidence: it was the last dig to be funded on the site, he had explored the area previously, the location of the steps to the tomb was only found when a boy delivering water to the team tripped over a stone that led to those steps.

However, really it is a story of filtering: Carter applied a systematic approach to exploring areas that had not yet been excavated or raided by tomb robbers in the past, the area they were digging that led to the boy falling over the stone had been excavated, including by Carter himself previously, but he wasn't satisfied it had been fully dug out.

He was far from random in his approach, instead collating and filtering information to choose only what was most relevant to him achieving his aims. It's likely he would have found the tomb anyway, it just happened quicker because he created the circumstances for this to happen.

Distilling – reducing, filtering – information is how we decide what to make use of and what to discard. Some argue that we live in an attention economy, where the time spent on information is currency: how will we choose to spend our time? We need to be aware too that in the process of filtering we are applying our biases as well as defining what is relevant to our work. For example, whether he actually said it or not, Steve Jobs is sometimes quoted as saying, 'If you need a task done quickly, find the laziest person to do it because they'll find all the shortcuts.' He was unquestionably a genius in technological innovation, but what are we choosing to filter out if this was his approach to work, and especially to people, while we celebrate what we can learn from his legacy? Not to mention that without understanding all the evidence we may be conflating success with behaviours that may not have been as responsible as they are assumed to have been.

Furthermore, there appears to be no evidence that Jobs actually said this. It's also attributed to Bill Gates and Walter Chrysler (again apparently without evidence). What does it say about our bias that we are so willing to believe certain people said certain things?

CONSIDER THIS

Once we have filtered information, we need to bind it together and find the narrative and the connections. Disparate information without shared context is just noise. Shared and expressed context is where meaning is found. If we think of the journey of Vincent Vega, John Travolta's character in *Pulp Fiction*, it's one of only loosely connected vignettes that slowly form together as the linkages and deeper connections are made. This is how our filtering of information works too: finding the common thread through what may at first appear unrelated moments and pieces of information and amplifying their value several times over in doing so.

Take a moment to think about where you filter information and inputs in your life to decide what's important. Is this a conscious process you follow, and when you're doing things for fun is it different from how you approach it for work? Ask yourself too if a more intentional approach would be beneficial, and what the behaviours are to support effective filtering.

Connect

To do this we must identify where connections exist and look for synergy.

Patterns are key. We already mentioned Great Ormond Street Hospital and their learning from Formula 1 teams. They looked beyond the obvious to find patterns of behaviour for role modelling – what are the patterns in your work that are found in other professions? Don't assume that patterns are always obvious, they can often be found in what at first seems disconnected.

We have seen this in learning: listening to a podcast on product design and often finding what is said can be enlightening but not necessarily obviously transferable. However, sometimes something will come back, a pattern will emerge, and a bridge can be built between the world of product designers and the world of learning and development. There may be no obvious parallels between the evolution of toothbrush handle design, its impact on bathroom manufacturing and the importance of evidence-based practice in learning, but it's very much there and provides an engaging and factual way of illustrating an important point and the impact of inefficient practices. (Rather than have us spoil it, see if you can find the story and make the links yourself!)

The ways in which connections can be made to help make a point seem more relevant, engaging and meaningful are many and don't have to be entirely serious – for example, David D'Souza, Membership Director of CIPD, has used in a conference that *Jurassic Park* is a film primarily about HR and HR failure. This enables an exploration of the roles and responsibilities of HR in a way that audiences will find both funny and memorable. The art is in finding the connection.

Stand-up comedians have described crafting jokes through this process of connections too. Take scenario A and filter it to the core features, then take apparently totally unrelated scenario B and do the same. The areas of commonality are where the joke is to be made.

TABLE 1.2A Joke scenarios

Scenario A Bouncy castles (core features)	Scenario B The economy (core features)
Plastic	Money
Parties	Finance
Inflatable	Banks
Children	Loans
No shoes	Deficit
Outdoors	***Inflation***
Fun	Interest

Joke: Why have bouncy castles got so expensive lately? I don't know, but it's probably something to do with inflation.

It's not a great joke but the idea is clear – the more we practise making connections, the better we get at instinctively seeing the links between the information we have. (And with practice, the better jokes we tell too!)

PAUSE

Take a few moments to engage with the detail of *Filter* and *Connect* in the table. Think about the ways in which you are already utilizing these skills and behaviours in aspects of your life.

TABLE 1.2B Filter and Connect: considerations for your story

Filter	Connect
Pan for gold and separate the nuggets	Recognizing: identify and reorganize connections
Find patterns in your context and in the adjacent community	Linking: build the bridge between your context and the adjacent community
Reduce to the core valuable elements – and explore how anything discarded might be used	Challenging: stress test what you save and use and what you dispose of
Change the way you look at something: look from a number of different perspectives, including the perspective of the adjacent community looking through the eyes of multiple stakeholders - not just assuming it is a universal experience!	Reframing: change the focus of what you are experiencing
Check facts – not choosing convenient or interesting over true, not forcing square pegs into round holes (but do trim square pegs to fit)	Navigating: choose a path and confidently embrace discomfort, don't be afraid of breaking the norm

ACTION

Work out what elements are important for you and your context and devise your plan of action, ensuring you think how you can apply it.

Now, take your outputs from *Filter* and *Connect* and move on to the next stage.

IAN SHAWCROFT, ENGINEER/PROJECT MANAGER, UK

Ian explains how his experience of bar work taught him the importance of listening and of adapting his communication

I had a few years in my 20s where I travelled all over the world and worked in a variety of jobs including working in bars. Without doubt the experience taught me a lot that set me up for success in later life, and that I am using today. Specifically it taught me about communication. Invariably in the places I worked there would be people worse off for drink! I needed to get information out of them at the bar and had to find a way without the other person taking offence – when alcohol is involved, things could (and sometimes did) take a turn for the worse. Tailoring my communication to the situation, looking at the full picture in front of me, thinking one or two steps ahead all helped, but so too did listening hard.

1.3

Foster and Cultivate

At the heart of *Foster* and *Cultivate* is the call to nurture and develop your thinking around the learning opportunities gained from exploring your adjacent community.

Foster

Have you ever watched a keen gardener? Regardless of the time of year there is lots to be done, be it getting the vegetable beds ready, sowing seeds, weeding, pruning, thinning, propagating and harvesting and then repeating the cycle. There is respect for the soil and a need to ensure it is a rich, fertile ground to maximize the yield, an act of putting back in order to harvest and repeat the rhythm.

As with gardening, so too with the arts. Listening to authors and actors talk about their approach to a particular role, scene or plot you will hear them reaching out to others and respecting the context they are operating in. Be it a film set in a hospital or a crime novel, both will have in the credits the support from the experts who help them focus, get in character and explore the context. Read an established author's credits and there is a rhythm there, acknowledgement of the people who helped get the book to market.

Anyone responsible for inducting anyone new into a role or organization (whether at work or volunteering) needs to consider how the rhythm of the role is explained and portrayed. There is a need to be explicit on whose job it is to introduce the new person to those rhythms to help them start with the best possible set-up. What does this mean for anyone wanting to learn from an adjacent community?

There is an opportunity to develop mutually engaged relationships with any adjacent community to benefit you in a number of ways. In the running group David is part of, there is a broad mix of people from different backgrounds and professions. The common ground is formed through running together. In nurturing the connections, insights from conversations can be enhanced and the commonality between what can appear to be different contexts can provide deep insights. One conversation about 10k split times turned into giving top tips for working overseas; a chance remark about being out of work while discussing upcoming races led to a CV-building session.

We are encouraging you to mine deeper in your adjacent communities to explore and map connections between multiple insights.

We are fans of viewing the world through 'holiday eyes'. When we go on holiday our senses are heightened – for instance, we notice the differences in light, differences in aromas. Novelty is striking, it links back to our flight-or-fight approach to how our ancient brain functions – however, we can make this work for us. Often you notice what appears to be something new on a return from holiday – a 'newly' painted gate on your street, for instance, that had in fact been painted some weeks before the holiday. You only notice the change as a result of the break. When we are fostering relationships with and within adjacent communities, we have the opportunity to do this through those holiday eyes.

When we view the world with heightened senses in this way, we can then disassemble and reassemble component parts of our personal interpretation of it, as in David's example with other runners, and explore deeper connections. These connections come from multiple perspectives which we can then reframe in our own context.

Talking about learning theory and leadership development with a physio recommended by the running club was one such opportunity. He does the physiotherapy in his spare time; his full-time job is as a director of customer services. The connection David has with him is now on three levels: running club, physio and linking professionalisms. If the relationship was viewed and developed through only one level (e.g. running) then a number of rich conversations would have been missed, but the running became a catalyst for deeper insight. The physio's questions on leadership development led to deeper thinking and reflecting.

In order to fully maximize this Fostering stage, we need to think about how we embrace Cultivate as a behaviour.

Cultivate

Being able to run any distance, whether at a local parkrun and jogging or if looking for a personal best time in a marathon, takes commitment, planning and focus. Making connections with diet, training, hydration and distance is important, and depending on what the goal is, there will be different demands. Building connections takes time, just like with gardening. We don't plant seeds and expect an instant harvest. As with those seeds, so with learning from communities – there is a need to fertilize relationships and any knowledge gained. How do we do this? Well, first with a sense of curiosity, as discussed earlier in Act 1. There needs to also be a sense of shared discovery, exploring what can be shared and learned. The 'fertilizer' has to have benefits for all parties.

There is a strong chance that within a community the relationships can be elevated to allow two or more disparate worlds – one of which will be your own, the other from the community – to come together for mutual benefit. In other words, you are growing with others and maybe even consciously (or subconsciously) seeking to grow others alongside you.

CONSIDER THIS

Very few things we will foster and cultivate in our life are simple or binary options or have guaranteed outcomes. Often there are phases of excitement and phases of needing the resilience to push through difficult times. There may be moments of looking outside for support or advice, and sometimes too having to acknowledge our efforts weren't applied in the most effective way and restarting with renewed insight.

PAUSE

Take a few moments to engage with the detail of *Foster* and *Cultivate* in the table. Reflect on the ways in which you already utilize these skills and behaviours in aspects of your life, for example.

TABLE 1.3 Foster and Cultivate: considerations for your story

Foster	Cultivate
Develop mutually engaged relationships with your adjacent communities Nurture the conversations you have to enhance and add context to insights	Fertilizing relationships and knowledge with curiosity and shared discovery Elevating relationships and bringing together two or more disparate worlds, including your own
Mine deeper, explore further and map connections between multiple insights	Growing with others as well as seeking to grow others.
Remember to maintain confident curiosity in what you do, keep looking at the world through 'holiday eyes'	Influence and incubate rather than indoctrinate
Disassemble and reassemble the component parts and explore connections from multiple perspectives to reframe in your context	

ACTION

Work out what elements are important for you and your context and devise your plan of action, ensuring you consider how you can apply it.

Now, take your outputs from *Foster* and *Cultivate* and move on to the next stage.

MARIANO GUTIERREZ ALARCON, ELEARNING SPECIALIST, FRANCE

Mariano explains how fostering the behaviours learned in a drama class improved his photography

In the 90s I was working as a freelance photojournalist shooting portraits of actors and actresses. During the shoots, I remember the awkward feeling of not being in control of the photoshoot and afterwards the results in print were equally underwhelming. My job as photographer demanded me to be in control of the photoshoot, but I did not know how to properly communicate with the actors.

It was then that I had the idea of taking drama lessons. My idea stemmed from the fact that in the photographer–actor relationship there was something that wasn't flowing, it was as if we did not 'speak' the same language. I realized then that in order to better understand and communicate with my subjects I needed to get in their shoes and become familiarized with their discipline, their language, so to speak.

It took me a lot of effort and will to do the two-year drama course, mostly because I never enjoyed doing theatre (and still don't). However, going through those two years of countless improvisations, understanding the role of conflict in theatre, the relationship between the conscious and the subconscious, the importance of being organic in order to achieve spontaneity, or to react to the real cues instead of preconceived ones, to name a few of the things I learned, these insights slowly migrated from the stage to the studio, and it totally changed my approach and my behaviour about making pictures. I ended up being able to proficiently manage the photoshoot and communicate with actors with a language we both were familiar with.

I remember one day at work a very famous (and equally timid) actress in the studio, she hated photoshoots, and I loved them. The conflict was set, the studio became a stage, we talked, we improvised and magically the trust needed to achieve a good picture was there and then... click click click click! Overall, my portraits gained in quality and depth, and the trust and rapport I was able to get with my subjects were totally transformed, to a point even I couldn't have imagined when I took my first steps in drama class.

1.4

Frame and Compose

Consolidate and prepare to share

We're now getting ready for our own 'opening night', so let's have a look at the way we *Frame* and *Compose* our learning and why this is important.

Frame

Nothing we are shown in art or drama is an accident. Everything is a conscious choice as to how it is framed and composed to be presented, with decisions made across myriad different elements to bring together what we may see for only a few seconds. Each of those elements exists in interplay with others. For example, a photographer needs to control the light seen by the camera. They can do this using the variables of the intensity of the light, the shutter speed and the aperture, and it is the way all are set together which ultimately dictates the end result.

Similarly, an artist choosing to paint a picture will have already chosen what they want to be present and how it will be arranged, both to be aesthetically pleasing and often to tell a story too. A theatre director choosing how to decorate a stage for a play will carefully decide what props will be visible at any time – nothing is surplus, everything is part of the story, whether it is actively used or not. At one end this is the 'Easter egg', the hidden thing you notice when you watch a film for the 20th time – nothing is just decoration. At the other end of the scale it's Sam Riley's declaration as Ian Curtis in the film *Control*, angrily stating, 'There's no such thing as background music' because everything that's created has been created for a reason and is deserving of attention. Framing and composition have been thought through in everything we see, whether we notice it or not.

Begin by deciding your picture and your context. In cinematography and theatre, the French phrase *mise-en-scène* is used, which broadly means 'setting the stage', and in the context of film is creating the most meaningful image you can in every frame that's shot. This attention to detail works for us in exploring what we take from an adjacent community too. In what we take and then share, what is it that we want our audience to go away with? What is it that we want them to feel, think, do as a consequence of what we are going to share with them? Most importantly, *why* do you want them to think, feel, do that in your context? What is it you are taking from another community to use in your work that is served by this? Think of a film or a TV show you have seen recently and isolate a single scene: how did it make you feel? What in it made you feel that way? How was the cinematography congruent with creating that feeling? Could it have been interpreted in any different way?

Interpretation is not manipulating something into your world and work: if it fits, it fits. Think of framing a photograph of a shop window decorated for Christmas. You can take a photograph of the window. You can move two steps to the right and take a picture showing that the doorway of that shop has someone homeless sleeping in it. Two different pictures of the same scene, framed slightly differently to tell a different story. This is not manipulating something, this is framing to choose what you wish to say. However, if you'd asked your friend to *pretend* to be homeless in the doorway so you could force your intent into something, that would be manipulation.

That moving two steps to the right is also where we shape and position as part of our framing, and it is equally well served by zooming in and zooming out. An optical effect of zooming in is to compress the scene (another stylistic choice made by photographers and cinematographers). This is also important in framing and how we choose to bring together the supporting elements in what we have learned from another community. It's important we zoom out and see all the elements of what we are learning in their own context, understanding the foundation they have come from and the environment in which they are typically used. Zooming in allows us to see the detail, explore the depth and identify the challenges and similarities from applying it in our own context.

Having framed the learning that we are building from outside our community we must prepare to share it, composing the work. We begin by planning what our story is. The 'why' behind using this and what led us to this point. This gives not just context but credibility too. Then we plan how the story will be told, setting our tone and pitch to ensure they are congruent, resonant and meaningful. The palette we use is also important to consider at this stage. Every film, every work of art, will have a palette (if you don't believe us, you can find a film's palette easily on the internet). These are the colours that are dominant in a film and set the tone. Colours have three main qualities – the hue (the colour itself), the saturation (the intensity of it), the brightness (how dark or light it is). Our use of information benefits from those three main qualities too – in film, colour is used to portray emotion and feeling. Depending on shade, red is passion or horror, pink in a film is typically representing a playful or overtly feminine scene, yellow is sickness or warmth, blue is cold or mysterious. What is the colour of our work, how intense is it, how light is it?

We must also decide the scale of how we will introduce the thinking of the adjacent community in our work. That is, whether it is the dominant aspect or if it is a small point to reinforce something larger.

To activate the most from Framing our learning, we need to embrace the behaviours in *Compose*.

Compose

The rhythm, colour and flow must also be mapped when framing our learning. What do we mean by this? The rhythm is the pace at which we present information: none of us can run at our fastest nonstop, and similarly none of us can process information or emotions at relentless intensity without some kind of break to avoid becoming overwhelmed. The way we present our work should follow these natural peaks and troughs and should be intentional in how we move people through states of attention, allowing time for reflection and, if necessary, recovery. If you watch the best presentations, you can identify the rhythm. A short presentation can be more intense and single-paced than a longer one; a longer one might start fast, slow down, pick up pace in the middle, slow down, then close with a pace dictated by the desired end result: slow for reflection, faster for call to action.

Watch or listen to some recorded presentations and see if you can map the pace and identify what makes it effective.

What's your rhythm?

CONSIDER THIS

Those of us of an age to remember the excitement of buying an album on vinyl, tape or CD will remember how the order of songs had a rhythm: the flow of the album would be a journey. The opener was almost always the catchiest song, the third song a slower song. The last song was sometimes the longest or a different tone from what had gone before. The first, second (often thought the best song on many albums) and third were often released as singles too, followed by two songs towards the end of the album. Think about the reasons for this approach – why did it work? What was the decision process behind it? Does it translate to your context?

The colour is the richness of our work. Is it full of metaphors, not to be flowery but because they add context, meaning and aid understanding, or is it plain and direct? What is the impression we are creating with the colour we bring?

And flow is the narrative, and how we flow between the different elements of our work. Is it abrupt, is it smooth, is it surprising or is it signposted so we know what is coming? There is no right or wrong, just a need to consider what is most appropriate for our audience and our intent.

So we must ask ourselves, how will the rhythm, colour and flow affect how what we share is perceived? You can see all these elements come together in many films. Watch, if you can, the trailer for the mountaineering film *Touching the Void*. Small elements are shown in close-up (zooming in), the music begins ominously, the palette is mostly white and black (to emphasize the cold), with colour rarely shown, mountains are shown (zooming out to wider context for the information), then drums and frantic camera work change the rhythm... framing and composition are chosen to disorient the viewer and create tension, emphasized by mixing footage from other parts of the film that seems to disrupt the narrative of the rest of the trailer. How does it make you feel? Why?

Having composed, we then have our call to action: how can we use this information, how can it be applied for maximum impact with the audience? This comes next.

II

PAUSE

Take a few moments to engage with the detail of *Frame* and *Compose* in the table. Reflect on the ways in which you are already utilizing these skills and behaviours in aspects of your life, for example.

TABLE 1.4 Frame and Compose: considerations for your story

Frame	Compose
Build your picture and context, for the why of you and your context	Creating: a story making sense from pitch and articulating
Identify the difference between your interpretation and the reality of the adjacent community	Deciding: the scale are you reinforcing, making a new point or explaining differently
Shape and position	Defining your 'makeup call' your call to action
Zoom in and zoom out	Emphasizing: your pallet and rhythm

ACTION

Work out what elements are important for you and your context and devise your plan of action, ensuring you explore how you can apply it.

Now, take your outputs from *Frame* and *Compose* and move on to the next stage.

JO BTEDDINI, LEARNING CONSULTANT, UAE

Jo describes how she has recognized the way in which indoor cycling benefits her creative thinking

As a learning designer I take a human-centred approach towards my work by keeping the beneficiary in the centre of my design thinking process. Therefore, I am always searching for what works best to maximize their learning experience and to help solve their problems. I do at times strive to visualize the learner's problems and generate creative ideas; however, I have discovered that indoor cycling has influenced my creativity and design thinking skills. Strangely, when attending virtual cycling classes, not only do I find myself immersed in the digitally created journeys and watching the scenic views go by, but I do somehow find the time and space to collect my thoughts and think 'outside the box' when using such a platform.

I think engaging in any sports activity promotes mental strength, enhances the cognitive function (https://www.healthline.com/health-news/playing-sports-makes-brain-more-healthy) and moreover helps designers to find inspiration outside one's self-context.

1.5

Format and Call

The essence of *Format* and *Call* in the framework is about making the learning from your adjacent community work for you. It is the opportunity to project your learning into your context. It is your curtain call and needs sharing, loudly!

Format

There is an ancient Papua New Guinea saying that can be translated as 'knowledge is only rumour until we feel it in our bones'. It has a rich depth and it works in the framework. We may know stuff, but do we always act on it? We may experience stuff, but do we always make the most of the opportunity it brings? No one thing we learn in one context can be fully 'lifted and shifted' into another context; however, we can work out what bits we adapt to take forward that make the best sense for us.

The stories we are sharing in this book are the learning moments we have got from our adjacent worlds; they have helped us develop our craft, they have been unique to us and our context. This is key in going back to our overall goal, the overall question we are aiming to answer for ourselves – how can we be learning role models in a way that adds value to our peers, customers, colleagues, friends and family?

There is deep learning from the film *Apollo 13*. One scene has a number of contexts: leadership, process change, organization design and even creative thinking. It is the scene where the carbon dioxide vents need attention. Gene Kranz, the NASA commander, urges his team to 'find a way to fit a square peg in a round hole, very quickly' to fix the problem. The team rises to the challenge, one character saying, 'We have to fit this, into this, using just this' as he points to the pile on the table, replicating the same materials the astronauts have on the spaceship. Another team member says, 'We are gonna need coffee!'

It is a story that works for those audiences exploring those contexts above and in asking them, 'Why have I shared this story?', they can see the relevance. However, it won't fit in other situations. For instance, in a 'how to write a business case proposal' piece of learning that example would not fit (although as David types his brain is challenging itself to make connections with the component elements of a business case and the items on the NASA table!). The key is, there has to be alignment: alignment to the context, alignment to the audience, alignment to the overall message being portrayed and ultimately the overall learning question being explored.

CONSIDER THIS

To what degree do you explain your formatting or allow your audience to work out the connections themselves (facilitated by you)? The actor's role is to portray their character in an engaging, believable way. How they introduce their characters may be explicitly worded or through subtle actions. Film critic Mark Kermode is a huge fan of 'show me, don't tell me', preferring the scene, rather than long narratives, to share the story.

In bringing Format to life, we explore the behaviours needed in Call.

Call

Think about any curtain call – a few moments before the curtain lifts, the getting ready on the set, the anticipation from both the audience as the theatre auditorium slowly descends into darkness and the actors wondering what sort of response they will get from the audience. Each performance is different, the actors vibing off the audience, the audience responding and making connections with what they are seeing on the set.

That getting ready part is 'the zone' for both the audience and the actors. The rituals of getting ready are similar for the audience in cinema. The routine of the adverts, the trailers, the mobile phone warning, the screen size altering, the classification rating. The actors of course are not able to see every audience, they don't get the same instant feedback.

How are your rituals informed by your learning? Or are they dictated to by traditions, introduced long ago? What are the calls for action you are giving your own audience? Just as importantly, what are the calls for action you are asking of yourself?

In the film *12 Angry Men* Henry Fonda's character holds up a mirror to each of the other 11 jurors, challenging them on how they have come to their decision. He unveils gaps in their knowledge and questions what they have observed in the trial. He highlights their pitfalls. This links to our word of caution: while we are advocating the learning from an adjacent community, harvesting the rich pickings, there is a need to recognize we cannot claim a universal truth if we have not uncovered all the details. We have strived to ensure the examples we share with you are focused on the things that have made us think and apply something in our context. We do not profess to be experts on the narrative of that film, nor do we have a detailed insight into the director's or scriptwriter's motivation for their work. We have seen something that has switched on that lightbulb for us. How important though is switching on that lightbulb?

There is a saying, 'if it ain't broke – don't fix it', meaning if something is working then why change it? There is also a counter-saying, 'if it ain't broke – break it', meaning systems and processes need to be stress tested and 'old ways of working' need to be challenged as the world around us changes. Those lightbulb moments where we get the learning from our adjacent communities may just be the ones that help us move, not only to new ways of thinking but to new ways of working.

We also need to remember that the opportunities from learning from adjacent communities are cyclical – things that we discover today, we may discard tomorrow because they no longer lead us to our goal. The trick is to keep pace with your learning, pause, review and take action regularly.

And share, loudly and widely! Share to allow others to see into your own intersectionality. Allow others to also find out more and help you dig deeper into the new learning. We encourage you to shout out and share your stories of learning from adjacent communities.

With this book we are sharing with the world examples we have used to make us more effective. Not just in our roles as employees, but also as humans interacting with others. One other word of caution: we are aware that many of the examples we have shared are not 'real-world' examples. Films by nature are largely works of fiction. The imaginations of the screenwriters, editors, producers and directors along with actors and audiences are all at play. There are scenes, for instance, in *84 Charing Cross Road* and *Mary Poppins Returns* where the route through the streets of London is not a route you could replicate in the sequence shown: one moment in St James's, the next St Paul's and the next Westminster, the next Tower Bridge is farcical on one level. We can learn from this too: the constraints of the reality as it is now shouldn't hold us back from creating a new reality for others.

Remember you are focusing on your learning, answering your learning questions and applying that in your context.

PAUSE

Take a few moments to engage with the detail of *Format* and *Call* in the table and how you can engage in the framework as a whole to maximize the learning from your adjacent community.

TABLE 1.5 Format and Call: considerations for your story

Format	Call
Bring the learning into your own context – format messages for your purpose	Harmonizing: remember this is not to appear clever. It must add value, be congruous and effective
Target messages and learning for different outputs, audiences and impacts	Introducing: is it implicit or explicitly referenced… is it something you do, or something you refer to?
Ensure alignment to your initial question	Scouting: be aware of pitfalls – what are the gaps in your knowledge that could expose you – ie don't claim a universal truth with a specific example because you are referencing something outside your area of specialism
[who/what/why and where of…] – what do we mean?	Shouting: assemble/compose/call out – roar – shout it!
Consider audience needs, engagement, expectations and profile	
Apply the learning to your messages and delivery	

ACTION

That is our five scenes. Before we move to the next Act, we encourage you to work on your own *Format* and *Call* actions and anchor your reflections to action by planning in your next steps.

The next part of the book will look at specific examples from the world of the arts to think about:

- yourself;
- your audience;
- the process you follow;
- and then taking that thinking deeper.

NIALL GAVIN, LEARNING MANAGER, UK

Niall shares his leadership takeaways from his dancing lessons

A colleague recently did a talk at work about relationships and what he called 'co-created spaces'. To illustrate his thinking he gave some examples, including this about navigating crowds in the street, which he described as 'the dance on the street'.

As someone who has been flirting with learning to dance for over 15 years and having worked in learning and development for far longer, I immediately connected those two concepts. And I've been thinking...

If we accept that learning takes place mostly in spaces that we co-create – be it face to face or virtually – and is essentially about action and response, then learning to dance surely invites us to consider the whole learner experience through a different lens.

My wife and I have been learning to dance socially for more than 15 years, with the inevitable breaks for things like house moves, illness, work changes, etc. But we're back into it again, with a new dance school, new steps and moves and more opportunities to put our learning into practice.

Why are we learning to dance? For fun, to have something we can do together that is outside of home, work, family, etc., to keep fit, to socialize. We have a desire to learn and we are motivated.

I'd suggest that the best way to learn how to dance is to do it. It has to be experienced, felt. Essentially, you, your partner, your teacher (and other learner couples, if you are in a group learning situation) are collaborating socially, taking (literally) small steps, in bite-sized stages, repeating/

practising (developing muscle memory) in a co-created – and safe – environment.

My colleague spoke of entering into these spaces with unconditional positive regard and set boundaries.

Again, in the context of learning to dance, those 'ground rules' play directly into the 'rules' of dancing. The leader has to learn to lead, and lead confidently. The partner has to learn to trust the leader to do just that (you can't both lead at the same time). A mutual, achievable goal will allow for mistakes and repeated attempts until the lesson's been learned and you can move on to other elements, such as technique and hold.

Indeed, in terms of leadership training, you couldn't do better than learning to dance. A good leader knows how to work with tension and resistance, both essential elements of managing people in the workplace and in navigating someone else through a routine and around the dance floor.

And there's always another new dance to learn. Don't take my word for it: get your dancing shoes on and get out there.

ACT 2

The thinking about

Setting the scene

In this Act we will look at specific examples from the world of the arts that have had an impact on us and where the framework has supported or enhanced our insights. We have structured them in the following areas:

- thinking about yourself;
- thinking about your audience;
- thinking about the process you follow;
- and then taking that thinking deeper.

None of these elements exists in isolation, of course. Everything we do – and everything we perceive – is a co-created experience between us and the others we are interacting with.

We can think of all these different areas as relationships:

- First, with ourselves, and how that is utilized both consciously and unconsciously to shape our view of the world and the view others have of us. In organization development there is a concept called 'self as an instrument'. It recognizes that as a practitioner we have significant influence in the direction of travel of a project and impact on its outcomes due to a range of things like own biases, values, knowledge, skills, attitudes and relationships.

- Second, with our audience and how this is a two-way interaction. This is not necessarily verbal but includes all the non-verbal signals we must be alive to and responsive towards. In this context we are using the term 'audience' to mean those people we interact with in the learning space, for example a delegate, student, employee, peer, coachee, mentee or a child in our family.
- Third, with the processes we follow. These need not be easy – often the best moments are generated from discomfort – but our processes must be congruent with us in a meaningful sense in order to feel natural. If they are forced, we will focus on the process, not the insight that comes from it.
- Fourth, with everything we do in our work. As will become apparent as you read through the book, the delivery 'event' itself is just one point on a continuum, not the main climactic moment it can be tempting to perceive it to be. Taking the framework into all aspects of our practice, not just how we deliver, supports us in having impact.

In the first Act we offer some questions within the framework that will help you identify what you can take from one arena and apply in another context. This second Act builds on that.

To highlight how we can develop ourselves to be better learning practitioners we have woven together a number of stories, insights from things we have seen, read and heard, and linked them to these relationships of ourselves, our audience and our processes. The themes chosen for the insights, *creativity*, *ending, being centred*, etc., are all things we have heard discussed in the world of L&D and which we believe can benefit from further exploration through the lens of the arts. Hence each example has a link back to our learning from this adjacent community of the arts (with a few slight detours along the way).

Why the arts?

David's overture described the scene at York St John University where the relationship between theatre performances and training was made. Those connecting threads got stronger when listening to actor interviews, and some of these connecting insights are mentioned in this Act.

The arts are a wide spectrum with many rich learning opportunities. Film, theatre, books, radio and museums are all covered in this Act. However, each of these fields has a variety of categories, each of which has its own area of deeper exploration. Take books, for example: novels, biographies, classical, fiction, crime, horror, erotica, business, self-help. The list is reminiscent of Polonius reeling off types of plays in Act II of *Hamlet*: 'tragedy, comedy, historical, pastoral, pastoral-comedy...' We barely scratch the surface here, but in doing so we encourage you to go as broad and as deep as you wish.

As with the arts, so with learning and the world of work. All our contexts of practice are different, as are the experiences and thoughts we bring with us alongside those overlaps, intersectionality and common understandings we carry too.

Reflection

In Act 1 we asked you to pause and reflect. Reflection is frequently talked about in ensuring that any learning is effective, that opportunity is taken to be in the moment, and to make sense of what you have heard, seen or felt. Our individual experiences of learning will be different from someone else's, even if two people have heard or read the same thing. It is because – and this will not come as any surprise – we are all different.

FIONA MCBRIDE, LEARNING PROFESSIONAL AND YOGA TEACHER, UK

Fiona shares her love of learning and what she has learned as a yoga teacher

I love learning and how it is a constant practice. It doesn't just happen in my professional life, but in all aspects of my life.

One of those aspects is yoga. During my yoga teacher training, I started to realize how the skills required for teaching yoga are similar to the skills required when helping others to learn.

A big part of yoga is tuning into the present moment to connect more deeply to yourself: your body, mind and breathing. It enables you to become reflective.

In our fast-paced working world, it is a rare thing to slow down and reflect.

Thing is... we need to slow down. We need time to think, process and be creative. So you'll not be surprised to hear, sometimes my next idea or 'that problem' I've been thinking through resolves itself when I'm on my yoga mat.

Over the past few years I've brought this into my work, for myself and others. I make time for slowing down, having a reflective practice a few times a week. When working with others I might add in five minutes for reflection in meetings/sessions I'm facilitating. It also has helped me to ask more questions, to support others to be reflective and notice what's going on for them in their work.

This Rumi (13th-century Persian poet, Islamic scholar) quote describes the experience delightfully: 'In silence there is eloquence. Stop weaving and see how the pattern improves.'

I love how I find learning in spaces away from the work. It can be wonderfully surprising.

We have different views, different influences and different life experiences. Just ask anyone whether *Die Hard* is a Christmas film or not and see what response you get. Some will think not while others will make the case.

CONSIDER THIS

Many movies are interpreted as Christmas films and can cause endless debate: *The Terminator* is another. What does this tell us about the human ability to interpret and find implicit messaging in different stories, different environments? What is the information that is being picked up in these stories, filtered, connected, with new meaning found and presented?

So how do we get from *The Terminator* and *Die Hard* to effective reflection?

Learning is more than having a 'nice' experience. In fact, we may sometimes learn just as much, if not more, from an experience that isn't 'nice'.

Where learning is at its most effective is when we can transfer it into our context and it has an impact on what we do, think, feel or say. Often the way we effectively transfer learning to our context is a consequence of how we have reflected on our experience. Reflection therefore is an important mechanism in the way we make connections.

Here are some tools that can help you develop your reflection further.

JOURNALING – PERSONAL TO YOU

The process of journaling is personal. There is no right or wrong; the important thing is just to do it. At its most basic it is free-flow writing whatever comes into your head. Some people like to do it on a screen. We like to write with a pen, and we have a pen, ink and a notebook just for journaling. If writing as the thoughts occur and develop doesn't appeal, then you can ask yourself prompting questions each day: what happened today? How did it make me feel? Why did it make me feel that? What will I do next with this, if anything?

The important thing is to go through a structured process of reflection. The way you do it, how messy it might be, even how coherent it might be, matters far less than the process itself and the journey it takes you on.

BLOGGING – SHARING WITH THE WORLD

Where journaling is often private, blogging is the opportunity to present your thinking to a wider audience. The best blogs are successful because they are structured, condensed and created with thought, like magazine articles. They can also be used to crowd-source information and thinking and feedback. This can amplify their effectiveness as a reflective tool: we can type our thoughts into a blog, we can publish, and we ask those who read it for their thinking and in doing so we can gain the wisdom of crowds.

A blog doesn't have to be profound or detailed, it's perfectly fine for it to be just you thinking out loud and working things out. The difference between blogging and journaling is mostly that others may read your thoughts and may comment on a blog, making it potentially a more conversational, collaborative means of reflection. For this reason it also requires a vulnerability and a preparedness to receive challenging feedback, whether fair or not.

CRITICAL FRIEND – HOLDING UP THE MIRROR

The most effective way of ensuring reflection happens is arguably through two things:

1 Creating time and space to undertake it.

2 Asking or being asked great questions.

The person in the role of your critical friend can be a peer, a manager, a mentor, a coach, within your circle or your profession or outside of it. The important element in any work with a critical friend is the trust you both have in that relationship.

It can be easy when we are busy to think that taking the time and space to undertake reflection is ineffective time, wasted time, unproductive time. This is a long way from the truth, however.

JENNY GOWANS, COMPANY DIRECTOR, UK

Jenny gives an insight into the importance of planning, regardless of triathlons or the world of work

I have completed triathlons on a national and international competitive stage. To get to that point it is more than having the right equipment, training, support and mental attitude. You have to plan and be prepared, looking at each detail including knowing the course details in depth, and your competition including their times, splits and strengths so you know who you are up against. Making the time to plan is so important. Don't underestimate the time needed to do something in any situation, it pays off.

We have already mentioned in the overture how we are fans of the 'what, so what, now what' approach to reflection. These are great questions to ask. Also 'tell me more…' and 'explain that in a bit more detail' or 'describe how that works for me' are brilliant probing questions that a critical friend can use.

BABS BURTON, RECRUITMENT COORDINATOR, UK

Babs shares how research helps both work and running

I never thought I would run a marathon but here I am writing about it. I started with running 5k many years ago and I dreamed of doing a half marathon, but the distance seemed too far away. However, I built up to it and completed my first half marathon in 2015. I did a few more afterwards; however, the thought of the marathon kept niggling at me, but it seemed such a huge leap and I didn't know where to start.

So with research, following a training plan, dedication to go out on the days I didn't feel like it, managing my time really well and a bit of belief, I

> ran the York marathon in 2019. It was hard but I loved it – I achieved something I had never thought possible.
>
> The marathon training gave me the tools, in my working life, to help me take on difficult challenges which I may have felt overwhelmed by before. I would ask myself questions such as, what do I need to achieve, when by, what do I need to do to get there, what is my plan...?

The success of this book for you depends on your viewpoint. We are asking you to explore *your* definition of each element we discuss and how it applies to you, not just how we or those we cite have applied it. Recently, when facilitating a masters programme, David described experiences of previous students. One or two commented that they had little or no time to study and yet the same students could cite plot lines from soap operas. One fellow learner challenged David, saying not to assume that there was no learning in soap operas. And indeed, there can be depth in the character development and social settings. While there was no issue there, that was not the learning point being offered. The story shared was not the story the learner was hearing. Have your story in mind as much as ours as you read further.

Reflection and the arts

Æsop's Fables tells a story with a moral; however, Æsop may or may not have written the fables, and he may or may not have been Greek or African. Regardless of the veracity of the legends that have built up around Æsop's identity, the moral of the stories that sit under the name is always for the reader to take away and do something with, and often the power in that moral is amplified by taking time to reflect.

It is perhaps telling that we often know the story and the moral but may not always follow the good advice. *The Hare and the Tortoise* may suggest that 'the race is not always to the swift', but do we always take the advice? Centuries later Covey tells us in his *7 Habits of Highly Effective People* to 'sharpen the saw', but do we follow that advice either?

Our intention for this Act is to share our stories from the rich pickings of the arts. We are light on advice but heavy on invitation to make connections. We share some of our personal learning about learning and ask you to reflect on what that might mean to you.

JULIE DRYBROUGH, ORGANIZATIONAL COACH, UK

Julie shares how reflective and reflexive writing gives her new perspectives

When David calls me to ask if I'll write something about how non-workplace activities inform my work practice, I'm like a kid in a sweetshop. I reel stuff off: learning dressmaking means I have to be precise, work slowly and remember maths. Sewing is a case study in YouTube theory-into-practice and proof of how just-in-time resources are brilliant for problem solving. How about paddleboarding? That's about practising balance and a calm mind – if my head races ahead or digs into old stuff on my board, I'm wobbling and off my feet in no time.

But it's writing I come back to, always. In 2012 much of my MSc journey was reflective practice – writing my truth, articulating my experience, sense-making the world through language and reading myself back in different contexts. It was through this that I experimented with a seven-year love affair with blogging – what happens when you share your thoughts beyond the privacy of your own head stuff? Turns out you share yourself in ways that open you to new people, new clients and new perspectives.

So now, this practice – reflective, reflexive writing, freeing people on the page to share their thoughts in the moment, then returning later to 'read' themselves and experience their world view differently – is a core tenet of how I work. Over the years, I've incorporated free-writing and wild-mind techniques, brought more story and metaphor to my writing practice and become very interested in the joy that writing can generate in the body... psycho/somatic practices that are so vital for wellbeing.

In 2021, I started Write Nights to get others involved in just writing for the hell of it, and in doing so learned the power of collective writing experiences.

And I never stop learning. My writing evolves as I do.

It's a life-long love.

2.1

Thinking about yourself

Setting the scene

If you are involved in developing people, be it as an L&D practitioner, HR officer, people manager, trainer, facilitator or (and perhaps especially) parent, you will find *how to do learning* is the staple of many L&D books. They will tell you about the technical aspects of working in L&D, about design, delivery, evaluation, analysis and the like. They will talk about communities, about performance, about coaching and mentoring as well as about digital and online ways of working in L&D.

What we have noticed in these books is that sometimes the 'how to grow as a learning practitioner' section is restricted to the technical knowledge of learning only. While many practitioners call for learning to look beyond this, there are limited examples of what this actually looks like.

This Act therefore takes the opportunity to explore you and your role in learning to drive your performance and that of your organization.

Thinking about yourself and acting

The overture gives an insight into how our inspiration came from exploring adjacent communities, along with what we can learn from film, stage, song and so on. It therefore makes sense that acting is the first thing we explore.

So, a question: in the world of facilitating learning and development, working with learners to gain new knowledge, build their skills base or think about their behaviours, is the facilitator an actor?

Are we acting as learning professionals? Jason Isaacs (2019) stated that 'acting is make-believe'. Does this definition mean what we are suggesting here is that L&D is somehow disingenuous?

No, what we want to do here is explore what is meant by *acting* especially within a learning context.

When talking about the film *Hotel Mumbai* in that same interview, Isaacs stresses, 'The job of an actor is to be in the situation, in the moment, and the job in a film like this is... to get your own ego out of the way, not to do any "tricksy" stuff – not do any stuff in the movie that you wouldn't see in real life.'

Isaacs was then questioned about the atmosphere on set, day in day out. He replied by stating he didn't want to compare the film set with anything like the real hostage situation of the real events of the hotel, but the crew and cast kept themselves in 'a state of trauma'. In other words, replicating the reality of the world of the characters they were portraying as much as possible. Relating to their world.

Director Anthony Maras kept the atmosphere as real as possible for the protagonists, replicating the conditions and sounds of the original 'heist'. Isaacs describes lack of banter between actors, no music playing at mealtimes and keeping themselves in an 'adrenalized state'. To support this Maras had speakers around the set, and the wider environment the actors lived and worked in 'would suddenly erupt with noises of screams, bombs or sounds of bullets'.

Isaacs adds that 'acting is imagination, tricking your imagination' and compares *Hotel Mumbai* with the film *Good* from 2008, in which he was also featured, where the backdrop was Nazi Germany in the 1930s. He comments, 'I owed it to the characters I was playing and the people who died in the holocaust.' This is where the power of the role of an actor to communicate an experience is so strong.

If we switch the role of the facilitator with that of the actor (or even director) then we need to ask how real the stage set we use must be. Have we made it as real as possible for the learners attending the event, be it online or face to face? While not every organization faces threats such as those in *Good* or *Hotel Mumbai* every day (although we recognize some do), the role of the facilitator is to make the learning event as real as possible for the learners. There has to be that insight, that dedication, that direction. Even with the darkest of material, Isaacs shares his belief that *Hotel Mumbai* is a film about 'hope and is made to be optimistic'. He goes on to add, 'It is no good just recreating trauma because who would want to go and see that?'

There is a brilliant quote from Trenfor that we have seen at a number of 'train the trainer' events. The quote goes along the lines of 'the best teachers are those who show you where to look but don't tell you what to see'. And this is what Isaacs and Maras are doing. It is a truly inspirational quote, encouraging you to think deeply about the role of a facilitator. However, it was only recently that we explored the source of this quote and asked who Trenfor is. What motivated him or her to say this? What was his or her story? The search was somewhat fruitless – there is a huge debate online about who he or she is or isn't. A number of online searches have been documented as not actually finding Trenfor. Is this inspirational quote another example of acting, someone providing a version of reality to share with a wider audience?

This could be dismissed as a self-indulgent rabbit hole, but it matters for a number of reasons. It demonstrates how reality can be constructed, potentially the power of fictional characters, how a story can spread, and perhaps too how willing we are to accept something if it is attributed to someone who sounds authoritative, and the risks of doing so.

And the concept of acting takes us to another place. That the learner in the session can have a bad day, turn up late, have a headache, request to leave early, take that phone call, reply to that email because they are so busy. Are these traits that the audience or the organization will allow to be displayed in the facilitator? Imagine the facilitator opening a session by saying, 'Sorry, late night last night, overslept this morning, had an argument with the other half and need to finish early today to design a webinar for another group.' Some of these things happen in facilitators' lives, but they have to be masked, managed, not acted upon in the moment with the audience but hidden from public view, in other words the facilitator as an actor existing in a role for an audience and creating an alternative reality for them in that moment.

Thinking about yourself and being centred

All of us have our 'lightbulb moments' where something completely obvious suddenly occurs to us and we wonder how it was hidden for so long. One of Steve's was attending a meeting at an environmental charity where everyone pulled out their laptops and notepads as normal and then the chair called for a minute of 'attuning'. With that everyone went quiet and we had a minute of silence, space to clear our heads from whatever we had been doing before and a moment to become fully present in the meeting which was about to begin. It was almost a moment of communal mindfulness before mindfulness became a more common term.

We hear many stories of the workplace where we are rushing from meeting to meeting, frantically typing out emails as we are in online meetings, and if we're lucky rushing to the bathroom before going into the next meeting, and then the cycle begins again. During the Covid-19 lockdown there was briefly talk that being online so much might provide opportunity for changed behaviours, but for some it seemed to make them worse, as if not having to rush geographically between meeting rooms created an expectation of immediate attendance on time. As one meme of the moment cruelly suggested, without the excuse of a train delaying arrival at a meeting the only reason for being late was now rudeness.

Another feature of how meetings are conducted online is the absence of so much small talk: when the majority of work interactions are scheduled, we lose some of the value in human connection and the insight and inspiration. In the physical world, that may come from conversations while queueing for coffee with a colleague from another department, or casually presenting a situation you're wrestling with outside the sometimes constraining practice of organized problem solving.

This behaviour of rushing and denying space for thinking and the absence of talking both formally and informally is not only highly inefficient, it also does a disservice to those who are relying on our knowledge and expertise.

So how do we break this cycle and stop our minds racing? How do we get our minds on track? And how do we bring our minds back into line when something goes wrong, or there's an unexpected intervention or interruption, for example during our delivery?

The idea of attuning everyone in the room, as happened in that charity meeting, is something that can work for ourselves as well as for others. In some respects it might be seen to play the same role as other aspects of delivery or work, for example where everyone in a learning space is brought into the room and explicitly connected to a common purpose or goal at the outset. Before even this, however, we can benefit from bringing *ourselves* into the room, centring our minds and ensuring we have the focus we need.

There are many techniques for this: visualization, mindfulness, focusing on our breathing, slowing down our thoughts, fixing our minds on the task at hand... and all have their time and moment for use depending on our personal preference.

Sports people and actors are great examples of those who require full concentration and attention for success. The role of attention in sport and its role in success has been studied extensively (Boutcher, 2008), and it's the same for actors, who must live in the roles they play while they are playing them and concentrate to not miss cues, whether those cues are written into the script or are others that occur and are congruent to their character to respond to. There is much we can learn from this. We may never need to completely transform our way of thinking and behaving in the way an actor does when they embody a character, but the ability to switch to 100 per cent focus in creating a mesmerizing different world, to believe something with such conviction we carry everyone who observes along with us, to be such that no one questions our commitment or identity... that is a level of confidence all of us could aspire to develop even while acknowledging that for many of us to just achieve a small percentage of this is enough to transform our work.

It could be said that if we believe in what we do enough then that conviction and commitment will come across, but that would be to deny the imposter syndrome that can hit many of us. We'd suggest instead that by learning from the way in which performers focus we can perhaps silence that negative voice that sits on our shoulders and keeps telling us there are others who are better or more knowledgeable than us.

One method actors use is to choose what to become aware of in the room and this becomes the anchor around which everything else exists in reference to. Combining this with the act of centring so the two things – the object and the centring – are associated with each other can amplify its effect (Klein, 2012). This is a remedy for stage fright too, where actors may choose an object to direct their attention to and be aware of (Hinckley, 2008). This also helps with avoiding distractions from others in the room, which may be important while acting in, say, Shakespeare's *Julius Caesar* where the disconnects between the 21st century and the 1st century BC might challenge an actor's concentration (for example, a mobile phone ringing in the middle of the '*et tu Brutus*' scene!).

Clearly this is not true for all of our work, however, because awareness of others is something that makes our work better rather than diminishing it. Others are a part of our world to be embraced, not ignored. So what might we choose to become aware of that supports our work and helps us attune and centre ourselves? Before delivering a session in a venue it might be something as simple as the layout of the room, or the location of items such as the pens, anything that brings us into the space, becomes an intentional process, and focuses us on the moment and stops our mind racing.

Similarly, before an online delivery, where arguably the stimulus is reduced as we stare into a camera and potentially do not see any other faces for the duration of our delivery, we might choose to bring our attention to an external stimulus.

Before learning sessions where Steve knows he will need to concentrate online for an extended period, he has a stress-squeezer next to his screen. He's never used it for stress, but has consciously developed the association between squeezing that a handful of times and focusing on the online meeting or delivery.

Alternatively, as a succession of meetings blur into one, it can be something different, such as standing and walking around the room between meetings and just asking about the outcomes we are looking for: that's a form of centring too, connecting to the moment and focusing to maximize the value we all bring.

So we'd argue that centring, or focusing before learning delivery, is something that we can build into our practice relatively easily. What happens if we need to do it *during* delivery though? If we lose our thread or forget where we are going?

In Shakespeare's time his actors might perform two or three different plays a day, which is incredible if we take a moment to think of how hard it is to learn the lines for one character, let alone for several. This is a practice that has been revived by The Globe Theatre in London in recent years, where the audience votes on one of several plays to be performed. Inevitably actors forget their lines. In an audience Q&A, Al Pacino recounted one such situation to Ruben Nepales (2018), recalling using lines from the wrong play while performing *Hamlet*. Realizing what he'd done, he deployed a trick from Shakespeare's time, which was to not panic but instead recite a few lines of his own, to keep talking to bring himself back into the moment rather than let his brain scramble for the correct lines and exacerbate the fear.

Many in the audience will not notice, and few if any of those who do notice will mind. Techniques actors use for bringing themselves back from the infectious laughter that can be inappropriate or prohibitive for a scene can be useful for us in our work too. Instead of 'going back into character' or trying to continue despite the loss of focus, they may re-centre and bring themselves back by concentrating on what is called the 'essential action' (Westbrook, 2018). This is because they have so broken the role and the focus on what comes next that their logical brain will reject anything that requires 'belief' in what they are doing, whereas an essential action – an act congruent with the character's motivation and also with themselves as an individual – is something that is 'them' and smooths the transition back into the role and focus.

Therefore, for us in our practice, returning to the *purpose* of what we're doing and concentrating on that and our actions in driving towards that purpose, as opposed to whatever situation has broken our concentration and trying to remedy that, may also be of benefit.

Depending on where we are, our audience may be less demanding than most actors experience, however, and if that is the case, there is nothing wrong in admitting that you have lost your way. This can be done in a professional manner that doesn't undermine you among those in the room. In other words, getting centred authentically and congruently!

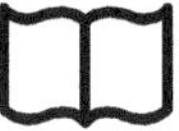

MICHELLE BATTISTA, CONTENT CURATOR, UK

Michelle shares what she has learned connecting to a community discussing the impact of the menopause to be able to manage it and the rest of life

I'm constantly sobbing, my moods are up and down, I'm anxious, I can't think straight and I'm so exhausted! What's happening to me? This is affecting my ability to function. I'm 44, people are telling me I'm too young for menopause. In fact, I went to see my GP aged 38 when things started wobbling. She said, 'You're far too young.' I ended up opting for anti-depressants. This, I now know from my community, is a common misdiagnosis for women experiencing menopausal symptoms.

Someone recommended the Balance app and this was a game-changer. You log symptoms, mood, food and sleep and the personalized data creates a report to share with your GP to start the conversation about menopause and treatment. It also includes articles, resources and a supportive community sharing their symptoms, experiences and solutions. This community has been key to recognizing, understanding, getting the right support and ongoing guidance. As well as medication and lifestyle changes, this community knowledge has encouraged me to make small adaptations to improve work life:

- Balancing work tasks to flex around symptoms: on days where I have fatigue, I shift tasks around so my energy is balanced, and take frequent short breaks.

- Memory and recall: I was struggling to recall information and focus. I started a weekly task list and I cross actions off as I complete them and capture notes from meetings that week so I can recall detail and actions.
- Raising awareness through content: I work on people management content and managers are crucial to supporting employees going through menopause, or they may be experiencing symptoms themselves, so I bring my knowledge and experience to raise awareness through learning.

While it's still not perfect, these small changes have impacted my productivity and sense of achievement, which is imperative to me and my wellbeing in the workplace.

Thinking about yourself and creativity

Here is a question for you: to what extent do you think you are creative and get your audience to engage in learning activities in a creative fashion? Where are you and your audience on the continuum 'I am creative–I am not creative'?

If you believe yourself to be creative, have you come across people saying, 'I am not creative'? How do you deal with the response? If you think you are not creative, then what makes you feel that?

There is a saying in L&D, 'steal with pride', generally meaning if you see a fellow L&Der doing some good work, then think about what you can take away and apply in your own context (although sometimes the 'your context' is not used and the results are hit and miss!).

We put ourselves towards the creative end of the spectrum, and love to build on other people's ideas and thoughts and see where they can be taken, and which elements can be amplified in addition to coming up with our own innovations.

One example of thinking about what can be taken from another world can loosely be called a 'JK Rowling approach to recaps and revisits'. By observing how many different ways Rowling summarizes at the end of each Harry Potter book and the recap at the start of the next, we were inspired to think about the different ways we could do recaps and revisits of learning sessions. Sometimes the summary was in Dumbledor's office, sometimes the hospital, sometimes on the train back to King's Cross. And the opening recap would be in the house in Privet Drive, in the garden, on the train to Hogwarts and once in the Muggle prime minister's office.

Doing things differently gives people an opportunity to undertake their own reflection and wonder what they can do as an alternative approach, though not everyone admittedly, but if we weave in activities and exercises that are relevant to the topic but not necessarily what the audience is expecting, this can spark their own creative insights.

Within our practice, we can sometimes become stale or mechanical and this will manifest itself to our audience. It is reported that the eminent Russian theatre performer Konstantin Stanislavski realized he had become mechanical in his performances. In order to change this, he included improvisation to encourage actors to create something new in each performance.

Stanislavski focused on what was at the centre of any tension within a performance. He talked about 'the rhythm of feelings'. The role of any facilitator is to realize the impact of their own feelings on the rest of the group. The mood they create can help focus on the real issues (when positive) or redirect focus on to the facilitator rather than the topic (when the mood from the facilitator is negative). One of these will enhance creativity, one will stifle it.

In design, we need to embrace the whole ensemble of those involved, not just the audience but their line managers and peer networks. How do we begin if we are at the 'I am not creative' end of the continuum? There are a number of things we can start to do to change this.

The first is to recognize our feelings when we do something different. A good test for this is to write your name and address on a piece of paper with your dominant writing hand and then replicate the activity writing with your non-dominant hand. Go on, have a go!

Did you notice the difference in the time it takes? Is the result neater or not? Forming the shapes of the letters and numbers, did you do a 5 and an 's' the right way or wrong way round? How was writing an 'e'? If it felt awkward, why? Another activity to encourage some creative thinking is to clean your teeth with the opposite hand. This can bring the same kind of response – it may feel awkward, using the brush may feel strange and the angles you reach may not be the same as with the other hand.

When you make these changes, you are noticing the difference, your instincts are more alert, and you are heighted to your routine and how it has changed. This is something you can work with in design and facilitation too. Asking people to do something different, instead of 'circle of death' introductions in face-to-face events where everyone sits in a circle and has their moment to talk, have a graffiti wall where people have to draw themselves.

Instead of the 'Can you hear me?' start to webinars we are all familiar with, ask 'What colour shoes and/or socks have you got on?' Instead of 'Can you see my slides?', ask 'Now why would I open this session with a picture of...?' Both spark something in your audience and make them alert that 'this is different'. Your challenge then is how you build on this.

The world of the arts is full of opportunity for creativity, and other adjacent communities can give equal if not more opportunity to embrace creativity.

Ultimately, creativity is about exploring and using what you have available and doing something different. Things we have done include use of outside spaces (in a variety of weathers), searches (a kind of treasure hunt), using a variety of objects to build process maps (like Monopoly houses, chocolate money, Lego and toy cars) and once using Shakespeare's *The Tempest* to frame a conversation on leadership after observing director Richard Olivier do it on a much larger scale. The audience was much smaller plus an extremely sceptical colleague, but one comment from a delegate was enough to realize it was the right thing to do – they recognized their world in Shakespeare and said, 'This is what we do in organizations!' Their reality had been replicated via Olivier and Shakespeare and a raging storm!

MICHELLE PARRY-SLATER, L&D DIRECTOR, UK

Michelle shares the value of Street Wisdom and shares her learning from it

Street Wisdom is a 'wanderful' walk – usually outside, but equally as useful in your garden or home. We so often walk only with purpose that to walk 'wanderfully', as founder David Pearl terms it, brings a new perspective to the thinking time that a walk offers.

On several occasions, I have enjoyed Street Wisdom as a participant, taking walks around new and familiar places in a new way. The process opens your mind to the possibilities and makes you realize the answers are everywhere, if you bother to look. The Street Wisdom facilitator's guidance questions get you really thinking in a stepped and preparatory way, which leads you to be fully in the present with your presenting problem, and of course to find answers for that problem from the streets you are in. The value of getting inspiration from around you is fulfilling.

I was so awed by my experiences of Street Wisdom that I now offer it as a practice in my work, dutifully offering the not-for-profit founder a donation each time my clients benefit from learning a technique which truly opens the world to answering their problems. As a facilitator for Street Wisdom I've really learned the joy of helping people focus on being present in the moment and to focus on the value of getting inspiration from what is around them. It has enabled a work perspective with a really different angle, encouraging people to be creative in a way that they perhaps never thought about.

The joy of facilitating Street Wisdom is the lightbulb moments that you witness in people taking physical exercise, being present in the moment and gaining more from their environs than they ever have before, even within their own home. It is an honour and quite inspirational.

www.streetwisdom.org

Thinking about yourself and failure

Actor Jon Hamm says, 'Don't be afraid to fail… it's the first step towards learning something and getting better at it.' Football manager Jose Mourinho has said something similar, paraphrasing Nelson Mandela with 'you never lose – you win or you learn' (Kilpatrick, 2019).

This mindset, that failure is an opportunity, is increasingly common in organizations that prize authenticity, honesty and forward-thinking approaches to development. At its most extreme is the 'church of fail', regular events where people shine a spotlight on the things that haven't worked, what they've learned from them and what they'll do differently next time. That almost celebration of failure is not appropriate for all perhaps, and for some it's simply a matter of accepting failure happens and creating an environment where honest reflection is taken as a collective learning opportunity and not an opportunity for blame. We all benefit from what goes wrong if the exploration of what happened is approached constructively, and creating a space for people to be open about failure benefits us far more than a pretence that failure never happens.

Failure comes in many forms and it's important that we keep perspective and don't misrepresent it. There's objective failure, for example: I did X to achieve Y but got Z. Then there's relative failure: I did X, wanted to achieve Y, and I did, but it could have been better.

Perhaps the biggest curse of the learning practitioner is the non-specific failure. That is, the room where only 60 per cent give feedback and 50 per cent of those that do think it was the best session they've ever been in; however, 10 per cent of attendees think it – or worse, you – wasn't value for money, or didn't meet their expectations. How do we rationalize this in a way that acknowledges how it makes us feel, the truth in the comments we've received and what we can learn from them, but also recognizes the successes? How do we consider all the contributory factors outside our control or ability to influence that led to each of those feedback scores?

Using those numbers above for a learning session of 10 people, do we worry that four didn't give feedback at all? That only three thought it was great? Many of us will fixate on the feedback of the single unhappy person.

Compartmentalizing is important. Separating our sense of self and identity from the perception or response of others, however hard that is. It is often said that the only people who never fail are the ones who never try. Another way of thinking about this is that if we want to achieve something we have to accept the possibility of not achieving it too: if it is something we want and have to work for then the possibility of failure will be there.

Acknowledging at the outset is what both prepares us for it and keeps us grounded. Yes, failure is uncomfortable, but it is our response to it that dictates whether it is an experience that helps us grow, be better like Jon Hamm suggests, or whether we allow societal norms of embarrassment to cause the failure to multiply within itself and become a failure to learn and develop too.

In *Performance Theatre and the Poetics of Failure* (2010), Sara Jane Bailes looks at intentional failure and how it refocuses us, and how the unexpected shift of attention can restructure reality and emphasize expertise. From the slapstick of Laurel and Hardy to the intentionally amateurish piano playing of Les Dawson, we can see this in the world of comedy, how intentional failure is a means to highlight skill. In a learning context we can be creative with this, from showing what goes wrong if we *don't* do something to openly admitting and recreating events where things didn't go as we wanted. It can be incredibly powerful to have an expert say 'I messed up and this is how I fixed it' when giving a case study.

Failure is also inclusive and could be thought of as role modelling, and there is a dishonesty in any pretence that anyone either becomes an expert or maintains expertise without failure occurring. In many respects we should encourage failure within our learning environments too: those who learn with us will be all the more resilient to failing in their roles if they have first failed in a safe environment. There are also many roles where we would not want people to fail while in a 'live' space – air traffic controllers, for example, should be allowed to fail as much as possible while learning from those failures in a setting that makes their practice far safer.

This then brings into question whether or not failure is even the right term. While initiatives like 'church of fail' are making steps to own the word and remove the negative connotation it has, it remains so loaded with negativity that for many of us working in spaces less accommodating we may never be in a position to propose it as a positive.

Steve once took part in a panel discussion on learning for a training function that daily dealt with life and death matters and mentioned in one of his answers the importance of learning from failure, only to be told that 'we never fail'. In this particular body, failure and language of failure were alien, so unless someone died – a very real possibility if things went wrong –it simply wasn't possible to fail.

Having reflected on this and spoken with one of the other panellists, Steve realized that this isn't a denial of things going wrong but a reframing, and a retaking of the negative space around what it means to fail. In this mindset, if something goes wrong it is just a part of the process, perhaps a deviation from expectation, but readjustments are made until the required outcome is reached. This is more than just semantics: the word 'failure' implies a finality, that something has ended and that a goal has been missed. This is unhelpful and can too often become a roadblock, a reason to turn around and go backwards rather than simply a reason to alter approach.

That's not to deny that going backwards may sometimes be necessary, but how often do we change path through pride or an unwillingness to face up to reality or fear of failing again when perhaps an honest and objective appraisal, a learning what went wrong, and small change of direction might be all that is needed?

Think too how few of us would call any of those who learn with us a 'failure' if they don't achieve what they set out to do. Rather than brand them so negatively we will take into account all the mitigating circumstances and how we could have done things differently to benefit them, we will work hard to help them achieve their goals and we will make adjustments to support them.

We should allow ourselves this same flexibility and respect when judging our own performance.

George Clooney encourages actors to keep going despite knockbacks – 'The only failure is not to try' (Bilmes, 2014) – and this is true in all walks of life. Failing isn't something going wrong or not achieving something, it's not putting ourselves in a situation where that isn't even a possibility. I'd suggest further than this too that failure actually comes only if we don't learn the lessons when our outcomes or expectations weren't met, and then if we don't alter our route to get closer next time.

So, failure is a redundant and unhelpful word that holds us back. You wouldn't be reading this book if failure was a word relevant to your practice because you are clearly working on development and you are keen to keep learning.

Keep 'not failing' – then look at the gap between expectation and reality and plot the path to close it.

STEVE BURTON, BUILDER, UK

Steve tells us what he has learned from running and 'failing'

When thinking 'what I learned from running':

- persistence and repetition are the route to success but being spontaneous is the route to happiness;
- to be comfortable, realistic and confident in my ability;
- believe in yourself, be yourself, be polite and accept others for who they are;
- when it's hard for you, it's hard for everybody, but getting past this is magic.

When thinking about 'am I going to fail?':

- listen to your body and the quiet voice, not the loud voice;
- eat, drink, sleep, rest when you want, not when scheduled;
- when you get lost, get un-lost;
- listen, not just hear, because people like to talk and you may just learn something;
- don't focus on the final goal, it's too big – break it down into manageable stages;
- if you're scared of cows don't let this stop you running through fields, they might not even be there – do it anyway and deal with them if they are.

Thinking about yourself and learning lines

Here is a question for the world of learning: is content designed for any learning session a 'script' to be learned by the trainer/facilitator? At different points in our careers we have had managers with different views. One manager was very much of the opinion that you had to learn a set of 'lines' – i.e. every time a certain course was delivered, there was a need to ensure that the same point was covered at exactly the same time. This was a challenge for anyone whose belief system errs towards the 'pulling' rather than 'pushing' aspect of L&D. We have trouble with pushing content as the default position. We strongly believe that we all know something about something and use that as our starting point.

One of the criticisms of the 'death by PowerPoint' approach to training is that the trainer/facilitator reads from the slide deck and not from the 'heart'. We believe it is a huge contributor to why there are low numbers on learning transfer (which in itself assumes learning has happened).

We have delivered a number of presentation skills training events and events and qualifications where the training asked for the delegates to give their own mini-delivery sessions. The advice to delegates to use prompt cards with a few words on, allowing them to talk around the topic, invariably fell on deaf ears. The need for the learner to have the security of everything they wanted to say far overrode the confidence they had in their memory and ability to talk and engage on their chosen topic. One example was, 'Why have you written on a card, "Hello everyone, my name is FIRST NAME SURNAME"?' The reply would often involve a 'well I am so nervous, I might forget!'.

The Washington Post (Farhi, 2012) featured an article that could not make up its mind on Bruce Springsteen's use of teleprompters for a concert. The article both defended and criticized in equal measure, the defence, one that many trainers may recognize, being that there was a huge back catalogue to remember, and the article argued that other famous singers use teleprompters (citing Paul McCartney and Elton John as examples). And yet the tone was that the teleprompter was a bit of a 'cheat sheet'. The article makes a link to US Republican party criticisms of (Democrat) President Barack Obama using teleprompters in speeches to remember lines and asks, is it unreasonable to expect an established singer to remember 40 songs, and is it unreasonable to ensure that the president of the United States makes sure each word he uses is without ambiguity?

There is a scene in Richard Curtis's *About Time* where Richard E Grant is the lead actor in a play and freezes and forgets his lines on the opening night. The audience are not impressed at all and the playwright is understandably very unimpressed too. Domhnall Gleeson plays the central hero in the story, who can travel back in time, and thus goes back to the start of the play and offers prompts to Grant's character. The play is a success and the playwright is hailed a genius.

The fantasy of time travel is not a luxury that L&D practitioners can rely on. But as with Springsteen, McCartney, Obama and Grant, do we in L&D *really* have to learn lines? It is perhaps not surprising that people new into the profession have the view that this is what we do. If they have experienced dull web sessions or a trainer reading PowerPoint slides, then they may well be concerned about having to learn all the content in training courses. In our experience, many courses come with extensive trainer notes, a veritable tome of information 'just in case you get a really obscure response – it is in here'. We confess, in the past we have been responsible too for some courses where trainer notes have exceeded what we would now deem appropriate.

The challenge for the designer to ensure the message deliverer has all the information they need offers many opportunities beyond writing it all down on a page to learn verbatim, however.

We would argue strongly that there is a need to engage in methods that allow for quick retrieval of information. This is where we can embrace lessons from *About Time* and think about our own teleprompters. Placing prompts around the room is a serious option. The website actorhub.co.uk echoes this, offering advice to 'make it like Olivia Newton-John' (Actor Hub, 2014). In other words, get 'physical' with memory retrieval. Dramaresource.com offers a more sober version of being 'physical' by encouraging movement for its readers who want to know how to learn lines, with a link to its 'scientifically proven benefits'.

This is good advice if you are in either the push or pull situations. Each session you deliver may have a clear aim and a set of objectives to pin the session content on to. How does the facilitator remember all the things to do with that objective? This in itself is a form of learning lines. Instead of scripted trainer notes, the task is to remember salient points for the learners.

Actor Hub also advocates the need to read scripts out loud. Not in your head, but actually out loud. When David started in L&D, his mentor advised him to read the training manuals out loud, and having a dog at the time, David spent many an hour in his front room over the years rehearsing conduct and discipline, customer service, new line managers, developing yourself and how to be a great mentor, all practised with just his dog as the audience!

Of course, the thing missing is the response from the audience. They hold the key – their insights to your facilitation will decide the next step. Actors and singers (and presidents) learn their lines to support them in the way they engage with the audience, in most cases creating an emotional depth and connection. So, what do you need to rehearse? Can you rehearse responses? Dramaresource.com offers a couple of tips that are transferable. First, they say, 'listen to what other actors are saying' and second, 'make a recording' (Farmer, nd).

Both are important. The other actors in workplace scenarios are the organization's employees and their stage is their day-to-day reality. Are you listening there? In terms of recording, we can ask to make a recording of any conversations we have with the learners in their environment. This allows playback and a deeper insight to their world, helping you to not learn lines but learn their context.

Anne Murphy Paul writes for the website Psychology Today and suggests that actors learning lines are actually 'searching for the intentions of the play's characters: why they do what they do, and especially why they say what they say... each word offers a hint of the speakers' motivations and desires' (Murphy Paul, 2012). She echoes earlier comments about movement to aid the learning, and 'doing it 'live'. 'For us this strengthens the need to go to where your audience works and sharing with them learning objectives, sharing elements of content, sharing thoughts on what activities within the session could look like, and how they would transfer back into their world.'

WENDY SOH, FREELANCE TRAINER, SINGAPORE

Wendy explains how karaoke helps her with her work in HR

Singing at karaoke is what I have enjoyed during leisure. Besides enjoying the music and practising voice projection, this has helped me to build self-esteem and confidence. Especially for a practising HR professional, voice projection during townhall and mass communications is important.

Besides, music also helps to further understand the emotions and how people react whenever there's a change in voice projection.

Karaoke singing also helps in building relationships with people around you. My network has expanded with this enjoyment.

Thinking about yourself and how you react

Dava Sobel in the brilliant book *Longitude* tells the story of John Harrison, a watchmaker who solved one of the greatest scientific problems of his age – how to measure longitude while at sea. Such was the problem that the British Parliament offered a prize ('The Longitude Prize') in 1714 and a huge £20,000 reward for anyone who could produce a proven workable solution. Harrison duly showed his working, but was not rewarded. Sobel tells a story of the establishment reacting against the Yorkshireman, the 'not our sort' approach (Sobel, 1995). However, enlisting the help of King George III, Harrison was finally awarded nearly all the prize money (some £1,250 short) though he was not given the coveted prize.

The story smacks of elitist, closed ranks and discriminatory attitudes. At every step at which Harrison met the conditions of the prize, the goalposts (via Acts of Parliament) changed. Harrison worked on the prize from his mid-20s around 1720 and received the final payment of his prize money at the age of 73, 10 years before his death. He gave 50 years of his life to one passion, producing proven results but being knocked back at every stage, given only small tokens of acknowledgement but not winning the coveted prize.

Sobel tells her story in a factual narrative from detailed research she undertook, but she appeals to the reader's emotions as she does so. The account of Harrison on the Longitude Prize website is fact based, although in the history of the prize, it stresses Harrison was working class, with little formal education, and omits to detail the goalpost changes or even credit him fully: 'Harrison came closest', it says.

The story is very powerful for David. Harrison lived and married in a town close to where David lived up to his 20s and as a child his parents would tell the story of the famous clock in the grounds of a stately home they would pass each time they visited his grandparents near Grimsby. So, his reaction on reading Sobel was one of outrage, dismay and yet relief that Harrison got some credit and an opportunity to enjoy knowing he was right.

The ending of Harrison's story is not the ending of the Longitude Prize and its website continues to offer prizes for solving the scientific problems of today. The website tells of the next steps after Harrison's death too, something Sobel starts to share at the end of her book, showing the reader that Harrison's story is not to be told in isolation from the man.

David wonders whether if his education background was different, would he react in the same way? In viewing the story through a gap of 350 years, was it fair or right to react this way, with outrage and dismay? Either way, he has an emotional connection to the story. This is just one example of how the arts can give us a strong emotional response and bond with a context, person and event outside our own experience. How we react to theatre and cinema experiences can vary from feeling uplifted to depressed and despairing, sad, happy, laughing out loud or crying. And those reactions can vary from person to person experiencing the same event.

Two cinematic experiences come to mind here. The first, after watching *About Time*, presenters Kermode and Mayo (2013) both comment on how many people came out of the cinema, took out their phones and rang their fathers to say 'I love you', something Mayo calls a visceral response to an emotional connection with the film, even though Kermode in his review says the film is 'deeply flawed, [but] it works!'.

The second comes after the screening of *Harry Potter and the Deathly Hallows: Part 2*. Kermode and Mayo describe discussing the film with their families as they came out of the cinema, commenting on it being the 'end of an era', a sadness that this film and book series had ended. The comment about the end of an era resonated with David. He watched the final film with his youngest child. His eldest two were away at university, and they had been through the previous seven films and all seven books together. It felt wrong to David that at the end they were not all there together. That ending of his experience of the story was not what he wanted it to be. It was messy, imperfect, and he reacted emotionally to it.

How do we link to learning within this? There is a series of elements. What do you want people to remember? What's the message you're going to close with? Thinking about cinematic endings... how do you want people to react? In the *About Time* example, an imperfect film gives audiences a reminder to do something (in this case phone their father). Is there sufficient reaction to your sessions to give a call to arms? How do you strike the balance between giving everything but also creating the impression that you have more to give if it is needed? Remember, it's not just your actions, it's the script and the narrative of what you do too.

Thinking about yourself and being an understudy

The role of an understudy, according to actor Michael Cortez, is one of the hardest tasks an actor faces. Imagine it: the audience has paid a small fortune to see the actor in the lead role. And they are not there. The understudy has to acknowledge that level of disappointment and deliver, *really* deliver, and also be themselves with their interpretation of the role, but not too distant from the way the lead would play the part. Bowie-Sell (2016) explored the concept of being an understudy with Cortez and five other actors for WhatsOnStage. She asked three questions:

- What is it like to understudy a role?
- Tell us about a time when you had to understudy at the last minute.
- Do you think understudies are underappreciated or is it part of the job?

There is a presupposition in the direction of the last question. The phrasing suggests that understudies are in fact under-appreciated and it is indeed part of the job: 'suck it up' almost. The answers for all three questions make fascinating reading from all the respondents, and there are some real gems of insights in them.

David O'Mahony in the same article comments on the role the producer plays in demonstrating trust in the allocation of actors to understudy roles. He also shares that actors in lead roles have discussed the pressure they face and commented, 'Oh, you're just a swing' with a derogatory slant, in other words, they are so low in the food chain they don't get the drive or have the talent for a great performance. O'Mahony calls these people 'incredibly naïve'.

His comments mirror comments we have heard about our profession: 'Oh, you work in training, you don't get what it's like in the real world' or 'I would love to do your job, it looks so easy' or worse, 'If you can do, do, if you can't, teach'. Statements which say a lot about the value others place on our role!

As we have mentioned when exploring 'lines', in designing any intervention we have often heard 'we need detailed trainer notes', often accompanied by the phrase 'what happens if you get chucked under a bus?'. The intent of this statement is to ensure that if anything happens to the main deliverer, an understudy can pick up the training and bang! – make the magic happen. This troubles us on a number of levels, not least in wondering just how many times are facilitators thrown under buses?

Questions need to be asked about the assumptions placed on the person delivering the learning and on the audience. What is the commission process for design, to what degree is there flexibility to allow the deliverer to put their own stories in the session to add context? If the learning is designed with the learner in mind, and the deliverer (and understudy, i.e. anyone who can step in at short notice if needed) is someone who is credible in that topic space, then to what degree do they need detailed notes?

As a designer we may not have a relationship with the deliverer or understudy, so we may not know their stories to allow them to improvise. Also, as a designer we may find our designs evolving and deviating from our plan. David Nicholls, author of *The Understudy*, shares in a *Guardian* article about how he has been responsible for the film adaptations of all his books. However, for a 2020 theatre production of *The Understudy* he is pleased to have nothing to do with it, saying, 'I don't have to police it'. A bold statement for something that he confesses to the writer of the article, Arifa Akbar, is 'the one [book] I yearn to re-write' (Akbar, 2020).

And then there is the concept that as both designers and facilitators of events, the role we play in the organization is one of an understudy in itself. We are representing a message from the organization, the drive for performance improvement, to increase skills, to be compliant, to be safe, to live our values, etc. We are the spokespeople within our organization for those standards we are writing or delivering. To what degree have we asked this audience how happy they are with entrusting their message to us?

Backstage (2022) advises, 'The most talented performers often get cast as swings. They can do everything and you can trust them, so you give them a huge amount of responsibility. If you're just starting out in the business, don't let your ego stand in the way… and forming relationships with a multitude of creatives. One job leads to another.

'If you're a performer of some stature and take an understudy position, check your ego. It's your job to serve the production. I've seen some understudies make the rehearsal all about them but remember: you are there to support the rest of the company! If you can't do this, you shouldn't take the job.

'Always be prepared! I've seen stand-bys go on at intermission as well as halfway through an act.'

Some wise words for L&D practitioners who are delivering an organization's message. There is also a range of advice from understudies to those considering the role (Bowie-Sell, 2016). There are some brilliant soundbites that work well for anyone in learning – well worth a deeper read.

Thinking about yourself and winging it

Winging it is what happens when you're put on the spot and have to perform without preparation or planning. To do it effectively requires several things to be in place. First, you can only wing it by building on experience you already have. For example, we have never been pilots or had any training, so winging it landing a 747 in a gale would be unlikely to go well. We have, however, delivered learning on presentation skills, so while we might not always fully enjoy the experience of being asked to talk to a room full of people about it 'off the cuff', we could probably wing it.

Second, to wing it effectively requires an anchoring position and a thread. Winging it needs a foundation to build from and a goal to get to. This is arguably what makes it different from improvisation where the goal can be uncertain but your experience allows you to build moment on moment and discover the goal. It's also different from blagging. You know when you are blagging because there is that feeling of being adrift, without the anchor or thread of winging it and without the sense of discovery that can come with improvisation.

As actor Christopher Walken is reputed to have said, 'You cannot improvise unless you know exactly what you are doing.'

To illustrate, if you asked us to stand up and talk for 10 minutes about presentation skills, we'd take a minute to find our anchor, based on our experience, the goal and the thread between the two. In this instance the anchor to hold everything in place would likely be 'audience experience'. The thread would be storytelling and how stories enhance or diminish that experience and we have stories of presentations we have seen and delivered ourselves that satisfy this criterion. And the goal would be for that thread to lead you to how you can leave your audience with your key message in a way that resonates and is memorable.

From that foundation, and with that thread in mind, we'd be apprehensive but fairly sure we could deliver through winging it with that minimal preparation. It's worth remembering too that the difference between blagging and winging is that with the latter the audience is on your side. If you're hiding from the audience that you're unprepared, that's blagging. If you're winging it, there's no shame in admitting it and getting the audience on your side with self-deprecation or a request for ideas. In fact, the request for ideas can even help you find your thread.

Winging it is something we should put ourselves in situations to do: it's part of growth, breaking us out of convention and allowing us to recognize depths to our knowledge and experience that we may not have been aware of. Both of us are privileged to take part in review panels for awards occasionally, and it is often striking how many submissions are at their strongest during the informal question and answer session over the scripted presentation they deliver. The passion, enthusiasm, deep thinking and compelling message will as often come through in this stage more than the presentation. This again illustrates how following lines can reduce the impact of delivery.

It's exhilarating too! It's not just being put on the spot by others, it's also putting ourselves on the spot. And it's not necessarily something big, it might just be that work conference call where someone says something about a subject we have some knowledge of – that's an opening for us to express that knowledge, not to show off but to support and help others, winging it to grow the conversation.

It's something that actors are required to do often, and some even say they are winging it all the time. They are often called upon to do something they have not done before (true of most parts they will play), which may trigger vulnerabilities and uncertainties and self-doubt about what they can do, but building on their experience, skills and knowledge they can deliver time and again, trusting that each moment will flow from the last and create a cohesive whole.

To do this they must create their anchor first and for some this process of winging it, of discovery as they play the character, is their preferred way of working. As with our description above, this anchor, that first impression, creates the starting point from which to build out the rest step by step.

As people professionals there are numerous lessons we can learn from the approach actors take so that we can become more comfortable with winging it. The first is to observe others, start to build our stories and even think how they might be used. A colleague of Sully, the pilot from the true-life film *Sully: Miracle on the Hudson*, when asked how his friend had known what to do in a crash situation, responded that he had been an air accident investigator so 'had more stories than anyone else' about what might work and what wouldn't. The more we immerse ourselves in our profession, the more stories we will have.

Second, we can trust the process, know that if we have our anchoring point and a goal, the flow between the two will happen, and with our knowledge and experience that anchor and goal will increasingly become second nature. If you're stuck, ask yourself the questions 'what is the problem people want to solve? How do they want to feel?'.

Third, we must put ourselves into situations where we can practise, expose ourselves to the discomfort it can cause and know that it's not lack of preparation that makes us uncomfortable – our working lives are our preparation – it's more often than not lack of script and the accompanying fear of loss of face or questioning of competence that creates our uncertainty.

Lastly, use the audience: don't have them as passive observers, interact with them, even if it is just adopting a conversational approach to your winging it rather than a presentational approach. You don't have to seek verbal responses if you don't wish to, but in everything we do, creating a connection is key to success, just as it is with actors.

Yourself and next steps

We have outlined in this section a few stories that have made us stop and think about the work we do. We have made connections with other walks of life. They have fuelled development actions and conversations with others to help us be better at what we do and who we are.

We debated whether we should put this 'yourself' section first or later on in this Act of the book. We decided on it going first: after all, if we want to nail our relationship with our audience and be on top of our processes and think more deeply about our work, then we have to be confident in who we are. There is a book by Vineet Nayar, *Employees First, Customers Second* (2010), in which he explains that if you treat your employees well and have them as your priority focus, then the customer will be delighted. Our approach to this Act echoes that principle: if you treat yourself right and focus on your own development, then your audiences will be delighted and your impact greater.

2.2

Thinking about your audience

Setting the scene

For the context of this book we have defined our audience as anyone we are supporting with their learning experiences. Our audiences can be individuals or groups. The location where we connect can be in their own setting or ours, or indeed somewhere less familiar for both parties. Familiarity with the location can be beneficial for a learning experience or it can be so loaded with prior information and expectation that it might need work to 'undo' before the learning can be most effective. The location can also be online, in person or on the phone. Some types of interventions are akin to a theatre performance where the presenter and the audience can see each other; for other types it is more like a cinema experience where the audience and the presenter do not interact directly. In some environments there will be two-way communication, in others there will not.

An audience isn't defined by the number of people but by their role. This is not always binary in our interactions with them – for example, in a more facilitated interaction the lines between the roles of audience and presenter are fluid, with all parties playing different roles at different points. A good facilitator will draw this out of those they are with.

While there are constants in the way we work with those in our audience, the way in which we communicate will adjust. Caroline Hopkins (2022) shares legendary BBC broadcaster Sir Terry Wogan's conversational approach, intentionally speaking as if to a single individual even when millions are listening. This won't always be appropriate for us in our practice, but we should always be mindful of what our audience needs in order for them to get the most out of our interaction with them.

Another consideration with our audience is the power dynamic. There's an implicit balance of power towards the presenter or leader of the space and session where the interaction is taking place. As we look at our audience we need to think of what assumptions and biases the audience may have as a consequence of the space we are in, the way we present in the sense of physical presence and style of working, and equally what assumptions and biases we may ourselves be bringing about the audience.

Thinking about your audience and acting

We have already looked at acting, but here we explore the concept further, looking through the lens of your audience.

CONSIDER THIS

Stanislavski, the Russian theatre practitioner, produced a fictional diary of Kostya, a first-year student (Markvoić, 2014). The diary addresses the assumptions that underpin the reality of acting that Kostya has been 'conditioned' to believe. Stanislavski calls it the 'system' and argues that there is a natural order of truth within theatre, and that truth when on stage is different from truth in real life. An actor cannot believe they are truly Macbeth, but they must believe the imagined creativity of it and be focused on finding the 'inner truth' that allows this expression.

If we accept the concept that there is a 'natural order of truth in theatre', then what is the natural order of truth in learning? Is the truth 'on stage' for us different from the truth in 'real life'? Many of the 2000-plus people we have interacted with in formal L&D roles would argue they were drawn into L&D to 'help people and allow them to be the best they can be', to share knowledge, to support people in meeting their potential. A further question might be whether this is what organizations and individuals want or indeed need to succeed. We may also wish to ask whether we are conforming to our own fantasy of what we think learning in an organization is and creating a disconnect between organizational and audience expectation and our 'inner truth'.

Further, how many people come into L&D with the strong desire to say, 'I want to drive organizational performance forward' and 'I want to challenge poor performance in individuals at all levels of the business' or 'I want to dive into the rich sources of data L&D can access'? And yet these are the things that are needed.

Similarly, if there is this disconnect between elements of our roles, there are many anecdotes about how few in an audience come to 'mandatory' compliance events with excitement and an attitude that they want to do it and will have a great experience.

How does our audience see us and our role? Simply by being in a position where we are on a stage (real or virtual) we are in a position of assumed authority in the context of our audience. Or perhaps if not authority, a position where expertise is taken as given. There will be expectations and assumptions made. Whether or not that is fair, or if it is our responsibility should we not meet those expectations and assumptions, is another conversation, but none of us can deny that they exist.

The reality is that many will be engaged and enthusiastic, some cynical, some disinterested. The audience will paint onto us many different thoughts coloured by their preconceptions, motivations and engagement with the event, whatever it is, before we've even begun.

The way in which the audience responds to us and our 'performance' is a significant driver of the success of our work. George Bernard Shaw defined the role of an actor as being to make the audience think real things are happening to real people (Quote Fancy, nd). In the context of learning professionals this translates to the lens the audience uses to view us being one through which they see authenticity and must see their world represented and aligned with ours. What we deliver must be believable for them. They are part of this relationship, not just passive recipients.

There is much to be said for thinking of the audience as our partner in the work of delivery. Part of our work is to create the permission, space and energy for this partnership so the audience sees themselves in this way. We can lead this, and use our skills and learning to influence, but we cannot force it. As John Cleese apparently said, 'When you do comedy, only the audience decides whether it is funny or not.'

So what is a 'good' audience and what role does the way in which we act play in that?

A 'good' audience is attentive because we have caught their imagination and interest. They are participating when we ask because we have energized them, made them feel safe to be on show alongside us, and we have created permission to co-own the moment with us.

This is no different from the arts. Consider stand-up comedy: a 'good' audience is one that engages when invited. Perhaps through heckling and other interaction they may tread the fine line between disrupting and enhancing the performance, expertly conducted by the comedian, who is creating the permission to co-own the moment, making them feel safe to participate. Where it goes wrong is where the comedian loses that control, either 'dying' on stage and getting no reaction at all or getting a negative response. They have failed to catch the interest of the audience, not kept them hooked or energized them, and rather than co-owning the space the audience has taken over.

LINDA ASHDOWN, ASSESSMENT MANAGER, UK

Linda shares the transferable elements from putting on a local pantomime

Driven by a desire to raise money for our local hospice, channel our love of theatre and create something with other parents at our children's school, my husband and I undertook directing a local pantomime.

Most of the people involved had not been on stage before and some were frankly terrified. We soon realized volunteer actors were just a small part of what we needed. We needed set designers and builders, wardrobe and props, lighting and sound, stage managers, publicity and fundraisers if we were to achieve our goal. All these players needed to be pulled together to create something special.

And create something special we did. Everyone who came was surprised by the high quality of the production and most importantly, with just four performances, we raised over £25,000 for our local hospice.

As an HR professional, what I hadn't expected was the personal 'payback' in terms of my learning and how I could utilize that in my daily practice.

So, what did I learn?

- How much confidence is a key part of performance. If you can help people believe they can do things, they will surprise themselves, uncovering hidden capabilities.
- Find the right roles for individuals and you will maximize the team performance. We spent time talking to people who wanted to be involved but didn't want to be on stage. By getting to know them properly we were able to uncover skills where they could really make a difference to the production.
- Having a unified goal that people care about really makes a difference. From the start everyone worked hard to minimize costs and raise income (tickets, sponsorship, raffles) to ensure we could maximize the amount we could deliver for the hospice. Everyone involved had hectic lives, but all found time to make the pantomime happen.

While my background in HR and teaching meant that these points were of course not new to me, the pantomime experience really brought them back into focus, helped me reflect and enabled me to bring fresh insight back into my work to enable me to drive performance and learning in others.

Thinking about your audience and creating a learning environment

There is an acting phrase, 'treading the boards'. Theatres Trust (nd) explores its origin from the 1700s where actors would bring their own planks of wood to set up a stage in order to perform. The history of theatre in the UK can be traced back to the Roman amphitheatres, copied from the theatres of the ancient Greeks, where moral stories were told.

Roman amphitheatres were open to the elements and had banked seating so all the audience could see as much as possible from their vantage point. However, there were some blind spots – those sat facing stage-left might find their view of stage-right restricted. In modern-day theatre settings, there is a clear pricing policy linked to the quality of the stage views. Those in the stalls or front rows of the dress circles will pay a premium price. Those with a restricted view, at the back or with an obstructed view will pay less, and this is made clear in the pricing plan. Audience members know that they get what they pay for. The actors know that some audience members will see more and some less. Two things come to mind for L&D: one in an online environment and the other in a venue-based environment.

In an online learning environment, live or pre-recorded, we can define the premium seats and the 'cheap seats'. These are linked with access to technology, its quality and the access to the facilitator through chat or camera functions or wider community platforms. In a venue-based environment, the use of 'theatre style' is a common layout option for L&D rooms and conference spaces. However, there are compromises – learners who get to the venue early may well opt to sit directly opposite the visual aid display. Those who sit closest to the facilitator's space are in a 50:50 lottery: will the facilitator block more near them or opposite them? The boards we tread in many instances are not those of the 1700s' actors, where they could lay out their space accordingly, but dictated to us by definitions handed down in decades of 'train the trainer' events and material and the layout of the room.

In Shakespeare's *Hamlet*, there is the line from Hamlet: 'The play's the thing where I will catch the conscience of the king.' But what sort of play, and why a play? Another character, Polonius, gives a list (a long list) of different types of plays, 'tragedy, comedy, historical, tragi-comedy, etc.'. These different types of plays produce a deep source of material for the L&D practitioner. There are options to create our storyboards in the design phase, thinking about the context in which we set out our own play for our audience.

In the 'play within a play' scene, Hamlet organizes his seating so he has the best view of the play along with views of his stepfather, Claudius. Hamlet has masterminded the event to ensure the play represents his theory about the death of his own father, which he believes Claudius is responsible for. This is a neat method of demonstrating ways in which the audience can sometimes take some control of the direction of events – or at least the way they see them – to gain insights from the learning without being directed by the facilitator.

In the UK in the 21st century it may be inconceivable that theatre as a form of entertainment can be outlawed, and yet in the civil war era of the 17th century, it was. Up until very recently there were no cinemas in the Kingdom of Saudi Arabia. The reason for the former was due to the threat of civil unrest where groups of people congregated, and with the Kingdom there are numerous debates as to why, with some external commentators speculating that the same reason was applied.

A common issue in train-the-trainer sessions is 'how to deal with disruptive learners'. The go-to answer is usually the same in theatre, cinema and learning venues in organizations and schools: remove the unruly element so the performance on the boards can go on. The history of theatre and audience relationship volatility takes some interesting twists and turns. In the early 1800s there was a decline in audience attendance that ran parallel with the economic issues of the time. Rural theatres closed and more people attended in the industrial towns as the populations moved into urban areas for employment. There was a clear 'no alcohol' policy, again to maintain control of the audience and stop disruption to the 'order' and messages within plays.

Interestingly, this led to the development of music halls, an alternative form of entertainment. Theatres became the domain of the privileged, whereas music halls were the domain of the working class and those performing within them were deemed inferior to theatre performers.

Is there a parallel here with 'traditional' approaches to L&D (i.e. training) and digital-based ones? Do some trainers view digital as a musical hall act and those supporting them as the 'rowdy, noisy masses who don't know any better'? Or vice versa?

In treading the boards, are you treading your own boards, creating your own space, or conforming to corporate layouts?

Thinking about your audience and hope

Hope creates comfort in insecurity, a balance in ambiguity and a vision – however hard it is to discern – that there is something more, something better than wherever we are at that moment.

Compare this to lack of hope, that sense that the present or worse is all there ever will be. The insecurity that comes from feeling we have no autonomy and no means to move beyond where we are.

Hope in L&D matters because there is uncertainty that often comes with stretching people and taking them from a position of comfort and into the challenge that can result from learning. It is part of our role to support turning that uncertainty and discomfort into aspiration and hope. Because if we're honest, we know that for many the idea of 'going on training' or 'doing a learning course' doesn't fill them with joy or optimism. Add 'mandatory' or 'compliance' into those phrases and some of your audience will feel their day may be ruined before it's even started!

Whether online or in a classroom, the motivations and aspirations for any group of learners are going to vary: from those who are committed to development at one end of the spectrum and who could perhaps be thought to already have 'high hope' for the learning experience, to those who are participating reluctantly or under the insistence of someone else, and whose expectation and hope may be lower.

In both cases our role is the same: to create a more unified perception and common state of mind at the outset and use this as a springboard to creating hope. There will be no set way to do this, but you can, for example, subvert what might be assumed 'dry' moments such as the discussion of learning objectives. This could be done using language to describe not what it is people will learn or be able to do differently but instead the impact it will enable them to have or the ways in which others' perceptions might change. Or you could even not talk about objectives at all. While the outcomes from learning that motivate someone may be personal, hope can nonetheless be generated through tapping into different expressions of those outcomes that will resonate broadly.

There is much we can learn from the arts in this. Think of *Star Wars*: *Episode IV*, which coincidentally is also called *A New Hope*. Luke's mission begins with boredom (no hope), becomes personal (finding Leia), becomes a cause (joining the rebel alliance), and from here hope is generated by chasing something bigger than his personal aims. Learning to use the Force is about helping the alliance. He then motivates Han Solo, first with money and then with reputation and by referencing the perception of others...

So taking this thinking, which of these will create more hope in a room of learners with their mixed and perhaps unsaid motivations?

By the end of this course you will be able to:

a. create a recruitment process which removes bias from CV sifting

or

b. recruit the best applicants for a role and create equality of opportunity within your organization

or

c. demonstrate leadership in your organization and role-model recruiting an inclusive, equitable and diverse workforce.

They could all have the same learning underpinning the outcome, and while option a) might be necessary for meeting some assessment criteria or objective analysis of the content, it is clear that options b) and c) are more aspirational, more resonant on a personal level, and as a consequence will be more likely to take learners from a position of nervous anticipation or reluctant participation and move them towards a position of aspiration and hope.

Another aspect to consider from cinema is how hope cannot be sustained over a long period of time. It must be constantly refreshed and it must at times take a hit in order, to paraphrase the famous *Star Wars* quote, 'to come back more powerful than you can possibly imagine'. It is not enough to have the opposite of hope at the outset, there must be a reminder of this too. Again, think *Star Wars* and the hits Luke's hope takes (and in turn the audience's, as we experience the film primarily through him):

- He begins with no hope.
- He gains hope when he finds Obi Wan.
- He loses hope when his aunt and uncle are killed.
- He gains hope when he finds Leia as a prisoner.
- He loses hope when he is in the compactor.
- He gains hope when they escape.
- He loses hope when Obi Wan is struck down.
- He gains hope when he joins with the alliance.
- He loses hope when the Death Star seems impregnable.

And so on. This isn't to suggest your learning should constantly pitch people into states of hopelessness, but instead that learning, like a story, may be effectively delivered through ensuring that each time a hope is met, some level of discomfort (and therefore generation of aspiration and new hope) is created. Almost like a computer game where each time a level is attained it is celebrated and a new, harder level (or stretch target) builds out of the skills just learned and demonstrated. Hope is then recreated over and again as the learning empowers people to see their way through to resolving the cause of discomfort.

Scriptwriters do this through creating conflict. That's not necessarily personal conflict but can be as simple – and as complex – as the tension that exists between two possible outcomes. Again, this can be in how you describe something, for example a scenario. We'll use the CV sifting and removing bias learning outcome above. Here's your standard case study:

> A manager has handed you a dozen CVs from people who have applied for a role she is advertising, and she says she has put them in order of her own preference based on what university they attended. Her experience is that candidates who attend a handful of universities do better in the role than anyone else. This learning will help you with your response.

This scenario is neutral – it has neither the hope nor the hopelessness that it needs to generate that hope. So how do we create hope? We create tension by creating conflict between different aspects of a story. Those don't have to be personal conflict, however – we can introduce time as a factor, for example. And ethics. And emotional peril. How about you describe that case study instead as:

> A manager has walked over to your desk. 'I'm really stressed,' she says, 'you can be a life-saver. I've left it to the last minute but I need a shortlist from these candidates.' She hands you a pile of CVs and explains that she has prioritized them.
>
> 'At the top are people who went to the same university as John, we know that makes them a good fit…' She tails off, seeing the look on your face. 'Look, I know it might not be how we're supposed to do it but it's the best way in the time we've got, and I don't think it's illegal either… is it?'
>
> She's worried, and you know she's under a lot of pressure to recruit and to hit challenging targets so it's vital the right person is found. It's not just her reputation on the line here, but yours too. She's waiting for an answer. How will you respond?
>
> Using the guidance of this learning you'll be able to meet her brief in a way that ensures the best hire is found from a diverse and inclusive pool of candidates.

Don't think of scenarios as a description of a transactional event, think instead of those scenarios as scenes in a film, involving real people and with real consequences. Create tension and risk, and create hope through the learning providing the route through this risk.

SARAH HAYDEN, WAREHOUSE OPERATIVE, UK

Sarah describes how volunteering has enabled her to gain transferable skills to support her career

Primarily I am a single mother to a five-year-old. As well as this, I work part time as a forklift driver in a warehouse which is going through redundancy. The warehouse is going to be moved around 100 miles away. It would be fair to say that life is difficult. It would be very easy to depend on others, however I try to rely on myself and my daughter, to show her that you can do anything if you set your mind to it.

When my daughter was a newborn, I started to go to a new parents' group, 'Bumps, Babies and Beyond'. It opened my eyes to the world of volunteering and supporting other parents. It also helped me make new parent friends and a new chapter in my life. It helped to occupy my mind while on maternity leave, but also I loved helping new parents who were, like me, struggling with parenting issues.

Volunteering gave me a new source of details and provided me with new skills to put on my CV, which I will be sending out soon, in hope of some job interviews.

Currently I am a forklift driver, but I am more than that, thanks to volunteering opening my eyes to a new chapter in my life.

Thinking about your audience and their 'journey'

'Journey' is a word that has, in Rebecca Nicholson's view (2017), ruined the concept of reality TV. She argues in her *Guardian* article that the word is overused. Indeed, if you are a watcher of reality TV, the word does appear in almost every question the presenter asks and every contestant's reply. So why have *journey* here?

'The journey' is the centre of many stories and plots within stories, the journey of the characters played out. Booker's (2017) *The Seven Basic Plots* explores the meaning of stories and why they are important to humans. This work was influenced heavily by others, including that of psychologist Carl Jung, leading to some criticizing Booker's work.

The journey is an important part of learning design. Who is the learning intervention intended for, what degree of thought for the audience is undertaken by the designer, to what end does the designer bring into their thinking the starting point of the audience, and how do they weave in the fact that the audience members may all have different starting points, views and demands of this learning journey? This may all sound a bit excessive for what some may think an everyday learning event such as 'customer service' or 'health and safety' is, but it is important to take a step back and reflect on this philosophical stance.

The inclusion of the journey here is not to encourage you to make every learning event a 'Dungeons and Dragons'-type odyssey, but to take into account the learners' reality.

Anyone who studies British history of the 1940s will come across the story of Dunkirk and the many soldiers stranded on the beach against an invading Nazi army, unable to get home. The story is retold in the multi-award-winning 2017 Christopher Nolan film *Dunkirk*. This film tells the journey from three perspectives: air, sea and land. And within each of these perspectives the timeline in the film is different: one hour, one day, one week. This is perhaps one of the most engaging aspects of the film, managing multiple complex narratives at the same time. It parallels the multiple complex narratives of organizations.

It is a useful exercise to ask to what degree learning interventions are complicit in being one-dimensional, ignoring a range of multiple competing elements.

Nolan (2017) explains that the film itself does not have a conventional ending. It is merely the overview of a set period of time. He also shares the two choices the soldiers seem to face: surrender or annihilation. The fact that this part of the depiction of events does not end in either is part of the film's brilliance. Nolan further explains how within the story there are many substories and that he had to sort out the myths that surround the events from the facts to create his script. He wanted to tell it from a subjective point of view, he wanted the audience to feel they were on that beach, they were in the cockpit of the aeroplane and in the boats at sea, he wanted his audience to be immersed in the journeys that were portrayed not only in the script but in the reality of the events in 1940. He also talked about 'stripping away' the usual devices of cinema; for instance, there were no stories of 'girlfriends back home' in the narrative, no 'generals around a table'. It was the soldiers on the beach, the pilots in the aeroplanes and the 'Sunday sailors' on the sea.

The lessons for L&D are layered here. The grounding in reality and the telling of a story from multiple recognizable perspectives offers a foundation and can make the experience one the audience will recognize and relate to even if they have no first-hand experience of what is shared.

And then there is the concept of trust and ensuring there is trust in the journey and being conscious of the extent to which we trust the learner to make their own sense of the journey. Similarly, being thoughtful about how the journey ends. It may not always be appropriate to have an ending that fits the (or our) narrative. At times, rather than dictate the ending, we, and the learner, may benefit from allowing them to be inspired to make their own sense, make their own ending and define their own next steps.

Nolan had to trust himself and had to get others to trust him. There were aspects of making *Dunkirk* that he could draw on from experience – the crowds on the beach, for instance, using many extras – but there were things he had not done before, such as the ships on the sea. The film was a success because the people around him trusted him to direct something that was new territory. Kermode sums up the success in his review of the film (Nolan, 2017): 'Christopher Nolan imagines that the audience is smart enough to keep up... and you know what – they are!'

Perhaps at times it is worth considering whether we in L&D trust our audience as much as Nolan does.

The journey plays out too in an article by travel writer Don George (2015). He shares his 'painful and exhilarating... but almost always begins with pain' approach to travel writing. He talks about how difficult the first steps of writing are, the drive and determination and time needed to start and to start at the right point. He describes the time, energy and effort needed to be a travel writer. George tells of his approach to one particular piece of writing when visiting Angkor Wat in Cambodia. He wrote three different versions from three perspectives, but it still wasn't working for him. He talks of how wanting to get it right paralyses him at times, thinking about what it should be rather than what it is. Again this reminds us of trust and the importance of being mindful whether we start to describe and design to what something 'should' be and how that has been decided, rather than what it is.

What would the learner want us to do? George goes on to say, 'And I learned once again that as travel writers guiding the journey our readers take, it is our responsibility to relive that journey in prose as passionately and profoundly as possible – to make sense of its meaning in a way that connects our story of a far-off place with the puzzle of the greater world.'

How would you write George's quote in the context of guiding the learner journey in your world?

Thinking about your audience and language

The language we use matters, and language is more complex than just the words we say.

Think of the different ways a statement such as 'you're so funny' can be said and heard: with joy, in laughter as an expression of genuine emotion to build someone up, with sarcasm, the kind of comment to cut someone down. Language is tone, intent, delivery and of course words too.

So what about those words? How often do we find what we say and what we think we mean isn't how others have interpreted what we have said? This is why scriptwriters, whether for stage or screen or politics, will spend hours and hours drafting and redrafting words to remove any ambiguity and ensure only one meaning can be taken from whatever is said. It is also why sports stars are reduced by media training to give stock answers, rendering all interviews largely useless as player after player in a football match gives almost identical answers about how 'it's nice to get a goal but really it's about the team winning, not my performance…'.

With film this is where the skill of a scriptwriter comes in: creating language that is naturalistic, compelling, informative and direct. If you hear some of the great film monologues, observe the rhythm of the words and the information they manage to convey. How much can you learn about character, context and environment from a few lines, well delivered with language carefully chosen? For example, the opening moments of Terrence Malick's *Thin Red Line*:

'What's this war in the heart of nature? Why does nature vie with itself? The land contend with the sea? Is there an avenging power in nature? Not one power, but two?

'I remember my mother when she was dying. Looked all shrunk up and grey. I asked her if she was afraid. She just shook her head. I was afraid to touch the death I seen in her.

'I heard people talk about immortality, but I ain't seen it…'.

The monologue continues and in around 60 seconds we gain an idea of the character – the man who speaks the words is religious, or at least has been and is questioning that faith, he has lost his mother, he is perhaps suffering his own existential crisis, and the words themselves have a rhythm and unforced poetry that is compelling.

We may not have the luxury of scripting our delivery and yet those who see us will be forming their own picture of us from the way we deliver our words. Or rather, we *might* script to an extent, but not fully. Our language must be alive, delivered in the moment, and while we may follow a structure, we must build the habit of expressing ourselves as we want to be heard. Some of these are obvious, we can often naturally pitch the complexity of our language to the room without too much conscious effort, but unconscious habits can still creep in. Phrases like 'you guys' can be a habit but can alienate a room of mixed gender.

Other language indicates our lack of confidence or a lack of awareness of the emotional power of words for those who receive them. For example, opening a training session with 'I hope you'll enjoy this course…' and 'I'll try to explain…'.

Compare those phrases to the more positive, driven alternatives, like 'On this course we'll enjoy exploring' or 'Together we're going to look at' and 'We'll explore' or 'My aim today is for us to unravel the complexity of…'. Be clear in your intention and the message you want those you are with to take away. After all, Arnold Schwarzenegger didn't say 'I'll try to be back', in *Jaws* no one was told they needed to 'try and get a bigger boat', and in *Field of Dreams* it wasn't 'If you build it they might come…'.

And above all, remember Yoda: 'Try not! Do or do not. There is no try.'

Intention is also important in the words we choose to join sentences. The different tone created by swapping every 'but' for 'and' is well known among motivational speakers. Compare the different tones: 'We need to do this, but it will be tough' or 'We need to do this, and it will be tough.'

We also cannot assume that the words we use mean the same things to all people, and emotions described by words aren't always analogous. Cassie Werber (2019) reported that in some languages 'anxiety' is closely linked to 'fear' whereas in other parts of the world 'anxiety' is closer to 'regret' or 'grief'. Meanwhile, being angry can mean anything from being envious to being hateful depending on which part of the world you come from. That is to say, if we describe a person as angry, someone's understanding of what is meant by that emotion might vary depending on where they are. Knowing your audience, their context and their background is clearly important.

Listen too to the language we receive from others in the room and what it tells us. What clues can we pick up about someone's state of mind and their response to the learning? And don't forget that language is unspoken as well as spoken. This is beyond body language and includes the language of silence, the quiet that you should resist the temptation to fill.

How will you use language to connect with your audience?

GUY GUMBRELL, ORGANIZATION DEVELOPMENT PROFESSIONAL, UK

Guy tells us how learning to communicate better with his son transfers to communicating better with others too

I am sure there is a hobby, sport or leisure activity in my experience somewhere that informs how I show up in the work environment, but what keeps coming back into my mind when I scan my life is the experience of being a parent. Many would say that parenting is a non-work activity on steroids, even though it doesn't always feel legitimate to associate it with leisure!

Our first son, Dominic, was born with Down's syndrome and autism. As he grew up and we grew to know him better, we realized that his autism was the greater challenge for all three of us. While Dominic has severe learning difficulties and a 'ceiling' to what he might be able to do in the 'conventional' world, he is significantly slowed down in his progress towards that ceiling by his struggle to process language and communicate.

Over the years he has learned to read, count and use a computer but it is still quite rare for him to vocalize what he wants or how he feels. Equally, it has been a slow journey for us, his parents, to learn how to be understood by Dominic. For instance, we have learned that the reply 'yes' to our question may in fact be a 'no' (or something more nuanced in between 'yes' and 'no'). Sometimes, 'yes' can even mean 'I don't know what the heck you are saying and I just want you to go away and leave me with the more interesting thing I'm focusing on at the moment'!

We have learned to gauge what Dominic might want by offering limited choice (say, between two options) to start communication, even if his final choice ends up somewhere different.

We have learned to allow long silence for his reply – and to not fill his silence with our mind-reading.

We have learned to give massive praise when he initiates communication (even if it hasn't always been on a topic we want to talk about).

How is this relevant to having great communication at work? Communication is a skill that involves more than the efficient production of sounds. It's about empathy, trust and silence as well as speech.

From my learning journey with Dominic I offer a few questions that have helped me reflect in the work environment on whether I'm enabling people to speak their truth to me:

- Might people be saying 'yes' to my question because it's an easier option than having a more 'difficult' conversation, and if that's true then why might that be so? How do I encourage each different person to speak their mind?
- Am I asking a question in an appropriate place, at the best time and at the right pace for the person I'm speaking to?
- When we speak about enabling and embracing diversity in the workplace, what are we doing as leaders to show that we include non-visible differences (such as dyslexia and other communication challenges) in this?

Thinking about your audience and understanding (about them)

To begin this it's important to think of what is meant by 'understand'. We can play here with semantics and imagine ourselves standing in service of our audience, or take a legal definition and take understanding to be about knowing, having knowledge and being in agreement with. We can also choose for these purposes one of the etymological roots of understanding to be from standing among, within and between others. All of these apply.

Why must we understand our audience? There's a saying for aspiring authors that they should write the book they want to read, and while this may be a good jumping-off point and create the psychological foundation for completing the hard work of writing a novel, it will not be one that will have impact or success unless it is a book others want to read too.

Returning to Jason Isaacs' interview (Isaacs, 2019). He was challenged on why he worked on *Hotel Mumbai* given it required a significant sacrifice of family time when the director, Anthony Maras, had only previously made a short film and this was his first full-length direction. Isaacs used the phrase 'it beggars belief' to demonstrate his admiration for the film Maras delivered, and explains how he researched the short film Maras was involved in and having done so 'had no idea if he had the skills to take on a [full-length] feature like this'. However, taking a risk is sometimes necessary: 'sometimes you have to roll the dice'.

Maras, in an interview by Paraag Shukla (2019), covers the need to be as authentic as possible in the portrayal of the real-life events. His motivations were twofold: first, to 'not make a fool of himself', and second, out of respect for the 1470 survivors, some of whom he had scheduled interviews with. He goes on to say in the same interview that 'you only get a sense of the matters of the heart when you speak to people'.

So how does this relate to understanding and knowing your audience?

Hotel Mumbai takes a terrifying, real-world event most will thankfully never experience and distils it to the human themes that underpin such events. It is powerful because although most people will never live through the moments depicted, Maras creates an immersive experience that enables those watching to feel the brutality and horror through the eyes of the characters.

So when we talk of understanding your audience, we mean many different things need to be taken into account: who and where they are, their thoughts and motivations and what they are looking for. We can't possibly know these things about everyone in our audience, but we *can* meet them where they need to be met. Reflect on Maras's approach to *Hotel Mumbai* and how certain human characteristics are constant in us all: curiosity, compassion, worry, seeking connection... if we can appeal to these, we will meet our audience on levels beyond the transactional giving and receiving of information.

Phoebe Waller-Bridge in the introduction to her 2017 reprint of the original script for the award-winning TV programme *Fleabag* shares insights on her approach to her audience. She confesses to being obsessed with audiences and how to engage with them, how to win them over, how to understand their reactions to given situations and characters. This drive and (in her words) 'obsessive' behaviour has led her to experiment to become a better writer and actor. Her motivation was to find 'new ways to put the audience at the centre of the experience'. Further, in the introduction she shares a range of what she calls 'big questions' about audience reaction and, more importantly for her, their emotional engagement with characters and situations. She is very aware of the audience's worlds and where they interact with her, and in the case of the TV version of *Fleabag* she shares how she deliberately set about connecting with the audience, regardless of where they were accessing the programme.

In closing her introduction, Waller-Bridge shares the secret of success in her world. It is the relationship with the audience; for her it is the ability to make the audience laugh. This for her is 'nailing it'. She can only achieve this through knowing and understanding her audience.

Further, no TV programme or film is released in its first version. There are read-throughs, pilots, test screenings, all of which may lead to changes big and small to achieve the aim. There is a clear intention, an ability to be open to experimentation and being driven to achieve the goals. Something echoed in the work of Waller-Bridge, Isaacs and Maras (and this book!).

We must be aware of our perception of the audience and understand this. What biases, preconceptions, judgements are we bringing to the work and how can we consciously mitigate (or even use) these in our work? We must be honest with ourselves and challenge ourselves to be mindful of how our thoughts about the audience will impact our work. Make a list of what you think you know about your audience. Ask what evidence you have for that, then seek evidence to populate the gaps.

CONSIDER THIS

The continuum of design in knowing your audience – are we designing for all, for the majority, for many or for one? Or do we design for one and create prompts for contextualization and transfer for all.

NIGEL HAYDEN, SCREEN PRINTER, UK

Nigel explains how for him his hobby of fishing has given him a different perspective on coaching new employees

I go fishing. Anyone who knew me as a 10-year-old will not quite believe you if they said fast forward 20 years and I will happily sit for hours just waiting for something to happen. I am a screen printer, working in a hot factory, close to hot air dryers. It gets intense and with the precision needed for our clients, the job can get stressful.

Fishing is my release. When the job gets heavy I imagine pitching up at a peg and seeing what the day has in store. It has taught me to chill out. Again if you ask anyone who knew me at 20 whether I could chill out by sitting next to a lake on a windy, rainy day, they would ask if they were talking about the same Nigel.

I coach new people – the industry turnover rates are high, pay is low. It can get repetitive. One view would be, 'Well, they are not going to stay long, what is the point?' But the point is, it is important... You could argue what is the point of any out-of-work activity, especially fishing – doing the same thing without knowing what the result will be, what is the point?

But there is always a point. Better to say 'ah well' than 'what if'.

Thinking about your audience and originality

Peter Howitt, director of the film *Sliding Doors*, had the idea when he walked into a busy road, almost got run over and thought 'what if?'. The premise of *Sliding Doors* was hailed as original by a number of critics (a couple of critics also thought the film became 'a little smug in its originality'). The film follows the parallel paths of a woman, Helen, played by Gwyneth Paltrow, catching or missing an underground train.

Original can have a couple of meanings – either 'being the first' or 'being unique'. In the case of *Sliding Doors*, it was both. However, being first is not always the same as being unique. Depending on your bias you may be expecting this section to be full of brand-new things shared here or uniquely created materials. Let us pose a question though: is it important to have an original idea? There is a much-used phrase in L&D, 'steal with pride', when someone sees another practitioner doing something good and then uses it in their own practice: an activity, an exercise, a story, a presenting style, a PowerPoint animation, a video, etc. Ideally, the L&D practitioner will transfer the activity into the new context; however, sometimes the trainer might just lift that great activity and drop it into their content with no context and no link back to the learner's reality, no debrief, and if learning lands then that's a bonus! 'Icebreakers' can be a classic example of this and something many of us are guilty of. Many will have seen a good icebreaker activity and copied it with no relevance to the learners' world or the content to be covered.

Haley Mlotek (2018), who interviewed Howitt on the 20th anniversary of *Sliding Doors'* release, observed, 'The film trusts the audience completely to understand this [film] is wish fulfilment in its purest form', the wish fulfilment being that opportunity to explore and 'check in with all our parallel selves, to see those near-misses and almost-was and what ifs'. Mlotek calls it 'movie magic'. This is something worth exploring within a learning context, near-misses and what ifs, not just for self-development opportunities but for wider organizational learning too. Imagine facilitating a group of senior leaders through a series of 'what ifs' and 'almost was' instead of four box models and long-established generic theory, and the different benefits the learning might have as a consequence.

We may not have the luxury of being able to combine both a first and a unique in what we do every time, but it is worth considering both these elements.

We advocate the use of pictures in slide decks. The visual connection with the topic or point is a great way to engage, asking the question of our audience, 'Why have I chosen this image for this topic?' It gets some great responses.

David has an example here.

> There is a picture that I have used a number of times to introduce the topic of evaluation. It is four drummers in uniform aligned. I chose it because learning evaluation needs to be aligned to a number of organizational things, in tune with measures and the learner's workplace. On asking the question 'why this image?' before any context is given, usually a few people in the group get the link with the image and the context I am introducing. However, at one event, a learner commented on the white gloves the drummers were wearing. She said we need to be respectful of the information we are collecting, it is precious. This was both a unique and a first interpretation of the image to the context, and one that was not only relevant but showed the power of the knowledge in the group.

If we want people to engage with our message, to be inspired to do something different back in their world as a result of that engagement, then we can benefit from being original. Something that is a first, something that is unique, something that is different is something that is memorable.

This is not just about originality for ourselves. The message and how we deliver it can also strip people of their identity, authenticity and originality if we are not careful. Have you ever sat on a delayed train and heard a bland corporate 'we apologize for the inconvenience' announcement? That announcer has been trained to say that. It's the result of a corporate training event or guidelines or manual – you can almost imagine it: 'Now, repeat, after me…' It is not very original, it is not very authentic and many times it goes against the grain of a train company recruitment material and organization values. If you are advertising your company as dynamic and looking for individuals with 'get up and go', why would you not harness that and work out a better way to convey the message? Why would you want to clone people's responses?

Just imagine the real-world life of the delayed train and how many people are on it and how many are relying on (and have others relying on them) being places at particular times.

In the film *Atonement*, directed by Joe Wright, there is a powerful scene on Dunkirk beach. The scene is approximately five minutes long. It captures the drama of what was happening in the French seaside town as the mainly British, allied and Commonwealth troops were stranded against the advancing Nazi army. What is powerful about this scene is that it captures the many strands and facets of what was happening and plays them all out in real time, captured in a single take: this is life. Many simultaneous events and dramas unfold at once, of which we see only a small fraction at any moment.

In a blog posting, Farah Cheded (2017) comments that while the evacuation was not itself in the film, that didn't matter, it was the effect on the individuals at that moment in time that was important, and that was shown. Imagine using this approach to work your way through the impact of a delayed train with maybe a thousand people on it. Would you still advocate 'apologies for the inconvenience' or would you advocate something more original, something that actually reflects the impact of the delay? If we could incorporate that sliding doors effect in our sessions, what would people gain?

Thinking about your audience and storytelling

'Are you sitting comfortably… then I'll begin…'. The opening words of a programme that started on BBC radio in January 1950 aimed at telling stories and nursery rhymes to children. However, stories are not just for children; stories are for everyone and produce a constant source of material for facilitators.

But does a story have to be true to be shared in a learning event? Mark Twain is alleged to have said, 'I have lived through some terrible things in my life, some of which actually happened.' This is echoed in the circumstances of *A Million Little Pieces* written by James Frey. Michelle Pauli in the *Guardian* (2006) shared how it was first marketed as a memoir of Frey's alcohol and drug addiction and recovery attempts. Later it was marketed as a 'semi-fictional novel'. The change in marketing tactics was due to a challenge of 'literary forgery', a claim that not *all* the events as Frey tells them happened. Nonetheless it is a powerful story and offers insight into Frey's world (and mind). There are links we can make and decisions we can act upon, or not.

The Psychologist (2016) offers insights into why humans of all ages and cultures engage with stories. They comment on the role of the hero in stories and say, 'A well-constructed hero should therefore allow us to travel the world in their shoes and learn important life lessons as a result.'

Before you get the impression that we are advocating 'let's just fill events up with stories', there needs to be a reason for the stories. And an acknowledgement of the degree of their truth and origin. Audiences need to know that you are following a set of 'rules' when engaging in stories. Cyriaque Lamar (2012) reports that Pixar have rules for their stories, including something that all of us communicating a message need to keep at the forefront of our mind: 'you gotta keep in mind what's interesting to you as an audience, not what's fun to do as a writer. They can be very different'. So while we as designers and facilitators may love a particular story within learning, we need to consider the relevance for the audience and ensure the stories are relevant to the point being made.

There are two stories that have come up a lot in different management and leadership courses that we have been a part of and handed down to others:

The first is the conversation between the US president John F Kennedy and a cleaner at NASA in the 1960s.

'What do you do here?' asks Kennedy.

'Mr President, I help put a man on the moon' comes the reply.

This story is told when talking about setting a clear, compelling vision that all can buy into.

The second is set in the 1950s and 1960s when NASA spent millions of dollars in the attempt to design a pen that would work in space (apparently pens cannot work in zero gravity!).

The Russians (who were competing for dominance in the 'space race') took a pencil.

This story is told when thinking about what is good enough: minimal viable products.

Now both could be accused of being urban myths, i.e. possibly not true. But they are just snippets – telling the stories in this succinct way doesn't give the whole picture, doesn't give the context for telling the story. So while another rule of Pixar is to ask, 'What is the essence of your story? [what's the] Most economical telling of it?', they argue that if you know this, then you can build the narrative out from there.

When telling the second story, mostly the audience would comment, 'Wow, why didn't the Americans do that?' or 'That is so simple'. A few would get the message's purpose, from the perspective intended: 'Do we need to do this, or can we do something different, cheaper?' A few would go off tangent for the purpose of telling the story. For instance, David once found himself in a bit of an unwieldy debate about 'communism versus capitalism' and was way out of his depth!

And then one delegate asked, 'Ah, but do you know *why* the Americans needed a pen and not a pencil?' It was at that point that David realized that not once in hearing or telling the story had he thought to do two things: 1, ask why the Americans needed a pen not a pencil, and 2, was the story even true?

Ciara Curtin (2007) offers some insight into why the pen/pencil situation happened. They argue the pencils themselves were incredibly expensive and the desire to find a cheaper (and more reliable) alternative drove the search for a pen. The Fisher Pen Company had designed a pen that could be used and sold them to NASA for more than $125 per item cheaper than the pencils, so the 'NASA spending millions on a pen', they argue, has indeed become an urban myth.

Andrew Clover, author of *Dad Rules* (2008), has a clear structure for the live performance of his stories. He begins with an introduction, 'This story will start with...' and signposts his story's ending with '... and will end with...'. He lays out the boundaries of the story, his equivalent of 'by the end of this session we will cover...'.

Which links with another Pixar rule: 'Why must you tell THIS story? What's the belief burning within you that your story feeds off of? That's the heart of it.' We need to ask ourselves whether the stories we tell actually align to the narrative of the learning session we are facilitating. Does it add value to the audience and does it help their ability to internalize the message within the story? So for instance, immediately after telling the cleaner/Mr President story, one delegate shouted, 'I wish I could get my staff to buy into our vision.' That was great, it led to a conversation of opportunities and barriers to this and important discovery questions: how did you know they were not bought in? How would you know if they were? What stories would you share within your organization?

Despite the successes with those stories, not everyone who hears the story hears the same message. In another group, the NASA cleaner story received a response of 'Well, that cleaner was clearly brainwashed and hand-picked to meet the president...'. Another person commented, 'If I had the money NASA had in my budget I could do some amazing things.' And yet another, 'Have you not got a more local and recent example?'

Jon Westernberg, a Sydney-based entrepreneur, advocates that 'storytelling is the greatest technology that humans have ever created'. He goes on to add, 'Storytelling is the basis for almost everything in our society, and the way we interact, build, communicate, live and dream all derives from it' (Westenberg, 2017).

For us the clear message from Westenberg, Pixar and Twain, along with a whole host of films seen and reviews heard, is it doesn't matter if the story is true or not, it is the skill of the facilitator to bring the story to life, relate it to the learner's context and allow the learner to build their own narrative around it.

In the words of Pixar, when finishing a story, 'let it go, even if it's not perfect. In an ideal world you have both [perfection and finished], but move on, do better next time.'

Thinking about your audience and multiple voices

We first came across the term 'zoo radio' when reading about the former Radio 1 DJ Chris Moyles. He had a self-brand strapline, 'the saviour of Radio 1', something that certainly irked some of the main-stream press. Moyles worked his way to the breakfast show in 2004, one of the most sought-after jobs in radio, with daily peak audiences of 9 million listeners.

The term zoo radio means a number of voices informally chatting among themselves to entertain the audience. This offers the listener the chance to tune into a number of voices and hear a variety of stories. It also gives the opportunity for the presenters to 'riff' off each other rather than prepare lots of scripts to read.

Zoo radio format has a place in L&D, especially in online-based sessions where the opportunity for the audience to hear multiple voices can add value to the listeners, and potentially a variety of views and insights. It also can help with attention span. Within face-to-face, day/two-day or more sessions, a zoo format can be incredibly expensive, but there are creative ways of letting this happen. In the design process, we can identify the subject matter experts or those with greater in-depth knowledge or skills in the topic area. Once identified, we can get them to be a part of the voice of the programme.

However, zoo radio can attract fierce critics. Penny Anderson wrote a scathing article in the *Guardian* (2008) that ended with a finger point at Moyles. She had an issue with the format and called the presenters and their zoo colleagues 'man-boys' even though there were a number of women who made up the 'posse'. In fact, Moyles's predecessor on the Radio 1 breakfast show was Sara Cox, and before that Zoe Ball, both of whom used the zoo format. Anderson says, 'The idea [of zoo radio] reached the UK with Steve Wright in the Afternoon with his posse of characters.' In fact, Wright actually used the concept on his breakfast show, some 10 years almost to the day before Moyles took up the coveted role.

Anderson was not alone in her decrying of Moyles. Other critics had issues with him and his group of commentators. However, as much as the critics hated him, Moyles has a comeback phrase: 'the haters will always hate'. He was incredibly successful and achieved the status of the longest-serving breakfast show DJ and hosted the longest show on radio (at the time), more than 51.5 hours, on 16–18 March 2011, raising money for the *Comic Relief* charity.

One of the key components of the zoo format was the audience. With the advent of messaging services on mobile devices, the audience provided an instant source of material, sometimes changing the course of the programme, with threads suggested by listeners running and running (again Moyles was an advocate of this; instances included the weekly checking in of Angelo, a man who was wanting to lose weight).

This for us is important in the role of L&D, in both design and delivery. Do we know the other voices, the other players? Do we know how, when and most importantly why they would interact with the session, and are we planning for them to be included as a key part of the session? The power of 'trust the process' in zoo format, that the audience will bring things to the event, is key here. Do we in L&D trust the process that the audience will engage and bring their thinking?

Zoo format itself has a link with a process practised more than 400 years ago. Zoo radio very much links in with the concept of 'cue scripts' which has been around since at least Shakespearean times. Cue scripts is where the actor gets themselves in the zone of their character, without necessarily knowing who else is contributing to their scene in terms of their dialogue, a kind of Shakespeare meets Moyles mash-up! In much the same way that in big-ticket films of the 21st century actors are not given the full script, nor were they in the 16th and 17th centuries. Shakespeare and his contemporaries gave actors key cues and lines, entrances and exits. An example in *Hamlet* is the line uttered by Claudius, 'What says Polonius?' The original actor playing Claudius had no idea what the actor playing Polonius would say.

As with *Hamlet*, so with L&D: just as the actors playing Claudius in those first performances did not have the full picture, neither do we in L&D. We do not have the full picture of what is happening in people's lives or the full story of who they interact with, who they are or what their issues are. What are our cue scripts for our audience and is our audience a part of the 'performance'? Do we consciously think they have something to contribute? Do we consider what knowledge and skills it takes for each of our audience members to undertake their role beyond a surface level of understanding? What is it we think they are in the learning event for? Are they willing participants who want to engage in our zoo format and pick up on the cues we give them or have we already made assumptions about who they are and their motivation or lack thereof?

The success of zoo radio and cue scripting was the freedom to explore with the audience and other actors. To recognize when to contribute and when to listen. When L&D fills sessions with one voice and lots of content, what is lost in the drive for increasing organizational performance through L&D?

Your audience and next steps

In this section we have explored the links between ourselves, our work and our audience and the ways in which those working in the arts have expressed these links. While the world of the arts may look very different from that of learning, it should not be hard to focus more on the similarities than on the differences as we have pulled out here.

To know our audience is to be effective in the work we do, otherwise, to put it bluntly, what is the point? We don't have to always delight them – sometimes our role is to challenge them, or to hold up a mirror. We must know them though, and we must be able to respond to them as their needs may change in the moment. We must know how to anticipate them, to read them and to know when to be guided and for us to learn from them.

2.3

Thinking about process

Setting the scene

What is 'process' in learning? *The Apprentice, X-Factor* and other programmes that have elimination rounds have contestants who talk about what they have learned from the process. Is learning a process, and what of the processes involved in making learning straightforward to access, evaluate and gain insights from?

Jane Hart from the Centre for Learning and Performance Technologies has stressed that 'you cannot design learning' (Hart, 2018). Indeed you cannot; learning is something personal, internal and as we have discussed it will be different for different people who receive the same message.

One process many learning practitioners faced throughout 2020 was to transfer face-to-face learning to online platforms. For a great number of learning professionals and organizations an online element to all learning delivery is now a core offering.

Online delivery for learning needs to adapt and refine approaches to reach a wider audience, to embrace new ways of thinking and acquire new skills to ensure the message is spread and contextualized for the learner.

The concept of process will be very much dependent on your context, the tools and resources you have at your disposal, the demands of your stakeholders and the knowledge you have to advance your organization's performance through learning.

Thinking about your process and making assumptions

In the film *Mary Poppins Returns* there is a section set in a music hall where Mary and Jack perform a duet called 'The Cover is Not the Book'. It goes on to describe what you will find if you read between the lines, that first impressions can be wrong. Take a moment and think, how many times have your first impressions about places, people, events been wrong? We form judgements and assumptions about people instantly; the ancient part of our brain is wired to do so to keep us safe. We may or may not need that function now in the 21st century but acknowledging its existence can be a big step in avoiding the mistakes that are inevitable in making assumptions.

Learning as a profession can be guilty of making assumptions. For example, we have been at conferences where a speaker will confidently assert assumed behavioural differences in millennials without any evidence whatsoever, or at best extrapolating from unrelated data, and many in the audience will note it down and likely repeat and perpetuate the assumption.

David says: I heard someone talk about assumptions within the context of body language and how we can get it wrong. They said that when body language changes, we have a visual cue, a clue to the fact that something happened, and it's up to us to find out what that is, rather than assume. So, for instance, when someone folds their arms, do we assume they are closing down or getting defensive? Or are they getting comfy? Or are they hugging themselves to keep warm? We have a visual cue (cues can of course be verbal too); it's up to us now to establish what is their reality.

Context helps us with assumptions and to what degree we make them. We heard someone recently tell a group of learners that 'digital learning is hard and scary'. When we questioned why, we discovered that *they* found digital learning 'hard and scary'. What this person had done was project their feelings onto their audience and assumed they would feel the same. They said they wanted to show empathy, but the audience may have been well versed in digital learning and empathy not needed in this way.

We may be hardwired in learning to react in a certain way, to not test out our assumptions, but rather in fact to embrace them and use assumptions to justify a dive into 'hero' mode to 'rescue' learners. After all, they *need* us or they wouldn't be here, right? Herb Stevenson's (2015) blog for Cleveland Consulting cited the Karpman Drama Triangle, a model of social, destructive interaction, as one of his key tools of working with business leaders. He paints a picture of 'rescuers' that some of us may recognize in others and perhaps ourselves 'believing they have all the answers and know the right solutions'. Whenever we talk about 'you should do this…' or 'what you need to do is…' we are in danger of being in the rescuer zone.

The dangers highlighted in this Drama Triangle play out in our design and delivery methods, especially when we use generic content. This could be the result of a poor analysis and can support explanations of why some generic training can get bad press. 'The trainer was unable to understand my context' could be one example of the trainer coming in with a rescuer approach. Stevenson goes on to get his clients to ask, 'Do I give and do things freely, or do I have expectations? The minute we expect things in return from people we are being dysfunctional.'

This raises a question: do we expect lots in return from our audience? Have we shared these expectations or have we assumed they know what our expectations of them are? A 'ground rules' approach is often seen at the start of learning sessions. There is a challenge with the word 'rules' juxtaposed with 'sharing insights freely'. The process at this juncture can be done just as effectively with a 'hopes and aspirations' rather than 'do's and don'ts/ground rules' approach.

In Kirsty Sedgman's (2016) article about theatre etiquette asking who decides the rules, she paints a picture of how times have changed, from 'rowdy' audiences being a part of the play to separating opera performances from plays, thus separating audience expectations on how to behave, creating a form of segregation to modify behaviours.

We are conditioned to shout 'behind you' in pantomime, but would we shout 'no, that's Polonius' as Hamlet kills his friend's father in mistake for his own stepfather at Stratford-upon-Avon's finest theatre?

Mark Kermode (2010) produced a list of rules, a code of conduct for cinema goers. The rules set out expectations for a deep immersive solo experience at the cinema, a set of expectations that have an assumed level of behaviour, of what is thought 'normal behaviour', i.e. if you don't follow this you are outside that norm, and not in a good way!

So what are the assumptions we can make in a learning environment? Some examples might be:

- People are going to be watching you. As with acting, it is you that people have come to see, and just like with acting that's often also not really true; it is the experience you give which has been the draw.
- Can we assume that not everyone will want to be there? The motivations behind the presence of people in the room will almost certainly vary.
- Your responsibility is to focus less on how you feel and more on how you make others feel, how you include them in the experience and take them with you.
- You will not know everything. Accepting this is not giving in to imposter syndrome but an act of humility that puts us in the frame of mind to accept challenge and learning from others.
- You will know enough.

We can also consider the element of unspoken contracting here as being assumed. By taking part in the learning you are delivering, people have entered into a contract with you, implicit or otherwise, that they will give you their attention and that you in turn will give them an experience to improve their practice or develop them in some way. That contract is also giving you their trust, and you in turn are giving them the benefit of your experience, expertise and knowledge.

Can we assume more than these things? Very probably, but how do we reduce the assumptions we are making to only those we can be certain of and avoid enforcing rules? In a way the collective of this book is our approach, and having an innate sense of curiosity of finding out what and who the audience is, what their reality looks like and checking ourselves when we have assumed.

It is not easy, but the sooner we actively remember that the book is indeed not the cover, the sooner we reduce the assumptions we make.

Thinking about your process and characters

We regularly work with people on designing for L&D resources. In these sessions we could use approaches and comments about human-centred design, giving a label and a theory to the design process for L&D activities. We could use empathy mapping as a heading and give lots of detail, or even personas and structured formulaic design grids, trainer notes templates and the like.

We used to do this. But we don't now!

We encourage people to think about the concept of storyboarding. Storyboarding can be a more effective way to consider the key players in the story, in other words the characters, the key protagonists. It is a great way to get any bias moved from subconscious to conscious.

If you are portraying people as heroes or villains or anything in between, how do you know this? Who *are* the main protagonists, what part do they have in the story, what is the journey you want them to go on, what is the starting point for them, are they all at the same start point, what are their traits, what are their strengths, their allowable traits and quirks, what are their struggles, their weak spots, their vulnerability, what do they know and do already?

How do you want them to feel at the end and when is the end? What will happen after they have left your part of the story? Are you there for a sequel or are you a 'one-off', a one-time-only offer?

When talking about designing courses and storyboarding and plotting character lines, David was once accused by a delegate of 'over-egging it', making design too complex. She added, 'I just open my PowerPoint and start typing.' The problem with the approach she advocated is that it can lead us down a path of what we, the designers, know rather than what the audience knows and the knowledge, skills and behaviour they need to embrace.

Bella Rose Pope (2019) blogs advice to budding authors, especially those exploring self-publishing. She says, 'A well-developed character needs a full back story.' This leads us to ask, do you have the full back story on your audience? Pope goes on to say, 'If you can't imagine your character as a real-life person, they're not quite complex enough to be well developed.' This is true for your characters in your design, along with the situations you are placing your audience in. If they cannot see the real life of the scenarios and activities you are offering, well, at best you may get 'That was a great day – thanks', at worst, 'What a waste of time that was – they know nothing about my world, the *real world*.' Pope goes on to say, 'You have to understand what type of character you are dealing with.'

This poses another interesting dimension. In our design, are we designing for character development at different speeds and realizations and engagement at different times? Or do we expect compliant clones once we have fed them some (great?) content? We have designed data protection sessions where we had clones being able to articulate the eight principles, but could they function back in their workplace with this knowledge? Could they work out what they needed to do in their job with this knowledge? Well, some could, some not so much, and some would struggle to recall one of those eight principles.

So, thinking about any 'train the trainer' type event, what is the storyboard of this course? Is it very much to turn out clones of the current deliverer? In some ways train the trainer does not encourage character development; it can pull out a constant supply of conformist ersatz androids, 'this is how we deal with happy sheets, this is how we do domestics, this is how we do an icebreaker, this is how we deal with difficult delegates (clearly a missed opportunity to work out character development here), this is how we deal with flipcharts, this is how we deal with people who use their phones in the session, this is how we send people back to the workplace...'.

In our compliance, regulatory training, do we factor in the narrative of the users, the character development, or do we just want people to be cloned in the knowledge they must gain and mandatorily get it at a time and place we dictate?

How do we deal with the Finns of the world? By Finn I mean the former Stormtrooper in *Star Wars: The Force Awakens*. He rebels against his cloning and joins in the resistance. In *Star Wars: The Rise of Skywalker* there is a wonderful moment where a fellow former Stormtrooper says, '*You're* FN-2187!' A point where two rebels realize that they share a common bond and their beliefs are what binds them. Who are your Finns and fellow liberated Stormtroopers and are they your heroes or villains? How do you deal with or design for this: is it a conscious part of your design, or do you continue on your PowerPoint slide and type away, putting everything you know about the topic in the session?

There is a different path. You could take stock and do a deep dive and work out just who your characters are and how the organization wants them to develop and perform.

This raises the question, how do you give them the space to do this? After all, which one of us conforms when told we *must* do something? Remember the airline briefings on what to do in an emergency – leave all personal belongings and follow the crew's instructions. Andrew Gold (2015) reported on people leaving a smoked-filled, 'nose-dived' landing with hand luggage. Will your audience feel compelled to leave their luggage behind or will they ignore all the content in your wonderful PowerPoint knowledge repository and do their own thing? And if they do their own thing, is that OK or will that put your organization and your L&D function at risk?

Thinking about your process and your entrance

An entrance is how the tone for what follows is set. In everything from the theatre to film to musicians on a stage – even buildings – the opening is what brings those present 'into the room', sets the emotional tone, brings focus and attention, and ultimately fast-tracks the process of engagement with whatever it is that we would like people to experience.

The entrance in delivering learning is of course no different.

Think of conference talks you may have seen. We've seen people come on stage to loud music, clapping their hands above their heads and trying to get the audience to join in, and we've seen the opposite too, people coming in and looking at the floor, silent, waiting for the audience to fall silent too. Both are effective because the speaker confidently holds the space and ensures that everyone present is on the same level and is sharing the moment.

Of course, it isn't necessary to enter in this way, it is just as effective to walk onto the stage and greet the audience in a friendly or light-hearted manner as the majority of speakers do: the important thing is that your entrance sets the tone and is congruent with the way you would like the audience to feel.

When presenting, whether to a room of 1,000 people or a room of 1 person or on a video call, there is much people will pick up from your entrance. Think about the impression you would like to create, the tone you'd like to set, the impact you'd like to have: those you are with need to view you as the expert, but confidence doesn't have to be expressed through swagger or through high energy, both aspects perhaps harder when people's view of you might be online on a small screen. Confidence can just as effectively be expressed through calmness, or the projection of authority from friendliness, from the way you take responsibility for including everyone in the room.

We were once told by a presenter that 'it doesn't matter what you say so much as the way you say it'. They were only half joking. The most meaningful message in the world ineffectively delivered can be lost, whereas in history we see all too often the impact of messages without real substance but well delivered. We can go further and say we're not sure there is a half-way here and a message well delivered but with 'um' and 'er' dropped into pauses creates uncertainty and disrupts the flow, which in turn affects credibility, whether that's unfair or not. Actors confidently express their lines and we believe them. Even lack of confidence is confidently expressed so as to be believable.

As an example of holding an audience, remember Gene Hackman's first moment on screen as Willy Wonka in *Charlie and the Chocolate Factory*? When he first appears he limps along a red carpet, taking his time, in no hurry, and silencing the crowd who have turned out to see him. At the end of the carpet he surprises them with a forward roll. Why? Well, having put all the audience members in the same emotional space, he jars them collectively to another space and in a way that delights them and keeps them on his side – he is unpredictable, in an engaging, fun way, and then he graciously, and immediately, makes it not about himself but about the children. And from this act of enigmatic charisma he has our attention from the start.

In films, characters are introduced quickly when they first appear, and often in a handful of words and gestures we know enough to make assumptions about the rest of the characters. We will often quickly know who is the hero, who is the villain and who is the victim.

What assumptions will people make from your words and gestures when you enter, and more importantly, what assumptions do you *want* them to make?

In the past the first an audience might know of you was from books or quotes in trade publications, but that is no longer true. Now many in the audience will arrive with pre-formed opinions from your social media and from any websites you appear on (or perhaps don't appear on too). This presents both a challenge and an opportunity, in that it presents space both to reinforce expectations and to confound them.

Think about this when planning how you might start your sessions. In many training environments you will be in the room as people arrive so there will be no big entrance; however, that doesn't preclude the ability to treat the start of the session as an entrance in its own right. Should that be the case, consider how you will create the distinction between the two parts of the session: the time before the learning delivery and the time during the learning delivery.

How will you create common mental and emotional space for those present? How will you give yourself permission to be the authority in the room and how will you make it safe for others to be generous and vulnerable with each other?

The Royal Shakespeare Company will often have actors performing in the round as the audience arrives, the actors already in character around the seats and aisles. We can think of this as similar to when we are in a room waiting for learners to enter and when they come in individually. The RSC uses this dynamic to their advantage, owning the space from the outset and already beginning, through subtle cues and interactions, to take control of the environment and the attention of those there. There is much we can learn from this and how we think about how to hold a space and those in it even when we are not the centre of attention.

Thinking about your process and feedback

Toby Jones (2017) observed, 'Actors constantly think they know how they are projected; the older I get, the more I am convinced this is not the case.' This quote took David back to an incident relatively early in his career when co-delivering with a colleague, observing at the end of the session that it had gone OK, not brilliantly, the timings were out of kilter. They shared 'nice working with you today' sentiments and then had a skim through the delegate feedback sheets. These were typical 1990s' 'happy sheets' with a 'rate the trainer' scale of 0–10 on them. There were some high scores. There was one that scored David a 6 and his colleague a 1. The colleague took this personally and raged against the delegate who produced this score.

David continues: His outburst took me by surprise. I had over the couple of years doing training had a range of ratings and was happy with the concept that not everyone thinks that as a trainer you are brilliant. I got that. It appeared my colleague didn't. He was older than me, and I had not learned the range of feedback skills I have at my disposal today. I could not tell him that there may have been a number of reasons behind the delegate's score, not least the fact that his session that should have run from 9 am to the first break, scheduled at 10.30, overran by some 50 minutes. He spent far too long on some slides, there was very limited interaction, and he waited until we got to the slide that said 'BREAK' before he said, 'OK, let's have a break.'

In Act 4 we give a list of books where you can dive into the technical aspects of the learning cycle, including evaluation, where the most common form is the learner's reaction to the learning, sometimes called a 'happy sheet', a kind of customer satisfaction 'rate our trainer' feedback. This is one of those areas in which we need to ask why we need it and if so, is there a better way to meet that need?

We would rather think about what feedback mechanisms we can weave throughout learning sessions. Katie Warriner's article (nd) for headspace.com discusses the concept of 'flow' with the example, 'a musician immediately knows when they have hit a wrong note'. This is very true! However, do we know which notes to play in sessions when we are delivering or designing? And if we play a wrong note, how do we know? Warriner goes on to comment about using feedback to make any adjustments to maintain flow. We can do this in the moment in learning too.

The chat function in webinars is great for getting some detailed feedback in the moment, as are the thumbs up/down symbols. They are great for check-ins: 'Have you heard of…?' or 'Have you experienced this…?' We design space for feedback in our sessions as integral parts of the structure, so it is not a forced part of the session. Rather than questions we ask for feedback as statements. These can include asking the learners to complete a section titled 'what I have loved'. And we deliberately use the word 'love' as opposed to 'liked'.

At this point it would be easy to default to an opposite question: 'what I didn't love'. However, what can get a greater response is 'what I want more of' and 'these are the questions I still have'. Both of these can give a much richer and deeper insight to the audience's thinking and what they need.

The actress Julie Andrews (2000) commented that she 'used to have a certain dislike of the audience, not as individual people, but as a giant body who was judging me'. Is there something here for L&D to reflect on? Andrews goes on to say, 'Of course, it wasn't really them judging me. It was me judging me. Once I got past that fear, it freed me up, not just when I was performing, but in other parts of my life.' Are trainers judging delegates on the feedback they receive?

Rhonda Blair (2015), at p-e-r-f-o-r-m-a-n-c-e.org, discusses empathy and this is relevant in both giving and receiving feedback. Blair is an American Professor of Theatre as well as an actor and director. She argues that 'as teachers we need to be empathetic with our students in order to meet them "where they live". The same is true for directors working with actors'.

Feedback in learning can be complex, steeped in tradition. As a fun mind exercise, consider how other functions in organizations might work if they also had the same kind of feedback relationship as learning. Few of us will have a finance team, for example, that will say after each payment of our salaries, 'Rate me on how well I have done the job I am paid to do.'

Toby Jones adds to his argument for actors to be realistic about their feedback by adding, 'When I look at myself on the screen, which I am duty bound to do, I look at it and it never looks like it felt.' Mayo asks Jones to clarify by asking, 'Disappointingly so or encouragingly so?' Jones replies, 'I have tried to be less disappointed by it, and just accept it is an occupational hazard.' He adds, 'It is what keeps you in the game.'

This is interesting when you link with learning practitioners who are in favour of being filmed and recorded or those who say, 'I look/sound awful'. If the latter is you, this is you giving feedback on yourself, but you look and sound how the world sees you and that needs to be embraced.

IAN PEGG, CHAIR, LOCAL EDUCATION AUTHORITY, UK

Ian shares the need for facts undertaking inclusion meetings

When chairing an exclusion or admission appeal where both the school head/senior management team and parents of the child are present there are a number of transferable skills to the wider world and work environments.

Evidence-based decision making is one of the key skills involved: analysing the appeal documentation from both parties, taking into consideration the regulations and then after presentation, using active listening skills, asking probing questions to clarify any points of ambiguity. Drawing together all this information allows you to make a balanced decision. This approach can be used in all aspects of life. Ensure you have the facts before you, where there are gaps balancing the probability against the decision, and ensure that the decision-making process is transparent.

In asking questions, you have to consider the ability of those in the hearing to understand what you are asking and how they may respond. You have a professional approach from the school, yet there are instances where the parents may not have English as their first language, therefore it is important to ensure questions are clear and understood and there is an opportunity for all to answer fairly using language at the level required.

It is important that all parties feel they have had ample opportunity to present their case, that they have been listened to and that they go away feeling they have had a fair hearing.

You are constantly learning and developing these skills, which then can be used across several other professions.

Thinking about your process and inspiration

Whoopi Goldberg (nd) says, 'We're here for a reason. I believe a bit of the reason is to throw little torches out to lead people through the dark.' It is a powerful quote and one that at first glance may not appear to be relevant to L&D. However, if we look a little more deeply, we may find just how relevant it actually is.

One of the things that can be an honour from working in L&D is that people will tell you their realities and will share insights that they may not do with other functions in the organization. As we have already discussed, we must be open and curious to hearing the realities, and we may have to draw them out.

In delivering corporate training programmes it can feel uneasy when delegates share their realities and tell us things that perhaps could be challenging or undermining of other colleagues. This is where reliance on course notes is no use, as often there is no stock response. From our own experience it took a long time to realize that very often there is no stock answer. Very often people who are sharing just want to be heard, or maybe are thinking aloud, working out how the material covered in the session will be applied in their reality.

This is something we must encourage, from time to time pressing pause on the session and saying, 'Tell me more...'.

L&D have the opportunity to develop this trusted relationship, not to tell tales or name names, but to give detailed feedback to the organization, be it the sponsor of the learning event, the relevant performance owner of the topic being covered or the senior leadership team.

So, is sharing a few insights on employees' realities enough to 'throw little torches and lead people out of the dark'? No, of course it isn't, but it is a start. There is an opportunity we must take in the design phase, or even before in the analysis phase, to understand people's reality, the people who will be attending our event or accessing our resources. Throwing information at people does not get business results, nor is it inspirational.

Casting director Donna Morong (2019) states that actors have 'a serious responsibility to communicate a part of the story and to bring it to life for the audience'. In other words, to be inspiring. This is once again something we can bring into our context. Morong discusses finding inspiration in adjacent communities and through 'being quiet, contemplating art at a leisurely pace' and switching off mobile devices when doing this.

Earlier we referred to 'holiday eyes'. This is something David advocated in the MBA module on innovation he used to deliver, encouraging students to notice the world in the same way that on holiday we notice sights, sounds, smells in a different way, being more aware.

How can we in the design of materials embrace the opportunity to look at the world through 'holiday eyes'? One strategy is the 'less is more' approach, not filling learning events with lots of content but allowing space and time for exploration and reflection.

As for that real-world feedback the learners give us in L&D, we could do as George Clooney advocates. He said in 2007, 'If celebrity is a credit card, then I am using it' (Huff Post, 2008) to highlight the war in Darfur to the United Nations, national newspapers and on diplomatic missions to China and Egypt. What he did was to find his voice and use it where it could gain impact. L&D could use its own equivalent to gain impact, to help shine a torch in the dark.

Brad Bird, the director for the Pixar film *The Incredibles*, has an approach to capitalizing on inspiration. He explains (McKinsey Quarterly, 2008) that the film had a particular challenge (animation with humans in them can be particularly tricky to pull off successfully). He needed a team who could deliver on this and looked for inspiration from employees who were most frustrated at Pixar. He told the technical leads who were sceptical that the animation could be done, 'Give us the black sheep, I want artists who are frustrated. I want the ones who have another way of doing things, but no one is listening.'

Bird, Goldberg and Clooney all recognized that for their inspiration, they needed to inspire others to act. Within L&D we have to recognize that the work we do needs to inspire our audience to act, but also we need to be inspired to arrange our work in a way that is inspirational, allowing people to see the light in the torch and to be inspired to share their story, to help their world, by either guiding them in the dark or sharing the light.

Thinking about your process and impactful delivery

Before we deliver any learning we need to know what our intent is, and we need to know what feeling we want those who receive that experience to have throughout and after we have delivered. There's a phrase attributed to the actor Douglas Fairbanks, that an actor is only as good as their last performance, and the same is true of us as we deliver learning: everyone we deliver to will have their perception built off those moments with us, regardless of how great our work has been previously or how great it may be in the future.

In short, we need to make sure that every time we deliver it is impactful.

What do we even mean by this? We take it to mean a sense that something useful, something that will change the way people think or act, perhaps even something profound has happened, that the delivery has in some way been memorable for those who have received it. Many of us will have seen conference talks that have left us thinking for many hours or even days after.

This is because of an impactful performance.

Another way to think of defining an impactful experience is to look at the opposite. How often have you seen a talk or been in a learning that has left you underwhelmed or in some way has not been memorable? Where you've been talked at, rather than talked with, lectured to and not involved? Where a script has been followed or a well-worn, over-rehearsed stream has come out from a well-meaning presenter who, with all the best intentions, has focused on their own delivery, not on the response of those who will be receiving it?

It should be said, we have been guilty of all these things too. There is no criticism in stating it.

When we deliver, those who are with us deserve to see the best of us and how we give them our best needs to be intentional. Not every part of our delivery can be 'high energy', for example, and not all of it should be reflective either. Our impact comes from intentionally managing the flow.

To try to maintain a constant level of high energy would be exhausting, and it would also be counterproductive. To achieve an effective end result relies on tides of emotion and energy, not a constant, high-intensity delivery. The best music, the best scripts, the best books all have light and dark, with the lighter all the more bright for the darkness that has preceded. The impact is amplified by the contrast.

This is harder the more times you deliver the same learning. How do you keep it fresh? You'll need to think back to what inspired you about it the first time you did it. Think about what character you are playing for those present – this isn't being deceptive, but just like an actor you need your audience to see you as passionate, engaged, inspirational and expert. Even if you have told the same anecdote so many times it has lost the intensity for you, you must ensure that those who hear it feel as if it still holds the same power for you.

So how will you structure your impactful delivery? It would be a mistake to think it requires a bombastic, loud opening or ending. You could have one, of course. But they are not absolutely necessary. We can learn here from TED talks. The 18 minutes given to a speaker must be used in full. In that time the speaker must hold the attention and interest of those present, they must – however many times they have rehearsed and delivered the talk before – have an energy that brings the room with them.

The film *Children of Men* has many incredibly impactful scenes. Avoiding any spoilers, in one scene Julianne Moore is in the front of a car, Clive Owen in the back as they are driven along a rural road in a forest. They are talking and playing a game when the car is suddenly attacked by men on motorbikes and others running out of the woods.

It's a tense, affecting scene that is utterly absorbing and ultimately horrifying. When we came out of the cinema it was the scene most spoken about in the group. We were discussing how it had been so effective. The soundtrack had just been the radio in the car that played a song that lasted the whole scene, jaunty and happy at first, matching the tone in the car, then by the end as it continued in the background, barely heard, a shocking juxtaposition. The ambient noise of the car, the people, the other vehicles and weapons had all been 'real' – there was no exaggerated explosion and the director had laid a tinnitus tone over the top to further create the immersion. It had been claustrophobic too – a lot of the scene was shot from inside the car, not just making it a tight space but also creating a sense of physical proximity to the actors.

Then one of the group hit the primary reason it was so powerful: typically in a scene like this the focus jumps from a close-up on someone at the front of a car to someone at the back, switching first-person perspectives. In this film, however, the camera panned, as if you, as the observer, were in the car and just turning your head. This was what made it so immersive. It created an implicit sense of presence, of it being in real time, of involvement. More than this, there was something in the speed of the panning being consistent – it had been passive, almost omnipotent, not frantic or panicked even as the others in the car 'with us' had been frantic. This contrast ramped up the tension even further. It was also all done in a single, unedited take.

You can find a 'making of' for this scene on the internet and as with so much, we can bring learning from it into our work. Enormous amounts of energy were expended in this one important but relatively brief scene to create that immersion, i.e. the impact on the audience required from this scene dictated the effort put into it, not the proportion of the film it took up. In your work, do you put the most effort into, say, the piece of learning that you'd like to have the most impact, or do you divide effort equally across the session, however long it may be?

For the film they began with the idea of what the scene should look like, what the desired outcome and impact were, then built it from there. They didn't start with the constraints of what existed or what had been done before, they started with what the end result had to be and worked backwards on how to achieve it, bringing in aspects and learning from other filmmaking and refining them to be fit for purpose. They knew it had to look like it was taking place in a car, but they didn't start with the idea of filming *in* a car.

The behind-the-scenes footage shows an adapted body of a car with no wheels and the roof cut off and a camera on a 360-degree spinning axis fitted where the roof had been. The interior of the car is modified to allow the camera to move while still appearing to be a recognizable, standard inside of small vehicle. The whole is then mounted on what is essentially a specially made trailer and driven along the road. There is perhaps something ironic in the claustrophobia and sense of isolation the scene creates when you consider a small family car has been made into a larger, more complex mode of transport requiring several operators to run, but as a viewer it's seamless, groundbreaking and worth all the effort that went into it.

The clarity, the being explicit in what it is we are doing, is more powerful if the preparation to make things simple has been done. A magician never reveals how they create their magic and similarly we don't need to show our working-out or all the steps we've taken in order for the impact to be effective and powerful. To be fully impactful you need to be conscious of all the different threads that go into your work right from the beginning to the end, and how you're going to pull them together to achieve that aim and then commit fully to do it.

Thinking about your process and meaning

What we mean to say and what others hear can be radically different. While this is awkward enough in social situations, it can be disastrous for the effectiveness of our practice as learning professionals.

We had a conversation with a learning practitioner after an event one evening when she told us how the event had made her think differently about her work. We asked her for more on what her big takeaway was and she paused before replying, 'I spend so much of my time going through the motions, and now I want to think about each step before I take it and remember why I'm doing it.'

That sense of going through the motions is a risk for all of us who find ourselves repeating the things we do, and while it is an indication of needing to keep things fresh, it is perhaps above all an indication that we need to reconnect with the purpose and meaning behind whatever it is we are doing.

The meaning we create about our learning is so much more than just about how we help people to *do*, it's also about how we make people *feel*. The story of the Ark of the Covenant and what happens with it in *Indiana Jones and the Raiders of the Lost Ark* is famously uninfluenced by anything Jones himself does, i.e. if he didn't exist the outcome would have been exactly the same: the Nazis would have found the ark, opened it up and all died. It could be argued this is an odd way to tell a story because the protagonist achieves nothing and gains nothing, his peril is short-lived and at no point is there any real sense his life is at risk because the jeopardy is carefully contained; however, the strength is in how the film makes people feel, not in the plot or the story or even arguably the characterization.

The same is true in the learning experiences we are responsible for. How we make people feel can be the primary way in which the meaning for the learning will be found, and with that meaning comes emotional engagement and far greater effectiveness in the learning. Think of two approaches to compliance training:

The first tells people the law about data protection, describes the penalties for non-compliance and goes through a series of predictable scenarios to assess their knowledge.

The second begins with a story of the consequences of non-compliance, not for the individual but for an innocent member of the public whose data is leaked. The learner is then taken through all the steps at which the leak could have been prevented and they are required to trigger the correct action. There is no assessment and the learner is given a quick guide at the end and links to resources to support them putting this learning into practice in their role.

Not only does this latter approach create meaning, it also connects with why people go to work. With the best will in the world few people are likely to go to work in, say, a financial call centre so they can manage people's data efficiently. Many more are likely to have as their motivation a desire to help people and ensure they are treated fairly.

This ties in too with the work of Simon Sinek exploring purpose (2011) and how by connecting with someone's purpose we create meaning behind what we do, and how that purpose, that 'why' we do something, is more important than the process of what we do or how we do it.

We must not be passive in this. This applies whether acting or in the way we approach learning, either as recipients or in the way we deliver: passivity denies engagement and engagement is where we find meaning. So we must be active in our approach and our thinking and ensure that we are intentional in the way we approach our material and those we are with.

So how do we approach our learning with the intent to create meaning? We can begin by creating a theme. This doesn't even have to be expressed but it needs to be something we hold in our head that is threaded through the learning. So establish your theme. If it's compliance, is the theme to create fear of doing something wrong, or to support people in doing something right? If it is quality control, is the theme to enforce a quality manual or to ensure people understand the impact on customers of *not* following standards? You could then find which of those will create the most meaning.

This theme should be chosen only once we have understood the purpose of the learning and the purpose of those who will be receiving it. How do we link what it is people need to do differently with what it is that drives them in their work and then find the overlap and connection between the two? Because this is where the learning exists.

Once we have a theme, choose a plot. Again, this is not something that has to be expressed, but it provides a means for us to map the learning into a narrative that can be followed, and a narrative that can be followed is far easier to find meaning within. It doesn't have to be a story, but there should be a natural progression between the different elements of the learning, from scene setting to examples and exercises, and a constant reinforcement of the theme through both subtle cues and explicit experiential examples.

Don't be afraid to call out the meaning either. It can be as simple as stating what people will be able to do differently as a consequence of the learning, not in terms of their ability but in terms of their impact. Meaning is less 'you can now describe the consequences of breaching our data protection policy' and far more 'you can now ensure customers and their families are protected from identity theft'.

Above all, to create meaning make the experience personal. As psychotherapist Carl Rogers (1961) said, 'What is most personal is most universal.'

Thinking about your process and quirks

A quirk can be seen as an oddity, quite often something to be dismissed or observed with curiosity. There is merit, however, in exploring quirks further and seeing what they teach us.

The impact of the Covid pandemic hit most communities across the globe. However, one off-shoot of the pandemic was the realization that innovation happened in a number of different and unexpected places, such as broadcasting. There is an annual European event whose aim is to 'test the limits of live television broadcast technology'. This event has innovation throughout, has a global TV and online stream audience of around 200 million viewers, a massive community and fan base across the globe, and is a pioneer for diversity and inclusion in some challenging markets. And as part of this community there is a rich learning vein too.

And yet, despite all this, Tom Hawking in *The New York Times* (2014) called it a 'cultural quirk'.

What is this event?

Well, the event I am talking about here is just one of an annual cycle of events that the European Broadcasting Union (EBU) organizes. The EBU has its roots in the International Broadcasting Union founded in 1925, where governments got together to agree (or mainly disagree) on broadcasting approaches for each country (EBU, nd). In the late 1930s and early 1940s it was pretty much under the control of the Nazis. Once the Second World War ended the drive for broadcasters across Europe to cooperate was strong; however, there was fear about domination, imbalance and government censorship and control. Alongside this, television technology was improving and advancing, thus making televisions cheaper for people to buy.

As a way of working on how to drive collaboration among broadcasters, share innovation in broadcasting and also promote harmony in a post-war Europe, in 1955 the EBU director, Marcel Bezençon, created the concept of bringing broadcasters together to focus on each of these things. He needed a platform for them to showcase advances in broadcasting. There were pressing needs, the desire and drive for reliable television links for mass events like the Olympics, World and European football events. These events happened every four years, and only the European Football tournament was guaranteed to be in Europe. Bezençon needed to create something to ensure European broadcasters did not get left behind by American and Soviet advances. For his solution he chose the format of a music contest based on the annual Italian Sanremo Song Festival. And so, in May 1956, the first Eurovision Song Contest happened (Eurovision.tv, nd). Just seven broadcasters took part. Imagine the broadcast technology needed in 1956 to beam an hour and 40 minutes of television live into the seven competing countries as well as three other member broadcasters taking the live pictures.

In October 1956 the BBC in the UK created 'The Festival of British Popular Songs'. Within this they used a format of voting. Each BBC region formed a jury and they voted for their favourite song. From 1957 onwards this format was used for the Eurovision Song Contest. The BBC also created other Eurovision firsts such as broadcasting in colour (1968), beaming the contest to Asia (1972), the 'flying points' of an electronic scoreboard and mass televoting (1998). It also has the dubious honour of being the only broadcaster to delay the contest by five weeks (1977, due to a camera crew strike) and have no filmed postcards (in Eurovision terms 'postcards' are short films that introduce each country's act). The BBC also came to the aid of the RTE in Ireland by lending them cameras that could film in colour for the 1971 contest in Dublin.

The contest is not celebrated by the mass media as an innovative broadcast showcase; in fact it has been derided. The parallels with learning functions in organizations can be seen here. Often the work of learning teams is under constant scrutiny and the value is challenged. Many of the comments in the *New York Times* article are trolled out relentlessly, and often falsely. From block voting to a lack of understanding about how attempts to fix results are managed, the myths about Eurovision are strong. Questions such as why Australia is allowed to enter can also be answered by anyone with a search engine – that people prefer to maintain their prejudice is telling!

One of the community groups of the contest is ESC Insight, which produces a podcast series. On 8 May 2020, as the contest-that-never-was due to Covid drew closer, Ewan Spence, the host, opened by stating, 'Let's have some fun… and play… the cards we've been dealt.' He went on to say, 'This is not where we planned to be this week… instead we have something else… we have the chance to shape [the Eurovision events of] tomorrow today. Events all over the world have had to think on their feet… the various communities have worked together to use technology…' (Spence, 2020). Demonstrating that even in the face of adversity, there is growth and opportunity if we choose to approach it with that mindset.

In the same way we might look at social history and innovation over the past 70 years through the evolution of the telephone, we might want to consider the innovation and evolution of the contest results scoreboard over the past 70 years at Eurovision, from telephone dial-in, long pointers, electronic and then virtual scoreboards, and 'flying' numbers to show the scores. For many the highlight is the scoring, seeing the results coming in and 'they voted for that?' remarks of the commentators.

David says: I have learned so much history from following the contest, which I covered in a blog post (Hayden, 2020), including:

- the genocide of Armenians in 1915, at the end of the Ottoman Empire;
- the 1944 Russian persecution of the Crimean Tatars in what is now a disputed area of Ukraine;
- the signalling of the start of the Portuguese Carnation Revolution in 1974;
- the power of the unions in the UK in the 1970s;
- the Alta controversy of the Norwegian building of hydro-electric power stations in the late 1970s and early 1980s on indigenous Sami lands;

- the impact of the war between, and in, the states of the former Yugoslavia in the mid-1990s.

In the blog post I share which songs link to my learning and other examples. Eurovision also made me aware of tensions between musicians and singers and those 'controlling the industry'. In 1977 the Austrian entry was all about the imbalance of control musicians have and how they feel they are just puppets. However, the press trolls out a clip of the group (Schmetterlinge) every time there is a 'how funny/strange/wrong/silly/irrelevant/out of touch/crazy Eurovision is'-type show or article. For every 'what was that?'-type song (where actually the writers, performers and broadcasters are making a statement) there is a wealth of songs that conform to popular thinking, but these are not shown in the 'how funny...' articles. The irony is the quirk is not with the songs but with the reporting media and the effort made to perpetuate the mockery rather than understand the event.

In the planning to put on the 2021 contest, the EBU actively consulted with other communities to learn from the experiences of Formula 1, world tennis and golf and how they worked to put on an event during a pandemic. This 'cultural quirk' is actually role-modelling looking beyond, learning from adjacent communities, and that learning benefitting many international outside broadcasts from the news to sport that we see.

What quirks are dismissed in our organization and how can we look more deeply into why they exist and what we can learn from them?

CHRIS BALDWIN, LEARNING MANAGER, UK

Chris continues the link with Formula 1 and shares how it manifests in his approach to work

The learning I have taken from Formula 1 racing... first, the mindset – it's all about performance and everything is done to improve results. Time isn't spent on nice to haves, or things which you should maybe be involved in, it's purely about the performance of the car and the driver.

Each thing which is done may only result in a tiny improvement, and by using the measures in place, they're able to analyse what went well and what didn't to improve next time. Not to appoint blame, but to support learning.

I've since learned these can be referred to as 'marginal gains', 'black box thinking' and 'growth mindset', which create a culture of continuous feedback and high performance.

Second, there is a multitude of measures, but ultimately only one matters – race position. All other measures are in place to support this, probably topped by lap time and top speed, but all are in place to improve the race position.

Last, the feedback culture is what drives improvement – you may be slower than other drivers because you brake too early for one corner, for example, but without the data and the feedback from your team, you would never know this. Feedback doesn't question your ability as a driver, or your commitment, or your previous achievements, and it doesn't criticize you personally, it just provides more information for you to use so you can continue to improve. It's not until you know you're braking too early that you can change your behaviour and consequently improve results.

So, how is this transferred?

We all have objectives, performance measures, success criteria or key performance indicators (KPIs), so by adopting the growth mindset we can improve fractionally every lap (or iteration) and learn from our mistakes.

Measures – evidence, data, statistics – are how we know whether we're improving or having an impact on performance. With data we can see whether we're making a difference, without it we're mostly just guessing.

We also need to seek out and provide feedback. It's not always easy at first, but role-model how to behave when you receive feedback and look for the ways you can use it to improve yourself and your work. Without it, you may be blind to the things only others can see.

Thinking about your process and others'

No one will hit the ground running on their first day. Everyone will have started somewhere, had a moment when they didn't know what they were doing, looked for inspiration and help. It is a mistake to look at anyone who is incredibly accomplished at what they do and think that they have achieved it purely because they are lucky or naturally gifted or haven't worked hard. This isn't just true for us in the context of a profession, but also when we change jobs – it is often that we go from being an expert and a high achiever to being new and starting again. From a high baseline perhaps, but with much to learn, even if just about the organization we have joined.

As just one example it can be inspiring to read the stories of successful comedians who seem effortlessly confident in their delivery. All have anecdotes of rough venues, of crowds where no jokes got a laugh, where they've been heckled and booed off stage, and most seem to have tales even after their success where they have had a crisis of confidence. Many will take a show on 'test runs' before a big tour and even once it is refined and every joke tested and rewritten, they will continue to iterate.

Some will use negative feedback to drive them onwards, even turn it into a positive with an exercise in reframing. Comedian Stewart Lee, knowing his target demographic will have formed their own opinion of certain sections of the media, will use quotes from those newspapers on his posters... '[Lee's routine] is a slime pit of bitterness... a tone of smug condescension...'. Not only is doing this reflective of his humour, but he knows it may bring a new audience who might be more attracted by the derision of a particular journalist whose views they also dislike than by a host of five-star reviews from newspapers they tend to agree with.

It might seem a stretch from that 'enemy of my enemy is my friend' approach to marketing a stand-up tour to then working in L&D, but you can take it into your practice too. An environment full of any group of people with similar roles will have a common challenge. This isn't (and shouldn't be!) a person but you will find a common challenge, a common drag on impact or potential that will perhaps unify people in purpose at least as much as a broadly generic, positively expressed outcome. Demonstrating understanding of that can be unifying and build connection.

Successful comedians keep learning too from the process others go through, and through analysing their own process. If you have a comedy club near you that has an established stand-up training course, have a look to see if you recognize any of the names that have gone through it at some point in their career. The one in Brighton, UK has household names Jimmy Carr, Shappi Khorsandi, Seann Walsh and Romesh Ranganathan among many others, the latter saying he felt like he'd hit a plateau until he went to learn more.

Even the people we look up to, perhaps *especially* the people we look up to, never stop learning and developing their skills. People who do well don't 'make it' and stop, they 'make it' because they know they can always learn more, and they look to others in their field or outside to see what they can take and shape and build on.

So how can you do this? Search for how others deliver learning. Be humble and vulnerable and ask for others to watch you and provide feedback. Find an adjacent community and do a deep drive into how they present or deliver a key message, find their videos on YouTube and analyse them for what works and what doesn't. TV presenters, circus ringmasters, podcast hosts...

One fun exercise can be to look at those who have been producing video content for a long time. Social media is full of influencers with a big back catalogue of content. Watch their first video and their most recent and see the growth, the difference. See if you can note what they've done differently and assess why they've done it that way. We all start somewhere – the most important thing is to start.

Another example you can look to is the way theatre was delivered during the Covid lockdown. Not so much the big stage productions but the plays written specifically for broadcast during this time, where actors would engage and play out the scenes over video calls. What did they do to keep it engaging? How did they manage to hold the attention of the audience – many of whom were probably suffering from video call fatigue anyway – and make it enjoyable?

Michael Sheen and David Tennant performed a play, *Staged*, in 15-minute episodes in 2020 in this way. Reading their comments on the process, one theme that comes through is that they wished to send up the inherent absurdity of the situation (Cremona, 2020). This is something we've taken into our own work where appropriate – acknowledge the environment you are in, call out the dynamic, especially if it is one that is unusual for some there. There is nothing wrong with doing this.

> 'I'm not going to lie, this is unusual... I can't see any of your faces and I'm talking at the light on my webcam...'
>
> 'If you'd told 10-year-old me I'd be in a room with a dozen people while a dozen more were on a screen waving at me from all over the world, I'd have wondered what kind of space age future we were living in.'

Bringing people into that feeling with you also helps create that unification and connection. See how others do it and look how to bring that into your world.

CONSIDER THIS

When considering process, we need to begin by asking, 'How will this benefit the audience?'

We all instinctively know when something we see tries too hard to be different, where choices are made to stand out but have no discernible benefit to what we think, feel, know, at the theatre, cinema or wherever else we experience it.

Ultimately, the audience will not care too much if your delivery isn't perfect: none of this is about what is important to you, it is about what is important to *them*.

It's not enough to be interesting or do something in an interesting way, it has to be compelling for the audience in a way that is contextualized and adds greater depth and impact for them.

Thinking about your process and being explicit

The writer Aaron Gansky has a list of must-do's when it comes to managing multiple plot lines in his novels. The full list is worthy of some thought for anyone designing any learning intervention. First he talks about introducing conflict and escalating that conflict (Gansky, 2022). Reading this, many people schooled in a traditional 'train the trainer' approach may be getting a little nervy… 'Conflict – what is that all about? Learning is supposed to be FUN! A non-threatening, safe space!' Gansky goes on to add the need to make space for resolving to varying degrees the conflict and then develop relationships and finally set up the action to come. This aligns with what we mentioned earlier about creating tension.

He also advocates that narrative in a novel has to move the scene forward – if it doesn't then cut it! (Reader, we have a file with over 20,000 words that have been cut!)

What he says here resonates in design activities. Far too many training courses begin their life in development with the expert loading up a PowerPoint deck and typing bullet points with, if we are lucky, the objectives being fitted in at the end. It is creating the deck from the perspective of what the trainer needs, not what the audience needs. We need to think more like Gansky – is what we are doing moving the learner forward?

CLAIRE HAYDEN, PUBLIC SECTOR WORKER, ENGLAND

Claire demonstrates both why contextual learning is important at work and transferring learning from voluntary work

I work outdoors for a large public sector organization. We have a number of mandatory training courses we have to go on. I went on one recently, manual handling. It was all focused on office-based approaches, nothing to help me empty an overflowing litter bin in a busy high street. At the end of the course I am no clearer on how to apply the techniques from that course.

However, as a volunteer for a local parkland, we meet up once a month and work with rangers from the local authority. Through them, I have had some training that I can directly apply in my workplace.

It kinda doesn't make much sense!

This is about the level and detail of instruction we give in the learning we create. There is a scene in *Rainman* where Dustin Hoffman stops walking when he sees the sign saying 'Don't walk' – the problem is, however, he is halfway across the road when he sees the sign. In our work, is the message sent the same as the message received or is there a disconnect from us not being explicit enough?

A confession from Steve: I once received an unsolicited sales email and I read it three times. The first time out of curiosity that it had got through my work spam filter. The second time to see if I could work out what it was they were selling and how it might be relevant to me. And the third time out of amusement before sharing select paragraphs with colleagues to see if anyone else could translate it (they couldn't).

At times we might joke about business jargon. How often are we guilty of this ourselves though? In many professions there is, for whatever reason, a default to a type of language that needs mental energy to convert to plain speaking. It's as if the role we do at work needs a unique set of words and phrases to be taken seriously. Or to put it another way, 'it's akin to it being incumbent upon the employment environment we operate within to maintain a requisite quality of expression and terminology to support sufficient gravitas for effective implementation'.

Speak plainly, clearly and using as few words as possible to avoid potential misunderstanding and keep moving the learner forward. This doesn't deny learners the joy of discovery, of course; it's all in how we create the learning exercise so the impact can be all the greater. What is important in clarity and in being explicit is that we work to keep things as simple as possible so the focus is on the learning that moves us forward, not on unravelling what is needed to even get going on the learning at all.

CHRIS SCHILLER, TRAINER AND COACH, UK

Chris explains how discipline learned in climbing supports him in his work, ensuring he can cut it

One of the things I have become acutely aware of over the years is how my approach to climbing and what I have learned from it has helped me in business. There are countless lessons, such as be really sure about the competence of the person you are with, whether it be on a climb or someone you are giving work to do on your behalf. But the biggest one for me relates to self-management. For example, it's way too easy to get excited and take on routes that are just beyond your capabilities.

Being a self-employed independent trainer and coach it is also way too easy to take on lots of interesting assignments even when you know you will be overstretching yourself. The discipline I learned from climbing that I apply to work is... sometimes you've got to be as good at saying 'no' and walking away as you are at doing your job.

Thinking about yourself and jamming

Some of the best outputs can come from having little structure – by breaking out of convention and having less time to think, we free up our creativity. Don't be afraid of allowing things to develop organically and seeing where they go... you can always pull things back if you need to and some spontaneous exercises can be fun too.

This may appear to contradict some of what we've already said about planning and preparation, but even spontaneity and removal of structure require planning, finding where and when it's appropriate to include it and how to manage it so it is focused.

Those of us who would buy (and perhaps still do) the latest album on vinyl, CD or cassette on the day of release will remember how important the cover notes were. Often the lyrics would be printed, sometimes a journalist would write a long flowery piece extolling the virtues and impact a musician or band had had. In one of those ways that it's only with hindsight we realize the impact a moment has had on us, sometimes those moments come back with new relevance.

Steve shares: I recall reading the notes in an album by the band James which explained how they wrote a lot of their songs through recording their jamming sessions where they'd play literally for hours in a free-form way. Then they'd listen back and pick out the bits they felt worked best and turn them into songs.

One of the many interesting insights from the multipart Beatles documentary *The Beatles: Get Back* released in 2021 was seeing that they had a not-dissimilar approach to writing some of their greatest songs. Paul might play and sing something, not always with lyrics at that point, George might join in, John would develop it over the top while Ringo kept time. What began as just playing with a catchy riff or out of an improvization of another song could end up as a classic piece of musical heritage beloved the world over. One of the striking aspects of this was that it appears they were pulling the song from somewhere; it arrived almost half-formed. The U2 singer Bono has said something similar before, along the lines of how they don't write songs; the songs already exist, they just tune into the frequency to receive them.

None of us is Lennon and McCartney, but all of us do have access to the same infinite pool of inspiration that comes from allowing our minds to wander and find their own path. There is no question that Lennon and McCartney wrote some songs they decided weren't good enough and perhaps weren't good enough; we only see and hear what they chose to share. They also had a day one, and a day one hundred, and a day one thousand where things didn't work. They didn't stop though, they created a space and a permission and a loose structure that allowed them to see where they would end up.

The world of music is full of stories like this. Ed Sheeran has said his way of working is to make things up as he goes along without much thought of process, and if it sounds good he'll keep working on it until it's finished. If it's not exciting enough for him to keep going then he'll discard it.

We can apply this in a number of ways. For example, when we are creating learning, allow ourselves to come up with ideas that don't work, that are silly, that aren't possible. List as many different ways we can think of to have impact, to create and deliver the experience for our learners. It may be that we end up where we began and that's fine because we've validated it, but it's equally likely we'll hit on something new or a way to adapt our thinking.

In the same way we can create space and permission for our learners to freestyle their thinking. One of the many benefits of the learning environment is that it is a safe space to fail, to try things we might not want to try when 'doing the doing' because the consequences are embarrassment, failure, financial and/or reputational cost. How often do we use that safe space to encourage people to push their thinking and test the boundaries though? How often do we see learning as an environment to tightly close down the parameters of what people do to predefined objectives and ways of doing things rather than to expand their thinking and encourage individuality and their own creativity that will help them navigate any challenges they'll face?

CONSIDER THIS

We may not always be the best, most objective judge of what is good and what can be discarded. I remember hearing an anecdote about musician Nick Cave spending an evening with the Pogues singer Shane MacGowan in his home. They were talking about music and playing each other half-finished songs when Cave rummaged through screwed-up bits of paper MacGowan had discarded in a corner of the room to see what was there. From this pile he pulled out 'Rainy Night in Soho' and after playing it on MacGowan's piano insisted it was kept and recorded. It's now a classic Pogues song and a favourite for many. How much embellishment there is in the story I don't know, but there is much truth in sometimes needing others to sense-check and give an opinion on whether we have something as good as we think, or sometimes not as good as we think!

RICHARD DAVIES, DIGITAL PRODUCTION MANAGER AND JAZZ MUSICIAN, UK

Richard brings this topic further to life and tells us how playing jazz has given him guidelines he applies at work too

As well as working in publishing for more years than I am now prepared to say I'm a part-time jazz musician, writing, recording and playing with other musicians. When it comes to the improvisation a lot of people will wrongfully assume that it's all just made up as we go along. Fortunately that is far from the case: there are rules even on so-called free-form playing and some of these also inform my day-to-day way of working. I could start talking about scales, chords and music theory but here is not the place. Instead consider this:

- Listen. When soloing always listen to the other musicians and react accordingly. They're listening to you so it's only polite. It also makes for a much better experience for the audience.
- No grandstanding: playing fast and showing off for no reason other than to demonstrate technique. It's impressive at first but it soon outstays its welcome.
- It's for the greater good. Your solo is only part of a greater piece of music. Ultimately you're a cog in an excellent well-oiled machine to produce a result.
- Make it interesting. Bring something different. Don't start on the root note. Play something wrong deliberately to see if it works – you can always fall back onto safe ground if it doesn't work.
- Quote from the greats. Don't be afraid to play a lick from one of the masters. It's worked before and there's a reason why those musicians are held in high esteem.
- Do the homework. Listen to the great musical works and learn the lessons.

Your process and next steps

In this section we've explored process and thinking consciously about the way we work, how we interface and interact with others and take their reality into account when working within our context. The process by which we do this as learning professionals is the means to make something happen. The process can be rigid and fixed or it can be loosely defined with only broad parameters.

Regardless, the process is not the end product; rather the process needs to *enable* the end product and processes defined for one context can rarely deliver results in another context.

Asking ourselves how fixed we are in our processes gives us an indication of how much we want to chain ourselves to them and how much we're prepared to flex and improvise to accommodate the context, reality and process others experience and perhaps need.

Look now at your processes and ask whether any can be tested and improved, which creates friction and drag, and which improves performance for you and for others.

2.4

Thinking more deeply

Setting the scene

In the last three sections of Act 2, we have explored the different ways in which you can apply learning from the arts and other fields into practice in the context of yourself, your audience and your process. It's also important to think more deeply about all of these in other areas of your work: take a step back and look at how our framework can support you in changing how you approach everything that you do in your work.

Why would you want to do this? We believe that the deeper the view we take of our work and ourselves, the more open we are to receiving insight from elsewhere, and that by expanding our reference points beyond the constraints of the immediate work we are doing, we can approach everything with a new focus.

As a practical example we can take sport. Choose a stadium-based event – athletics, football, rugby... any of them. Now, anyone who has been to one of these events and stood in the crowd will know that many social conventions are disregarded. Not always positively, but positive expressions too. See a goal scored at a football match, especially an important one or one where there is rivalry or not much time left to add to the drama, and there is a spontaneous outpouring of emotion and joy and a breaking down of social boundaries that doesn't exist anywhere else.

The design of stadia is still based on the Roman circuses where part of the logic was to create a different world where the normal rules didn't apply, and by creating space to 'let off steam' an implicit agreement was reached with the crowd that once back on the streets the normal rules would again apply. This implicit agreement still exists today.

How much of that do we carry into our learning events? That there is a barrier created between the world of the learning room, that safe space to fail and to develop ourselves, and the 'real' world? How can we make that implicit change of behaviour go explicitly beyond the artificial environment we are making?

As we have discussed, it is important to keep challenging our assumptions as we develop our practice. Do we really need to tell everyone the learning outcomes at the start of a piece of learning? Don't just assume it's needed because it's the done thing. Take again what we see elsewhere: *Harry Potter* books don't tell you what is coming next in each chapter; by contrast *The Pilgrim's Progress*, a fantastic 17th-century piece of literature, is not diminished because each chapter starts with a summary of what is coming. The film *Midsommar* tells you the entire story in the first five minutes if you look for it. If you see it, the whole film is more horrifying because the sense of dread is amplified. If you don't see it, then it's horrifying because the unknown is shocking each time it is revealed.

Keep thinking more deeply, keep asking why decisions have been made, and keep coming back to your work and asking what you can bring back to change your own decisions and viewpoints.

Thinking more deeply about 'trainertainment'

NB: this section refers to a colloquial term and concept of trainers purely aiming to entertain their audience, with no link to context or workplace performance. It is not intended to detract from or defame the work of the Texas, US-based company Trainertainment.net, which works to provide coaching and training for those in the entertainment business.

We have seen sessions where the presenter has held the audience captive in the palm of their hand, telling a compelling, engaging story, using a range of emotions to elicit the relevant reaction. However, once the session ended, the absence of a call to action or clarity of next steps and performance impact calls into question what has been left and what has been taken away.

Have you found yourself in this scenario? If so, then you may have experienced 'trainertainment' where the focus of the presenter has wavered from delivering the learning. There are varying forms of trainertainment:

- the wannabe show person/presenter (which is ironic given many of the themes in this book!);
- the 'it's all about me, just me and only me' presenter;
- the control freak;
- the 'I am here to see you have a good time, but not necessarily learn – I want 10s on the happy sheet' presenter.

Samuel L Jackson's character in *Pulp Fiction* has a wonderful line: 'Oh, I'm sorry, did I break your concentration?' (IMDb, nd).

This quote takes us back to a few people in each of the groups above that have come across demonstrating their own unique trainertainment approach.

A challenge with the concept of this book could be that we are encouraging many of the things you see in pure trainertainers. Lots of references to acting and the skills around that profession. There is a difference between this and trainertainment, however. This book has at its heart what we can learn from an adjacent community to drive performance and engagement of employees in organizations going through learning events, and we have chosen the arts because it is packed with deep learning for us.

Where contexts are clearly different, the similarities are also stark. Theatre actors have documented examples about stopping performances as audience members' phones have rung; however, in the workplace L&D is a disruptive function – it very often takes people away from their role in the organization. Work doesn't stop for L&D.

The people in our learning sessions are busy, the people they interact with are busy too and may be dependent on them. Companies need decisions made and mobile phones make us so easily accessible, and even with the best intentions, learners can be interrupted. If we are not mindful of how to manage this then the disruption has gone full circle on itself.

There are trainers in a face-to-face setting who have had a 'phone creche', though this raises the question of treating people with trust as adult learners. Some presenters tell the audience that questions will *only* be taken at the end of the performance and to wait until the relevant slide appears if they have any.

Jesse Scinto (2014) states in *Fast Company* that not involving the audience is a mistake: 'Whenever we listen to our audience we learn.' Scinto goes on to say, 'We become… more persuasive.' She encourages her readers to 'tear down the fourth wall'.

The fourth wall is a reference to an invisible barrier between actors and their audience, an invisible wall separating the story from the real world. Advice for filmmakers and theatre producers discusses the power that breaking the fourth wall can bring, along with the challenges. Lannom (2020), writing for *StudioBinder*, offers, 'If you do it wrong, you will… pull the viewer out of the story… if you do it right, you can connect with your audience and elevate your material' and advises asking, 'How real do I want my project to be?'

This last sentence is at the heart of why trainertainment can fail so spectacularly. The story may be worth a listen, but how real is it in the context of those hearing it? In the *Guardian*, Natasha Tripney (2008) writes about the wall and says, 'It is understandable why they'd want to minimize the uncertainty that comes with audience involvement. After all, by drawing the audience into things in this way they're introducing another volatile element into the already precarious experience of performing live.'

Is Tripney articulating some of the fears of trainertainers in involving the audience? The erosion, in their eyes, of their authority on the topic?

CHARLIE WESSON, L&D CONSULTANT UK

Charlie shares her story outlining emotional intelligence and asks, 'Is it a nice to have or an essential skill?'

Emotional intelligence (EI) skills help me most as an L&D professional. Goleman (1995) splits EI into Empathy (the most natural for me), Self-awareness, Relationship management, Motivation and Self-regulation. Acquiring these skills will be a lifelong learning journey and the last three take effort and focus. Learning more about myself, my motivations, triggers and values is key to regulating my behaviour at work and home. It's also critical for relationships and as the author Robin Sharma says, 'The business of business is relationships.'

Challenging life experiences forced me to develop parts of my EI, like empathy, at a young age (not just as a caring older sibling). As a teenager with elderly (but stubborn) relatives, the difference between sympathy and empathy was not lost on me as they strove to remain independent. Volunteering once a week at a school for pupils with special educational needs taught me about the hurdles some children must go through and highlighted that not everyone is starting from the same place.

Prioritizing my wellbeing through self-awareness and self-regulation has helped me keep going through times of family illness, grief and loss. Discussing these experiences has made me feel more connected to my colleagues than any 'after-work drinks' ever would. As the saying goes, 'The most personal is the most universal.'

How does emotional intelligence help at work? To perform well and have an impact on what I do, I need to understand barriers, communicate effectively, and know the best actions to take by getting to know my colleagues and connecting with them. Meeting the learner where they are and not where I want them to be allows me to create more effective and successful learning initiatives. I can't control what people do but I can motivate them, inspire them and challenge them by controlling my actions.

Thinking more deeply about being ubiquitous

The arts are everywhere: online and in our homes, in our offices, our cars, on our phones and computers. They are as varied as they are eclectic. And we cannot agree on what is good, what we like and don't like. If you have read to this point, you will have either nodded away at some of our links to the arts or tutted very loudly and shaken your head at some references. Taste is something that is very much up for debate, a point of huge disagreement. We as authors don't always agree either and this is one of the strengths of our relationship, professionally and personally!

There is a wonderful scene in *Abigail's Party* where Beverly and Laurence argue over the print 'The Wings of Love', which ends (plot spoiler from the 1977 film) in Laurence having a fatal heart attack. 'The Wings of Love' was something of a 1970s' UK cult classic and it appeared on many people's walls. The heart attack in the play was caused by a clear difference in taste – Laurence was more Shakespeare and Van Gough and thought the print was mass produced and just cheap 'porn'. Beverly was a fan and argued vehemently in its favour. The original 'The Wings of Love' was created by artist Stephen Pearson around 1972 and inspired variations by other artists and printmakers – an online search will show some of these.

Just as the arts are everywhere, there is a strong ubiquitous sense of people's views. Pick any social media channel and you are faced with millions and millions of views, some unique, some common, and a huge number polarized. In any news show you will be inundated with people's views and examples of poor journalism: the default 'how do you feel about...' and worse, 'what does this mean to you...' questions that allow for the multiplication of views, not facts, on top of an already flooded market of views.

And yet in L&D at times we also churn out versions of our own mass-produced, dusted-down content. Sometimes with no thought to the original. How many management development and leadership programmes, for instance, churn out Maslow's Hierarchy of Needs as a pyramid without ever stopping to think, 'What did Maslow really say and do?'

As with L&D, film, music and theatre, the Covid pandemic brought about a need to change to maintain a relationship with audiences. David Peisner in *The New York Times* (2020) wrote, 'Since the concert industry shut down in mid-March, the livestream has become ubiquitous… [for example] Keith Urban played in his warehouse with his wife, Nicole Kidman, dancing in and out of the frame.'

There can be a sense that unless we have a loud voice in the conversation we might be missing out or be anonymous, the value judgement being that having a presence is important. But can we be ubiquitous… do we need to be? And can we say no, and if we do, what does that mean and what is that like?

Thinking more deeply about the ending

David writes: As a child I encountered a fair bit of bullying. I have a stigmatism in my left eye and when I am tired, well, it goes all over the place. A prime target for teenagers to signal and then single out anyone who is different. Add to this I was not particularly good at football; in a northern comprehensive school that was unthinkable (no coordination thanks to the wonky eye). So, I escaped in books. Characters became my friends; I would be on their adventures with them, side by side. And when the book ended, I always wanted to know 'what happened next?'.

I am not alone in my thirst for wanting to know what happened next. Film and book sequels are a constant source of debate. Is *Back to the Future II* any good, do we need a *Toy Story 4* (yes we did), what about *Star Wars I, II, III* (best not to linger too long on that) and is the ending to *Star Wars IX* the end? Was it better just to leave the successful original or satisfy the audience's thirst for a sequel (along with the box office bucks)? And that is just films. TV and books do this too.

In the mid to late 1970s there was a glossy American TV series, *Rich Man, Poor Man*. I loved it so much that when it ended, I bought the book (Shaw, 1969). But in the book there is a sister, Gretchen. Gretchen was not worthy of being included as a character in the TV series. Why? Irwin Shaw, the author of *Rich Man, Poor Man*, wrote a sequel (Shaw, 1977), the ending of the first book, the aftermath of the French Riviera tragedy, launching the narrative for the second, *Beggarman, Thief*.

And then the TV adaptation of the sequel. How would they work with the changes from book one that impacted on book two? But again, I had a shock. This time the script writer removed Rudy from the story. Arguably *the* central character, removed in this adaptation. Why?

Now pause: think about how learning sessions often end and the way we announce the closing section. We may give a recap of what we intended to cover, sometimes we may even get a round of applause! But how do we and our audience then exit the session? Some will be rushing to grab their phones, some rushing to meet another deadline (another meeting or in a face-to-face world running for the train or to catch up with a colleague), some might linger, wanting to discuss the topic further and go over key points.

Of course, we have done the end-of-session happy sheet, or if online, after the goodbyes, the screen has a handy link to a survey. Is this part of the exit, the looking at the numbers and that ego-satisfying 'was the trainer any good?'?

But what have the delegates left with? And does this link with the airbrushing of Gretchen and Rudy?

First, the removal of huge chunks of narrative to fit a schedule, a neat time slot for prime-time viewing. In learning we have a specific time slot. Second, the reimagining of the original story and the way one ending can be a new beginning to continue the narrative. In learning, we have an opportunity to help our audience explore their role in multi-dimensional complex organization concepts.

Third, the concept of the series, run over a number of episodes, each episode having its own cliff-hanger ending. (In fact, the cliff-hanger to grip the audience is so commonplace it even appears before advert breaks on programmes that show people building their dream house... 'will they run out of budget... can they weather the storm... and then Covid hit, the site was closed, will this ever finish?' It is formulaic to hook the viewer.)

Where film, TV and books may have clearly defined endings at times, some have very ambiguous ones. *The Italian Job* is one such example – did they or didn't they get the gold off the overhanging bus? Or what happened when the bus stopped in *The Graduate*? In the book *The French Lieutenant's Woman*, John Fowles gives the reader three ambiguous endings. In learning sessions, does the ending launch into a 'what will you do next?' handover?

The end of the course, event, programme, session, whatever your word of choice is, is not the end of the learning, ever. The learners have exited the session but this is just the beginning. Actively seeking what happened next is a core component of Brinkerhoff's Success Case Study methodology (Brinkerhoff, 2003).

HANNAH PELL, LEARNING SOLUTIONS EXECUTIVE, UK

Hannah tells how baking transfers to workplace organization and time management

Baking is something I've been interested in since I was a child clinging to my nan's knees and dipping my fingers into everything I could reach. Back then I was only in it for the perks of licking the spoon, but as I got older I was fascinated by the alchemy of it. The thrill of transforming the unassuming raw ingredients into the glorious 'gold' that is cake.

It's the first memory I have of learning, aside from being in school, and it lends itself to developing a plethora of skills I've needed in B2B learning solutions. The ingredients are my stakeholders, the method is our process, the cake is the learning intervention being created as the final product and I'm the baker bringing it all together.

Just like in the workplace, you need patience and trust in baking. Do not open that oven early. Trust the ingredients are doing what they're meant to and check in when it's appropriate.

Time management and preparation are also key. Did you prep the ingredients in advance so everything is at the same temperature before starting? Have you allowed enough time for each stage of the method? If not, then rash decisions like turning up the heat to bake it faster, or not allowing sufficient cooling time, will result in the cake being a burnt, collapsed mess that people won't enjoy.

Lastly, I've continuously learned from my mistakes to improve the final product. Why did this cake not turn out right and what can I do to avoid that outcome next time?

I have applied all these talents to my work at the CIPD. So next time you reach for the mixing bowl you might just be enhancing your organization skills, and remember to celebrate your accomplishments with a well-deserved slice of cake.

Thinking more deeply about emotion

We can be prone to assigning value to emotions. We can think of them as good/bad/positive/negative when objectivity requires us to acknowledge the emotion for what it is, feel into it, question that subjective value we've given it, and accept it.

When characters are created in fiction there is an understanding that in order to have depth you must acknowledge all aspects of a person, but in that acknowledgement there is no sense that a destructive emotion is necessarily 'bad' in the conventional sense. This is perhaps why biographies can be so fascinating: they give us a sense of a 'whole person' where previously we may often only have been aware of the facets they chose to reveal (or we chose to see).

It's the same with emotion in presenting. Our nervousness comes from our desire to do well, from our worry of not doing well, of being exposed, of being mocked or considered a fraud. It isn't negative or bad; our nervousness is a reflection of the things we value.

It's important to recognize this, how the way we feel about something isn't created in a vacuum but is instead a consequence of the experiences we have had in the past, the values we have in the present, and our aspirations and fears for the future. It's also important we see them in the context of others and how we create emotion in them.

We can be conscious about this when presenting. We can think about what the emotional response is that we want to receive and about how we generate it. There are basic innate human responses to situations – happiness, anger, fear, desire, curiosity and so on... how can we be intentional about creating these?

Much of what we have already explored will support this idea of creating an emotional response while managing our own. Throughout we have looked at where the arts can provide us with inspiration for connecting more deeply with those we engage with, whether working in a formal learning environment or an informal setting. One of the most impressive things for me is how actors in the theatre can repeat performances over and over again, sometimes more than once a day, and maintain that sense of newness and impact. Michael Chekhov developed a 'psycho-physical' approach to acting which helps with this, in which the character is kept distinct from the actor, with the actor creating and experiencing an 'inner event' which is then seen by the audience as it is expressed (Michael Chekhov Acting Studio, nd). What inner events can we call on to keep our stories fresh if we have told them many times?

Emotion is so important because it creates engagement with learning. It creates connection, and it is human and therefore authentic and recognizable. In the early days of corporate training it was a running joke how every course could be passed because the questions were so binary and easy. You didn't need to do the training course to know, for example, that if you see a colleague stealing money from the till you should report it.

Life is messy, it is emotionally laden and the difficult decisions we make are often difficult because they require resolving emotional conflict. Our learning should reflect this; the way we deliver our learning should recognize that there is a challenge and so mental and emotional energy is consumed. We should also acknowledge this in others and the impact emotional expression has on us and give ourselves time to recover.

Steve writes: Some great practical learning I have experienced included role play of a challenging conversation. It was so good because it called on emotions and generated an emotional response.

Role play is not always appropriate in learning, I believe it has its place, however. This particular conversation was as a manager working with an underperforming team member. Each person only knew their part of the story. I was a manager who had a team complaining about an individual not pulling their weight. Someone else played the part of someone who was struggling with work because their partner had recently been diagnosed with a serious illness but, crucially, they were not yet ready to tell anyone.

It was an emotive, powerful and affecting learning experience. Even though we'd been set up for it and a safe space was created for the conversation and we knew this topic would come up as an example (as L&D professionals we have an ethical and social duty of care), it was still tough.

After the role play we were brought back into the room, 12 of us who had gone through the same session in six pairs. The trainer had rearranged the room into a horseshoe shape of seats with herself in the middle, immediately changing the tone from one where we'd sat at tables before the exercise, clearly a space for attention in a learning environment, into a space for talk, openness and thoughtfulness.

As we sat down she invited us to check in, to say how we were feeling if we wanted to, 'an invitation to talk, not an obligation to talk'. At first there was silence, then one by one we all opened up, not about what we'd learned from a process point of view or from how we'd kept to script and reached a positive outcome, but instead about what we'd felt. Those of us in the manager role spoke of how we'd navigated successfully or otherwise the resistance to talk we'd come up against, the frustration perhaps, and the efforts to make a human connection, to reach emotionally into ourselves to connect with the other person.

Those playing the part of the underperforming colleague played back how they'd felt, not about the story but about the responses they'd had, how they'd been made to feel by those in the manager role.

After this checking-in we had a break and then started the next part of the learning with a deeper understanding of ourselves and those we were sharing the session with.

We have a responsibility as learning professionals to both inspire and connect with emotion and to acknowledge its impact on people including ourselves, creating a space for people to opt in and opt out if they wish, to feel safe and empowered.

How will you do this?

AARON HEARNE, COMMUNITY AND OPERATIONS MANAGER, UK

Aaron tells us how he transferred his experience in setting up a charity and making emotional connections into volunteer management

I am going to share my experience as a volunteer and how that has positively shaped the way I approach my job and career. For context, my story begins with my relationship with my brother, the most caring, intelligent and witty person I have ever known. Liam was not just my brother, he was my best friend. In 2012 I tragically found my brother, who committed suicide at the age of 14.

As with any loss of a loved one, it directly impacted my life and those around me. In his honour, I began The Liam Charity, a fundraising awareness group, supporting the NSPCC's Childline service. Over the past 10 years I have been privileged to participate in many campaigns, highlighting the importance of their work as well as creating new memories of Liam through fundraising activity which has raised more than £280,000.

During this journey I decided to leave my job as an accountant to pursue a career in volunteer management. The key thing I learned from this experience, which I have taken into my job, is understanding someone's 'why' and how that can fundamentally make the difference in every interaction. I often say (controversially) that there is no such thing as a selfless act in volunteering or fundraising. This is because, although it is not a financial transaction, it is an emotional transaction. The sense of belonging, making a difference, positively impacting someone else's life or achieving personal goals outside the constraints of our 9 to 5s are all part of the emotional transaction, in exchange for our time. For me, I had all of these and many more, and my main 'why' was always ensuring that my brother was remembered for who he was, not how he left. My relationship manager always knew this, so every interaction with her was perfect, where others fell short of the mark. The impact we made on the lives of young people was a beautiful by-product of this 'why'.

Thinking more deeply about perception

How much do we assume about a person because of the way they move, the way they sound or what we perceive and imagine about them from the signals and cues we receive?

The Laban method of movement focuses on body, movement and expression, how in its simplest form an image can be created through movement, and also how an actor can connect with the body of their character rather than their own (Laban's Efforts in Action, nd). This supports an actor or a dancer in transmitting a feeling or emotion to an audience with the smallest and subtlest of displays.

Many of us will be well practised at reading and interpreting body language and for many of those we work with the way in which we present ourselves will be important – an open stance, the energy we use and so on. It would be a mistake, however, to imagine the reading of our body language is universally the same. There may be many reasons why those we are with may not be able to interpret or see us, and we must ensure the perceptions we create are universal through using every mechanism we have at our disposal.

Part of this will come naturally from being congruent: a high-energy physical presence and a slow-paced delivery are incongruent, will confuse those picking up all aspects of our delivery, and will create very different experiences for those responding to only one element of what we are doing.

Additionally we can explore other props we have that create perceptions, beyond sets and environments. Think of sound. A radio drama will create a fully rounded character without any visual stimulus but through story, expression, sound effects. Think about audio books and novels – the way in which our work is presented won't always be us on a platform, at the front of the room or on a video call, and while we must consider how we and our work are perceived across all those mediums, our work may also be written. If a presentation is recorded, have we thought how it will appear if it is transmitted with subtitles or will those subtitles cut off a key part of an image? Do we know how our work will sound with reading software? Are we over-reliant on a visual piece of messaging that will be lost on some of our audience?

It would perhaps be a mistake to overly choreograph our movement, but we should nonetheless be conscious of it. We could be sitting or standing, moving or static. If we're on a screen our background is important too, and we need to consider how our background might look to those with visual impairment (e.g. a blurred or cluttered background might be problematic).

With the advent of hybrid conferences and hybrid learning, the presentation style has changed too and this is something that needs to be adapted for. We both like to walk around when presenting, at the front of the room if necessary; however, if the room is set up cabaret style we might sometimes walk around the tables too.

When chairing a Q&A session it feels natural to face the person being asked questions and the audience too. Hybrid work can require a fixed camera and bringing in lecterns, which may be uncomfortably restrictive and send imposter syndrome into overdrive. A chaired Q&A can mean sitting in a row facing cameras and the audience, which feels unnatural but works for the audience.

Being conscious of the perception each of these different set-ups and environments creates is critical and should play into our work. Being behind a lectern creates a different sense as a presenter and for the audience – it immediately throws up a barrier. Subverting that by engaging the audience and perhaps making it explicit that you're *not* seeing it as a barrier can change this in positive ways.

Lastly, we must not let our perception stop us from hearing others. Whether through unconscious bias or otherwise we should never assume that our perception is a universal or even common truth shared by all, and we must be open and humble to hearing how others perceive things.

NEIL COSGROVE, CUSTOMER SERVICE DIRECTOR, ENGLAND

Neil takes lessons from creating perfect pizza into his role engaging his audience

I'm a 20-year tenured customer service leader, meaning large teams to motivate and keep engaged and a strong customer-centric approach to work.

In my spare time I've enjoyed developing my skills as a pizza chef for my family and friends. Making a great home-made pizza that leaves your diners hungry for more has many 'secrets', not only for pizza making itself; it nicely summarizes some transferable workplace lessons:

- Buy a quality oven.
    - Translated: the physical environment in which you host your staff and customers needs to be fit for purpose. Buy once, buy well. And keep it well looked after.
- Get the best ingredients. Quality over quantity. Complement flavours carefully.
    - Translated: seek high-quality people with standout characteristics or skills. Recruit with serious consideration for how they'll fit together to make one successful team.
- A home-made, fully risen base holds the whole thing together. If the base is poor, nobody says how great the toppings are.
    - Translated: the foundations of a successful (customer service) team come from doing the basics really well. Before building bespoke customer solutions (the toppings), the base has to be great to please everyone.
- If you overfill the pizza (are greedy with the toppings), your whole pizza sticks to the oven, doesn't cook and you end up with a mess.
    - Translated: don't overload your staff with tasks that leave them over-burdened and unable to serve effectively. Enable teams to deliver just one or two things (toppings) once, and well. Two perfectly served-up solutions (pizzas) will land better than one sub-par mess.
- Ask the customer how they enjoyed their pizza – what could be improved?
    - Translated: feedback helps you validate your service. Learn what works well and what needs to be refined by asking. Better still if you can get your customer self-serving (building their own pizza).

Thinking more deeply about the importance of kudos

Another adjacent community that David belongs to is a running club, and he uses the fitness app Strava – at the heart of Strava is the ability to give others kudos.

Kudos works in a similar way to liking or favouriting a post on any social media. It's effectively a quick thumbs-up to congratulate someone on what you believe was a noteworthy activity. You can see who has given you the kudos and how many thumbs-ups you have received, and you can share kudos throughout the feed that shows you the activity of those you follow. While Strava specifically encourages kudos for noteworthy activity, my experience with my small group of followers is that every activity becomes noteworthy.

Is every L&D activity noteworthy? And what do we mean by noteworthy?

As with many things we experience, the noteworthiness (or not) of an activity will be a mix of objective and subjective, of value judgements and feedback. As with David's earlier story of the stand-in, an activity can be noteworthy for everyone in entirely different ways. An experience also doesn't have to be positive to be of note, and kudos does not have to be direct.

For us in L&D the kudos we give and receive is important validation and positive feedback. It is rare to see credits for creating learning, but it is equally rare that it has been created in anything other than a team effort. For ourselves, creating a piece of learning may involve us, someone managing a contractual arrangement, someone scheduling work with internal and external teams, a design team and coding/build team, a quality team, a pilot group and so on... and that's just those directly involved. Indirectly there will be a finance team, marketing, customer insights....

Sharing kudos with all those connected is important, as is making sure it goes to the right people.

Steve shares his examples of kudos: One group I volunteer with sends 'thank you' messages each year to those who volunteer. They also send a message to the families of those volunteers thanking them for enabling that volunteering. I give a few days a year to them and it means a lot that they recognize not just my time but the time my wife and daughter *don't* have me around for and how their role in enabling and supporting me to volunteer is just as valuable as my physical contribution in person. That the group recognizes this means more than their gratitude to me personally.

What of receiving kudos? It's OK to be proud and happy and gracious. We can too often be dismissive and self-deprecating, but to do so diminishes the person giving feedback and belittles their experience and the impact. It honours them to take the positive feedback and thank them. It is subjective and again a value judgement, but I'd argue there is nothing more important in our work than having a positive impact.

One thing we may wish to consider in our work is how often kudos comes from being outside of our comfort zone, from pushing outside the familiar and breaking conventions and expectations. It is a truism of Hollywood that it is when actors take on an unexpected role that their likelihood of winning plaudits is likely to be higher – a well-built Christian Bale losing weight to be emaciated in *The Machinist*, Charlize Theron becoming a serial killer in *Monster*, Robin Williams taking on the sinister role in *One Hour Photo* and Tom Hanks almost unrecognizable in *Elvis*. We're not suggesting you reinvent yourself to get kudos, but there's strength in recognizing that challenging the norm and what people might expect from something you are doing is an act of professional courage that can bring many rewards.

To finish on giving kudos, ensure it isn't an afterthought but is central to what you are doing. It is simply the right thing to do to recognize and be grateful. It is much more powerful towards the end of a session to thank those who have contributed, whether they are in the room or not, and *then* do your closing piece. This brings the kudos into the session, adding value and impact.

For comparison, when a programme ends and the cast list gets shrunk to advertise the next programme, how much attention do you pay to those being given kudos through the credits? How many people (perhaps none without a personal or professional connection) make the effort to read the greatly reduced text? Similarly, most of us have left a cinema while the credits roll at the end of a film. Then think of tricks used to get people to stay to the end and how this makes the giving of kudos part of the film, not something bolted on at the end because it has to be. For example, *Ferris Bueller's Day Off* and the 'it's over, go home' at the end of the credits breaking the fourth wall, or how Marvel films are now well known for ending the story during the 'normal' time of the film then starting the next story and essentially trailing the next film at the end of the credits, guaranteeing audience attention.

In fact, one Marvel film ended the story, had some credits, had a scene that wrapped up one loose end from the film, had more credits, then a scene to generate excitement about the next film in the series right at the close. This creates impact with the kudos and segments different elements to add to their memorability. How does this apply to our work? An effective flow might be:

- finish the core of the learning *[the main film]*;
- thank everyone in the room (virtual or physical) and those others who have contributed *[first credits – meaningful because it isn't while everyone is packing up their things]*;
- ask for reflections/thoughts/feelings – essentially a checking-out process with people, creating space for them to talk *[additional scene]*;
- finish and invite everyone to pack up, then ask them to hold on for 30 seconds *[final credits]*;
- give the 'to take this further' resources, show where a community of practice exists, etc. – make this a downloadable/photographable/shareable/printed resource *[final scene]*.

LIOR LOCHER, ARTIST (ALSO LEARNING CONSULTANT, COACH AND AUTHOR), UK

Lior shares a story linking artistic practice and harnessing the energy from it, earning our kudos

Having an artistic practice is a form of problem-solving unlike any other I've come across. It's like going from flat black and white to 3D in colour with sound. I hadn't realized how mentally restrained I was, and now there is a lightness and a depth at the same time. It brought body and soul back into how I work and I needed that.

Art is about honouring and perfecting your craft, doing the work (whatever it is you actually do). And then showing up with it in public, sharing it with others. That is the bit you can control: the work and the showing up. Sure, you will get reactions and they will vary, and people will or will not enter into co-creating what happens next. But that's not your part of the work, that is theirs. That realization was liberating.

Art is putting spirit into matter. You take an idea and make it material. The act of creation. And then, by existing, the new changes the course of the world a little bit, like all new things do as they shake up a system. You put a pin into the world where it itches the most and then that energy can go somewhere useful.

Art is always uncharted territory. A form of research-in-action, you do something and reflect and refine, as you create your way into something that didn't exist before you started and that likely came out differently than you initially envisioned. The process is every waterfall project manager's worst nightmare. It is glorious. It also terrifies me, and I need to work through that every time. Stretching practice in more ways than one.

The way our world is going, we will need that more than ever.

Thinking more deeply about knowledge

To what degree does a trainer or facilitator or manager need to know about the topic they are encouraging their learners to embrace? It may appear a daft question at first glance, but think about it for a while from two perspectives.

First, if we are expected to be the most expert in everything to enable us to transmit that knowledge, it is doing a disservice to the role of *teaching* and becomes simply about knowledge transfer. Steve recalls a maths teacher saying to his class studying for GCSEs that there was already someone there who was more capable than she was. At the time this seemed bizarre but in hindsight the humility in that recognition is telling: she rightly perceived her role as stewardship of that ability, guiding through the principles and ensuring it was focused and continued. She didn't need to know how to do maths at a level of complexity beyond what she was required to teach, but she did need to know how to recognize and harness that ability, to facilitate and guide its development and ensure it was encouraged.

That incredibly able boy subsequently got extra tuition through the school to complete A-levels not normally offered, supported by that same teacher, and went on to get a First from Oxford. That his teacher wasn't as capable as him didn't hold him back at all.

Second, when talking about her role as Queen Anne in *The Favourite*, Olivia Colman (2018) said, 'I don't do any research – I trust the writer has done all the relevant research.' How does this apply to us in our work? How often is what we are delivering or referencing or calling upon created by someone with more expertise than us? For me it is regularly, as Newton said, standing on the shoulders of giants. This entire book is written through learning and curating from others with greater expertise and knowledge in many areas than our own. Recognizing our strengths and our role, whether as manager, trainer or facilitator, is of great importance – a manager doesn't need to be able to do everything that every member of their team does. They simply need to understand the impact of that work and the questions to ask to support and guide it.

As trainers it can be helpful to position this at the outset. It can be tempting to list our experience and credentials almost as a way of justifying our presence and giving people confidence. There is much to credit in acknowledging the expertise in the room too. 'That's me, I know there are people here whose experience and stories will give a different perspective from mine too and I'm looking forward to hearing them.'

Vulnerability is a strength when training and being able to admit to not knowing an answer is authenticity and also builds trust. As with all we do, we must do so in a way that aligns with the expectations of our audience or we create an incongruence that can damage our credibility and the impact of what we are doing.

There are ways to do this. An ad-libbing actor will never say they don't know what comes next; they'll retain character, find a way to keep that co-created relationship with the audience uninterrupted, and they'll maintain congruence. Ways we can do this while training are, for example:

- 'That isn't within my experience, how about others in the room? Can anyone share their experience?' – which is a facilitative approach.
- 'Tell me more about what has brought that question' – this won't always be appropriate but sometimes the question asked is less about knowledge and more about a behavioural piece either in the person asking the question or the scenario they are describing.
- 'That's outside my area to confidently respond to, though I have colleagues/resources/research that go into this. After this session let me pick up with them and get back to you' – this is essentially saying you don't know, but it is doing so constructively and while maintaining the congruent position of expertise that keeps the rest of the session impactful.

It is rare that anyone in the room is there to trip you up. By taking a moment to consider your response, not thinking you have to reply in less than a second (in fact, often visibly reflecting before answering is taken as a positive) and consciously answering in a way that is supportive, helpful and honest benefits everyone.

The famous saying is that knowledge is power. That's true, but it shouldn't be seen purely in the sense of knowledge acquisition. Self-knowledge, and knowledge and humility to recognize what we don't know, is perhaps the greatest power of all.

KRYSTYNA GADD, LEARNING CONSULTANT, UK

Krystyna tells us how her hobby has shown her how a preferred way of learning isn't always the most appropriate way to gain the knowledge she needs

How my weaving has impacted my work life… I have had many hobbies over the years and my preference has always been to have a go and if I get stuck, then read a book, watch a video or even go on a course.

This has not been a bad strategy in the past, but I have found with weaving, my 'gung ho' attitude has led to me coming unstuck at times. Weaving brings together many skills, including maths and a little engineering, depending on the type of loom you have. That is one of the reasons why I love it so much. My latest loom is called a magic dobby and it requires patience and some forward planning, as well as understanding the limitations of this equipment.

I love to set myself a challenge in most things that I do and my latest is to weave enough fabric to sew a garment to wear. I have learned so much:

- If I take the time to thoroughly acquaint myself with a new piece of equipment before I embark on a large project, I understand its strengths and limitations.
- Understanding fundamentals about your fabric structure can help you to overcome any equipment limitations.
- I need to learn more about the theory of weaving instead of leaping headfirst into a major project.

In my field of work, I have often pondered about preferred learning styles and this is a perfect example of how my preferred style does *not* help me perform my best. What I really should do is:

- study a little more theory;
- create small practice pieces to build up skill and knowledge;
- plan carefully on big projects;
- reflect at each stage to see where I might recognize my progress or errors.

Thinking more deeply about communication

Communication, you would think with all the practice humans have, would be easy. However, view many social media conversations and it appears the choices are purely binary.

When James McAvoy (2021) was asked about what he learned from Forest Whitaker while working on the film *The Last King of Scotland*, he said, 'I find you learn more by watching – I don't think anyone can teach you anything – but you can learn stuff... You learn through watching other people... And by respecting others you let them in... and they start to work on you without even knowing it.'

He went on to talk about Joe Wright, the director of *Atonement*, and that his skill was 'knowing how to communicate with people who do acting – it sounds rudimental – but... I often think it is difficult for directors to get up to speed with what it is we do and how we go about doing it'. McAvoy went on to talk about the difference between an actor who has worked on 50 films and a director who had maybe directed only 10 films: 'How does he know what actors do? However, Joe Wright, who been an actor, was in the theatre and worked with actors all his life, knew how to talk to actors and how to get them to do what he wanted them to do. He knew how to talk to us, how to ask what he wanted from us and he also knew how to lead us there without even knowing we were being led there... Joe is a natural on a film set and that is where he becomes his highest self.'

McAvoy's insights here offer a question for anyone delivering a learning programme or line manager developing an employee: do you know how to talk to others, others whose role you have not done? There is a skill in this. Great facilitators and coaches have those skills.

RITA ISAAC DE MATOS, L&D COORDINATOR, UK

Rita explains how she takes skills learned in a book club into her work, specifically reading about relationships and how to communicate with others

In 2018 I joined a book club with a very particular theme: polyamorous relationships and the need to learn how to better communicate in poly and ethically non-monogamous settings. I was curious and had several poly friends, so I wanted to know more about it.

This extracurricular activity became one of the best sources of content on non-violent communication, communication styles and group dynamics I could ever have tapped into. It effectively made me a better people manager and communicator. I've used some of these books as references to help people improve their communication skills when wanting to define how they come across to others, to hold performance management meetings successfully and even to coach some of my line reports into development.

Ethical non-monogamy is all about consent, respect and effective communication, so it's easy to understand how so many of the concepts on how to communicate clearly and negotiate that are valuable in polyamory contexts were so easy to transfer to work, especially when giving and receiving feedback more effectively.

The skills developed through this area of my life are at play in having me be my best at work every day, at the CIPD, when working and communicating with stakeholders and supporting people's and managers' development. I would 100 per cent recommend expanding your library to include some titles on non-monogamy and communication needs if you want to improve your communication skills, come across intentionally, give and receive feedback, and overall understand others and build better relationships.

Thinking more deeply about the script

As we have said elsewhere, nothing we have suggested so far should be taken to suggest that anything we do in learning and development is acting. This applies too to scripting: we do not suggest or believe that everything that is said should be scripted.

We do however think it is important to map out the broad sense of what it is you need and want to say, what the key touchpoints are, the rough timings and sequence of these, and this then becomes a guide.

Film-makers have their own approaches to scripting and even the biggest blockbusters will have words changed in the moment, improvised or just altered to better fit how the actor sees the character. Harrison Ford famously challenged George Lucas over his dialogue and the difference between a written script and a spoken one. Ken Loach is reputed to not reveal the full script to actors, instead doing it scene by scene. Actors won't always know what others in the scene will say, keeping a naturalistic and real response that requires a level of trust from the actors that must take enormous effort: to enter a piece of work with just a back story for your character but not knowing the storyline for the film, whether your character is a major part or a minor part, what will happen to them and so on.

Other scripts are developed collaboratively – *Breaking Bad*, for example – and comedy scripts will have multiple read throughs before being finalized.

So how do we approach the idea of scripts that aren't scripts? Of broad themes? Of remembering to cover the right topics while allowing the flexibility to respond to what is required from those we are with?

There are two common approaches. The first is the idea of the 'memory palace' where a mental journey is taken through a room. This is practised so the same sequence is always followed, allowing us to drop out and drop back in again at any given point. Some actors apply a similar technique. For a long Shakespearean monologue, for example, the lines can be rehearsed through positioning Post-it notes with the lines on throughout the actor's house. They'll be positioned somewhere that the routine is always the same – for example, the first line on their alarm clock, the second on the bathroom mirror, the third on the kettle and so on. Every day the actor memorizes the sequence and order of the lines and this is reinforced through the routine, enabling easy recall.

In a far less complex way we can apply the same principle to the way we remember the key themes we wish to hit during a day.

Visual cues can be used too, an image or an icon on a slide rather than words. This doesn't even have to be obvious to anyone but us. If we're in a physical space we can arrange cues around the room.

Facilitation will be different again. Where training and the delivery of learning will require us to often be the focus of sharing, a facilitated discussion relies on our ability to bring the focus onto others and draw from them. Scripting is definitely inappropriate for much of this – though it can be useful to have a script to set up at the outset and position boundaries – however, it can be useful again to be mindful of what themes you're looking to draw out and how you can provide cues for these to ensure the conversation is rich and meaningful and contextually appropriate for all.

So when we talk about scripting we mean less in the sense of remembering line by line what needs to be said and more being conscious and mindful about the themes and broad areas to cover, being considerate of the language we are going to use, ensuring our examples are culturally and contextually appropriate and meaningful. It's less 'this is what I'm going to say' and more 'this is how I'm going to say it and the sequence I'll be saying it in'.

MEG PEPPIN, ORGANIZATION DEVELOPMENT CONSULTANT, UK

Meg links patterns as we grow, those boundaries that appear and what that means for her approach to work

An underpinning principle of organization development (OD) is something we call 'use of self'. As Nancy Kline once said to me, 'people learn you'.

Exploring the impact of being the youngest child has been one area I have thought about as part of strengthening my capacity to utilize myself more fully. Perhaps being called 'the baby' well into my 50s might explain why sometimes I get frustrated and angry waiting for 'people (the grown-ups?) to sort things. Some of the 'they should' I notice my internal voice being indignant about (little Meg feeling unable to say her bit), well, that can make me judgemental. Echoes from early years projecting themselves onto me now.

If I'm impatient (wanting to be seen to get things done like the grown-ups), I might move on just a bit too early, lose a valuable insight. If I'm anxious to be heard ('listen to *me*), it might mean I interrupt and cut someone short. Just a little bit.

If I'm genuinely interested in others, they know that, they *feel* it and it allows them to perhaps be more open to expressing themselves. If I am able to still my own thoughts so others can fully explore their own, then they will get that insight.

Old patterns that served us as children do not necessarily serve us as adults. I am no longer 'the baby' or the youngest. More often the oldest!

I meet people where they are, not where I think they 'should' be. I'm interested in what they think and genuinely see their thoughts as valid without needing to persuade them (very often!) to mine. I was told recently by a client that the 'big thing' people got from working with me was that they felt I was really being me. That then invites them to be them. They learn from me because I have been shedding those outer layers that are made up of assumptions that aren't true.

Thank you Nancy.

Thinking more deeply and next steps

In this section we have explored thinking more deeply, about how some of the things we perhaps take for granted and just 'do' are worthy of more consideration, and how with some of what we underestimate ourselves in we can instead benefit from recognizing where others are in relation to ourselves.

To think more deeply about our work and all the elements of it is to be a true learning and development professional. If we are not thinking more deeply, how do we know where to develop? How do we know where to focus our energy and attention on learning? As we have developed this chapter, the theme of giving back and sharing has run as a thread throughout, something we didn't anticipate. Perhaps this is indicative of what thinking more deeply inspires: a humble recognition of where we learn and benefit from others, and a recognition of what we can and must give back ourselves to enable other people.

ACT 3

The thinking beyond

Setting the scene

In Act 1 we shared with you our framework, looking at the actions (*Find, Filter, Foster, Frame* and *Format*) along with the corresponding behaviours to drive those actions (*Curious, Connect, Cultivate, Compose* and *Call*).

FIGURE 3.0 A structure to format your adjacent learning story

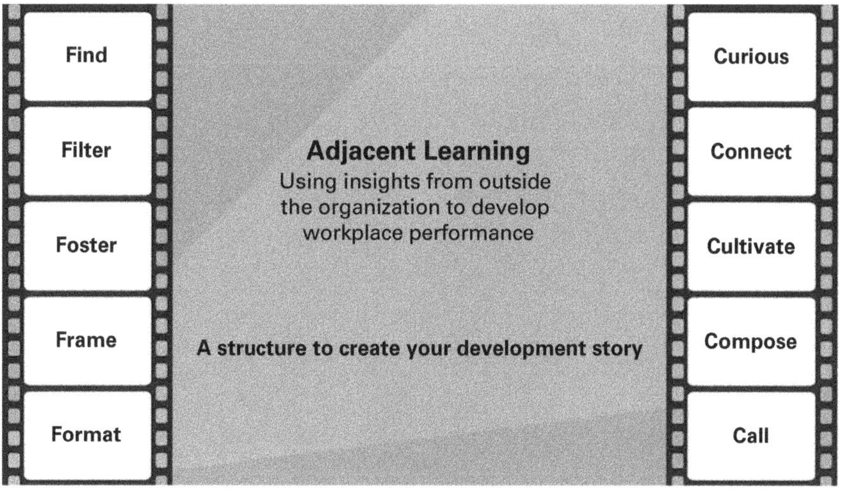

Find
Filter
Foster
Frame
Format

Adjacent Learning
Using insights from outside the organization to develop workplace performance

A structure to create your development story

Curious
Connect
Cultivate
Compose
Call

In Act 2 we shared a range of stories both from across the world of the arts and from our network. Here, we shared how the framework can be used in conjunction with a formal development plan. We introduced you to three tools for reflection (blogs, journals, critical friend). This Act will provide structure for your approach to reflection and explore how you may want to formally develop actions from outside your 'day job' into the world of work.

When pausing and deciding what action to take we consider a similar approach to that used when writing a play using the following steps. View them as threads that woven together create a storyboard template for you.

1. Create your plot.
2. Create an interesting subplot.
3. Consider the environment for the story – can it transpose? (*Romeo and Juliet* famously being presented in many different environments and periods of history.)
4. Develop the ideas and create interesting characters to inhabit them.
5. Decide the structure.
6. Decide how you want it to look.
7. Know your audience.

Here is our suggested template for those seven threads. The threads may be different lengths and have different colours, some may be thicker than others, some may come from another picture and be reused and repurposed. We have aligned them to our five areas of the framework and then created a series of questions for reflection. Using this storyboard template will allow for the construction of a reflection journal or blog entry, or it can be used when working with a critical friend.

We asked a few people in our network to share their story via the template we created. Most we sent out, but three we did conversationally.

We are sharing these here. As you can see, some stayed true to the questions we suggested and some went off piste, making their own

TABLE 3.0 The framework and blueprint for your storyboard

	Create your plot • What is your motivation? • What's the driving force behind the discoveries you are making? Create an interesting subplot • What is your connection, or why did you choose the adjacent community that you did? • Are there twists and turns that add interest or depth of understanding?
	Consider the environment for the story • What are the links between your plot and the world you inhabit? • How are these connections drawn? • Will others be able to transpose them into their context?
	Develop the ideas and create interesting characters to inhabit them • How can you build on what you have so far? • What needs to be amplified, and is there anything which benefits from reduction?
	Decide the structure • What is the rhythm, flow and colour of your output? • What is the narrative journey? • How much, if at all, is the process part of the story? Know how you want it to look • What is the format for your output? • How will it be most effectively delivered to resonate with people in the broadest number of contexts? • What needs to be added? What needs to be subtracted?
	Know your audience • Who will receive this? • How will they receive it? • How do you want them to feel/act/think differently after?

sense of their story, while others made tenuous links to the template. For us that is the beauty of the template – it can create a starting point that could lead you to some fantastic discovery.

3.1

Journal responses

Naomi Stanford

Here, Naomi Stanford, organization design professional UK and author of a range of books and blogs on organization design, shares her insight from diving into regenerative horticulture. You can follow each of the threads Naomi weaves into her story here.

TABLE 3.1A Naomi Stanford's storyboard so far

	I wonder how many organizations are looking to get novel and valuable insights into their strategies, policies and operational delivery, from the growing regenerative horticulture and agriculture movement. I'm getting curious about this as I delve more into the study of regenerative horticulture. The thrust of this movement is the conservation and rehabilitation of the soil. The report, *Soil Health: A security threat profile* (nd) tells us, 'Soil is the forgotten everything to humanity. It is the medium that feeds us, clothes us and (traditionally at least) houses us. Yet the past fifty or so years... we have disregarded the importance of soil, treating it purely as a blotting paper into which plants can place their roots.' Writer Robin Wall Kimmerer, quoted in the report, said, 'This is our work as humans in this time. To build good soil in our gardens, to build good soil culturally and socially, and to create potential for the future.' As I learn more about soil (part of a horticulture path I am pursuing as a career change), I am seeing multiple parallels and new perspectives on organizational life and learning. For example, on the parallels: • Soil is a medium for growth, thriving, productivity • Soil is rich in interdependent ecosystems • Soil health requires thoughtful nurturing, not thoughtless degradation

(continued)

TABLE 3.1A (Continued)

	Substitute 'An organization" for 'Soil' and you see the parallels. What's intriguing is that in learning about regenerative horticulture, I am seeding new approaches to my organizational work. I am asking myself the question – in what ways is my organization like soil, how can I keep it regenerating healthily and not degrading?
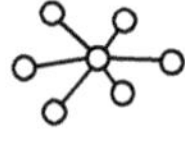	Regenerative horticulture methods eschew mechanistic approaches to growing plants that focus on improving the efficiency of one specific part of the system: yield, size, durability, growth rate, decorative merit, and so on. Treating one part of the soil ecosystem by, for example, adding nitrogen, potassium or phosphorus, results in dangerous imbalances to the trillions of microscopic organisms working together as the soil food web. The system of a farm, vegetable plot or garden, sits within and relies on interactions with the larger natural system. For example, the crops and plants need insects to pollinate, surface and groundwater to irrigate, microbes to cycle nutrients, and soil to provide a strong and fertile growth medium. Caroline Grindrod (nd), regenerative agriculture expert and founder of rootsofnature.co.uk, notes that, 'Through a rapidly emerging world of plant research from a more holistic and biology focussed lens, we can understand that many of the diseases and vulnerabilities of our modern cropping systems stem from poor plant nutrition arising from dysfunctional soil health.' What, I ask myself, are the diseases and vulnerabilities of our modern organizational systems and what do they stem from? What is the poor nutrition that feeds our organizations? In answer, what springs to mind, as an example, is the 'disease' of inequitable pay systems: Domonic Rushe shared an Institute for Policy Studies Report in the *Guardian* (2022) on 300 top US companies which found CEOs making an average of $10.6m, with the median worker getting $23,968. In May 2022 the UK's Office for National Statistics reported that across employees as a whole, pay for the top 10 per cent of earners rose by 11.1 per cent in the year to March, compared with a median of 5.5 per cent and just 0.9 per cent for the bottom 10 per cent of earners.
	Causing the loss of a functional soil food web and the resulting vulnerable and disease-prone plants and animals are practices including tillage (the preparation of soil by mechanical agitation of various types, such as digging, stirring, and overturning), leaving soil bare and exposed, use of artificial fertilizers, use of pesticides, the use of antibiotics, a low diversity of species and overgrazing caused by badly managed livestock.

(continued)

TABLE 3.1A (Continued)

It is not hard to think of loss of organizational functionality through this lens. Organizational tillage includes agitation by competing projects, changes in strategies, high employee turnover, adoption of fads of the moment, and others. Organizational soil is left bare and exposed by power plays, management inattention, wrong metrics, and other factors. Use of fertilizers, pesticides and antibiotics is paralleled in organizations by training programmes, performance management systems, and treatment of symptoms, not underlying causes. We are all familiar with the view that lack of diversity in organizations is unhealthy, and many employees are hampered in their work efforts by being badly managed, as reported by Mark Allen (2019).

As Grindrod says, the more we damage the soil food web, the more we must lean on energy-hungry and environmentally damaging artificial fertilizers, pesticides and animal medications to treat the symptoms of sick plants and livestock caused by deficient soils, resulting in the costs of production going up, and the nutrient quality of our food plummeting. So it is with organizations, though it is not the quality of our food that plummets, but our productivity, wellbeing and resilience.

To help redress the decades of soil degradation practices, regenerative agriculture and horticulture practitioners adopt principles that treat the soil as a complex series of interlocking ecosystems with elements that cannot be 'treated' independently. The questions below are some starter organizational questions that each principle triggered for me.

Minimize repetitive soil disturbance (tillage) = where and how are we disturbing things?

Keep the soil covered with organic material (to minimize erosion) = where are we exposed and vulnerable? Where/how are we eroding things e.g. trust?

Maintain a living plant in the soil all year round = where are we/are we not seeding, nurturing, encouraging people and practices?

Maximize diversity in crops, pasture plants and habitats = where are we good/less good at developing diversity of workforce members, ideas, behaviours, experiences?

Integrate livestock or wild animals = who helps us deliver our products and services who we don't include? E.g. contractors in our training courses, delivery drivers who might want to use our restaurants?

(*continued*)

TABLE 3.1A (Continued)

Think how organizations might beneficially regenerate adapting, adopting and living principles similar to those of agriculture/horticulture regeneration. But, before launching into a prescription on this, consider the point that 'Every environment across the world is unique and supports a different range of habitats and potential agricultural/horticultural options. The rich diversity of our global cultures has emerged under the particular influences of what food and fibre can be locally and sustainably produced.

Applying this to organizations suggests that the detail of what regenerates one organization's 'soil' may not be the detail that regenerates another organization's 'soil', knowing the organization you are working with is a pre-requisite, and getting in consultants to produce speedy solutions to problems may not result in healthy regeneration. (Note: I am not viewing 'regeneration' and 'transformation' as synonymous. I am highly sceptical of transformation projects).

Soil regeneration is a long-term ongoing activity usually done by rotating land use. One farmer, for example, talks of 5–7-year rotation cycles of grasses, legumes, root crops and grazing cattle. I wonder how long-term rotation could benefit organizations? What would it look like? What would form the rotation – people, processes, practices, policies... ?

Regenerative farming and horticulture can produce great food locally and at scale, while greatly accelerating carbon drawdown, regenerating biodiversity, and managing precipitation to provide greater drought resilience and better flood protection.

It seems to me that the principles and practices of soil regeneration are readily adaptable for organizational use, will bring new insights and perspectives to conventional ways of thinking about organizational life and issues, and will result in benefits of resilience, organizational and employee wellbeing and meeting ESG aspirations.

Andy Lancaster

Andy, learning professional and author UK, uses his storyboard to share his voyage in volunteering.

TABLE 3.1B Andy Lancaster's storyboard so far

	When I look back at my career, many have selflessly provided time to support my journey, through a willingness to give freely from what they had. To that end, about a decade ago I was motivated to set aside time to volunteer. My subsequent volunteering voyage has led me into unfamiliar waters such as supporting a homeless drop-in and a charity supporting young people struggling with difficult issues. Volunteering provides an amazing opportunity to engage with adjacent communities. My recent involvement has been in supporting the global fight against leprosy. Whilst an ancient disease, globally there are more than 200,000 new cases a year. Although curable, millions of people worldwide live with the effects of the disease, from physical disability to mental health problems, poverty and discrimination. My connection with this community came by chance. For years, my mother had been a supporter of a charity working with people living with leprosy to attain healing, dignity and life in all its fullness. In a passing conversation she noted they were looking to recruit trustees including one with an HR-Learning background, my specialism. It fired my curiosity. I knew nothing about leprosy but had experience in one of the trustee areas being sought. I applied and was surprised to be appointed to serve on the Board. It's been life changing.
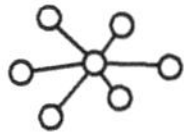	In thinking about engaging with adjacent communities, our spheres of influence can seem limited by our existing knowledge or experience. Involvement in radically different disciplines can appear out of reach. From my experience, it may be productive to take time to explore the spheres of influence of those with whom we already have shared connections. That means taking a genuine interest and curiosity in what those around us are involved with. The fact is that we are only one step from intriguing, unchartered waters. By investing a little time in understanding the reach of our network, we will find advocates to encourage us in our journey.

(continued)

TABLE 3.1B (Continued)

	My volunteering voyage into an adjacent community focused on leprosy has cultivated relationships and learning opportunities in diverse specialisms including healthcare, tropical diseases, patient rehabilitation, cultural insights, third-world infrastructure, project appraisals and management, inclusion and stigma, safeguarding and fundraising, to mention but a few. In cultivating new relationships there is overt learning as trustees share perspectives to shape the board strategy and decisions and by 'osmosis' where ideas and insights permeate my thinking as we simply spend time together. My learning opportunities have increased exponentially and I'm frequently able to apply valuable insights in my job.
	This adjacent community and learning environment offers structure and informality. In my busy life, fixed board and committee meetings ensure engagement, reading and thinking. The rhythm of the board diary ensures I sharpen my thinking with papers to read, reports to help write, and discussions to prepare for. But then, there are valuable informal get-togethers, where a lack of agenda enables creative conversations. And, in framing the output of the community, there are the life-changing opportunities to visit the programmes and projects. How powerful to recognize first-hand the massive impact of adding a small contribution to the mix.
	In taking a voyage into volunteering, I am confident that we all have valuable experiences to share. My encouragement to others is to recognize the impact that contributing a few hours a month, or year, can have. What may seem obvious to us can be a radical solution for others. Take time to think about what motivates you and be curious about what others close to you are involved in; it will help map out life-changing learning opportunities. And, what's been fascinating is that in every attempt I have made to give back, I have always ended up gaining!

Hilary Karpinski

Hilary Karpinski is an operations director in the third sector and had links with county women's and girls' Rugby Union in a volunteer capacity in the UK. Here Hilary's storyboard looks at the first part of the framework

Young girls (12–16) participating in rugby union across Yorkshire were almost non-existent unless there was a link to a sibling or a dad already playing. So, boosting numbers and engaging more females in such a rewarding activity was a baffling challenge, exacerbated further by how to retain them to develop, with most giving adverse peer pressure as the reason for not playing or for dropping out.

With no precedents in place and little support (due to lack of understanding) from a male-dominated committee, I opted for the 'trial and error' approach, ideas ranging from free kit incentives to covering travel costs, promoting health benefits and meeting new friends. However, without a doubt the breakthrough came with bringing in positive role models/peer supporters – essentially turning the one thing that stopped them playing on its head using 'trusted' allies telling 'lived experiences'. The solution was right in front of me, cost neutral, and enabled established players to give something back.

Taking this learning into the work environment....

My current role brings me face to face with challenges from people in our communities who are considered 'the hardest to reach' and not engaging in any support through statutory authorities such as the council or the NHS. If you understand this demographic group, you know that this is mostly due to lack of trust in or fear of anyone they see as 'in a position of authority'. The role of my organization is to locate these people and work to help them re-engage on their journey towards improved health and wealth. Taking my rugby experiences, I have developed peer support help delivered not through officials or trainers but through people they know, trust and look up to in their own communities who themselves have been on a similar journey and make no judgements or assumptions, offering only genuine empathy and understanding.

This approach has seen successful far beyond costly programmes delivered by statutory bodies which are unrelatable to their audience. Simultaneously, as an advocate for these groups, I also regularly find myself in need of a convincing argument to change or influence a policy decision with senior leaders and have concluded that nothing makes them sit up and listen like the reality of a case study describing real lived experience to contextualize impact.

I strongly believe in the benefits of 'lived experience' and the value of role models and continue to apply these to many scenarios, not least in a current project I am developing around reverse mentoring.

Steve George

Here Steve George's storyboard shows how the framework has put a more formal way of thinking on his development and academic interest in psychology.

TABLE 3.1C Steve George's storyboard so far

Create your plot

My motivation to maintain professional development in psychology nearly 30 years after my university degree in the subject is due to the number of ways I apply what I learned then, and how much more I have yet to learn that will be both interesting and practically applicable in my work. That order is important: it has to be interesting first and foremost.

On a personal level it's to keep my interest, avoid becoming stale, and also simply from curiosity. On a professional level I'm driven to find new ways of expressing and sharing expertise and to find new ways of working that make me better at my job.

Create an interesting subplot

I studied psychology at university, embarrassingly because I didn't know what else to study. My first choice was history, but I wasn't expected to get the grades I needed to study this at Sussex University, a place I really wanted to go to; however, I was accepted for psychology. In the end my results were good enough for history (surprising me as much as anyone else!) but I decided to stick with psychology. It's been one of those quirks of fate I'm forever grateful for, particularly given in the past few years I've taken up studying psychology in more depth again.

For me the twists and turns have come from seeing learning increasingly adopt – and sometimes misappropriate – psychology and neuroscience. Neuroscience was approximately 15 per cent of my degree. This adoption is particularly evident in work around the validity of psychometric testing, but in unconscious bias particularly. I was writing essays on both subjects in the mid-'90s and now seeing the extent to which they've entered the mainstream corporate lexicon as if fresh ideas to an extent, when they were already mature concepts in another field, has been an education for me in terms of adjacent communities and what we can bring from them.

Consider the environment for the story

Psychology is full of research and profound insights that are repackaged and applied to work on behavioural science, learning, organizational dynamics and more. Identifying what is contextually appropriate without making generalizations is part of the skill of using adjacent communities, and that applies as much to bringing in learning from an academic discipline such as psychology, as it does from any others.

(continued)

TABLE 3.1C (Continued)

The way I make the connections is often direct: research in psychology has shown X, that has a direct relationship to the work I'm doing, and therefore I can reference it or use it or demonstrate the influence and impact of that research. There will also be indirect connections. For example, when studying counselling techniques for working with adolescents I came across a reference to encouraging those receiving the counselling to consider 'hacks' for boosting dopamine, serotonin and oxytocin... all things worth taking into account when creating an optimal learning experience.

Absolutely. Psychology – and simplified, practical ways of expressing the learning from it – are at heart of several advances in learning practice in recent years.

Develop the ideas and create interesting characters to inhabit them

Much as with unconscious bias becoming a mainstream conversation a long time after it was an area of academic study, sometimes building on what we have is more a matter of looking back at what we *had*. This is what I find myself doing increasingly: reading the digested summaries of current research while looking into the theories and concepts that have stood the test of time and research repeatability.

Evidence needs to be amplified, alongside understanding and stating of the nuances and factors that contributed to the results in the research. This in turn will lead to the benefit of reduction from blanket statements that fail to take into account context, environment and other factors that influence outcomes.

Decide the structure

A variety of approaches, but if I explicitly refer to psychology in my work it might be with reference to an outrageous experiment before the time of ethics committees or to debunk some received wisdom that has gained traction. The intent with both is the same: to challenge people to look at the evidence behind what they are doing and to not accept something must be true just because it has become the dominant orthodoxy. This then provides the gateway to evidence-based work and its appropriate use. One fun one is Stanley Milgram's obedience experiment. The evidence has been reassessed and fresh conclusions drawn that question the original findings with different, challenging new insights. Albert Mehrabian's work on non-verbal communication is another. Despite his own best efforts to debunk the way it's been misquoted and misused the myths are still prevalent.

Learning about ourselves and others by referencing the research that tells us more, and making sure that we ourselves understand what it is we are talking about.

The process is part of the story because without it the evidence cannot be reliable and our understanding will be flawed.

(continued)

TABLE 3.1C (Continued)

	Know how you want it to look Typically a presentation for peers or at an event, though sometimes it will be introduced into a conversation to address a challenge or validate an approach in a piece of learning work. Typically by presenting information that will be new to many, compelling, evidence-based and practical. Also sometimes by taking something many people will believe to be true and challenging it. This is both engaging, and evidence of the value of using academic research appropriately in our work. At present all my reading comes from a few select sources – the British Psychology Society and a handful of journals. I need to broaden my reading to other, less obvious but equally rigorous sources.
	**Know your audience** Mostly those who work in L&D, OD&D and HR. Sometimes explicitly through presentations and writing; sometimes it will be implicitly applied in the learning they do that I have had some part in creating. If the information has been explicitly shared I want them to feel empowered and as if they've learned something new, valuable and interesting and ideally an anecdote to tell friends and colleagues too! If it's shared implicitly I'd want them to feel they've just had a very engaging and beneficial learning experience. Even better if they then try to deconstruct what made it work for them.

David Hayden

Here David gives a little more depth on how the framework has shaped his thinking on producing this book in his storyboard.

TABLE 3.1D David Hayden's storyboard so far

Create your plot

My motivation for writing this book comes from a few different sources. The idea was clearly laid out in the overture of the book and includes the distilling of those 'that can apply in my context' moments as well as helping other practitioners work out how to get the most out of other communities they are a part of.

To consider how to be a better practitioner by making links with topics that may or may not seem to be connected at first glance; to help with the 'whole person' at work agenda.

Create an interesting subplot

The arts was really a community that chose me; it was the moment at York St Johns and listening to some film critic podcasts that the momentum gained... in a number of training sessions I used to use the example from *A big boy did it and ran away* – so really it chose me!

The twists and turns are one of the things I have liked most about this – some like Linda Ashdown and Richard Davies (whose stories are in the book) really helped, but then listening across the L&D profession to what was not being talked about was a key element that added depth – every time someone said 'we need to learn more from other professions' I immediately tuned in....

Consider the environment for the story

Very much a spectator to some elements of the arts, but that spectator approach comes in a few formats... the arts can be an immersive experience – be it as a reader, an audience member or having a conversation with an actor, singer or musician. There have been some links previously unknown that writing this book has uncovered.

The connections are a mix of explicit and some very loose and a few tenuous... but the primary connection has been to the practice of learning more about learning, be it how people learn, how they approach learning if they are learning themselves or supporting others on a learning quest.

The whole premise of the book is about helping others transpose this into their context.

Develop the ideas and create interesting characters to inhabit them

There is much we have not covered that could have filled another book – keeping it succinct is a challenge; not wanting to lose some ideas has been a tension with what to keep and what to prune. Each element not in the book has some significant examples of learning from another community.

An explicit link to performance in the workplace – because the workplace is such a varied place dependent on context, sector and country, performance looks very different in some settings.

(continued)

TABLE 3.1D (Continued)

	**Decide the structure** There has been a mix of jamming, freestyling, of improvisation, of solo, of harmony, and plenty of bum notes along the way... The flow has been sporadic... the colour is vivid most of the time, but there have been times where it is very much like grey storm clouds. Learning about learning by looking outside of learning and what can be brought back. Not a fan of a process-first approach, but totally see why that is needed; the process was organic, but once tapped into supported the rhythm. *Know how you want it to look.* This book is the format for the output and we have ideas and plans – we are currently talking about the gap between writing and its publication and then post publication – lots of opportunity to consider different media.
	**Know your audience** Primarily L&D practitioners, HR practitioners and then people managers with a strong interest in learning... and ultimately anyone in learning. To look closer at their adjacent communities and what learning they gain – and shout about how they are applying it....

3.2

Critical friend responses

We used the critical friend approach to a few of our network where we met up and had a conversation to explore where their adjacent learning has taken them. As you read the stories from Nathaniel, Jake and Matt, see if you can spot how they link to the framework.

Nathaniel Redcliffe

Nathaniel Redcliffe, author of *Greener Grass*, and David Hayden met up in July 2022. Nathaniel is also a theatre practitioner at the local hospital in the town they live in, and both are members of the same running club.

David asked about the process of writing *Greener Grass* and this sparked a number of subsequent avenues of conversation. Here is a precis of the meeting and some of the links to the framework that fall out of it.

Process of writing *Greener Grass*

During lockdown I had spare time on my hands and seized the opportunity. I went for it and wrote the book. The plot was based on a screenplay I had written about 15 years earlier in my last days at school.

I started out with a skeleton of what the narrative would be and then added some flesh on the bones, creating bullet points for the direction of travel for each player and the plot. My intention at the start was to get it out and for people to enjoy reading it.

Inspiration

Rob Grant's books, US crime drama, programmes like *The Wire* and early (unpublished) attempts at writing (which on reflection could be seen as a rip-off of *Hot Fuzz*!) all contributed; however, the backdrop of my teens was the backdrop of the book. I didn't read much but Rob Grant's solo novels and Stephen King's *Green Mile* are favourites that will have inspired somewhere.

Formal training to write

None other than secondary school English. I left school and started working at the local council, undertaking a customer service apprenticeship within the IT team.

Links with running

Running is a stress releaser, creating endorphins and reducing anxiety. At a recent away run after a stressful day it was the perfect antidote! Writing *Greener Grass* has had a similar impact for me.

Post-published thoughts

There is a whole degree of vulnerability; it is almost as if I have bled on the pages. People who have bought it, friends, friends' parents, colleagues at work, doctors, people in the running club. A mixture of nervousness and anxiousness at their thoughts: will they like it? Will they think I hold all the views of the characters?

Plans for the book

Of course I want it to do well, for people to like it, for it to get popular. I have the skeleton of a follow-up.

David's review of *Greener Grass*

Reflecting on the conversation, David drew a number of parallels to the framework and the opportunity that Nathaniel has to tap into his adjacent communities to help with promotion of *Greener Grass*. The obvious ones, the different work communities at the hospital, the members of the running club, family, friends, people he did the walk with to Everest Base camp recently for his 30th birthday, are all potential communities and networks he can target to help with the promotion.

It was interesting to observe Nathaniel talking about the process of writing and the plans for the book. There was a wonderful moment of vulnerability when I commented that I had a really strong emotional response to the writing, an observation on how sometimes we are just not prepared for feedback. To be clear, the characters of Dan and Joe in the early chapters could almost be one of my friends, Andy Haines, and myself – Andy the handsome, confident, toned, slim Joe and me the fat, insecure Dan. Andy died way too young, but it was his face I was seeing as I read it.

I recognized the setting: it was a northern town, and the contrast between the streets that the 10-year-old Dan and Joe walked and the 16-year-olds walked was described in a way I could relate to.

To dive deeper into a review is impossible without giving away the trajectory they walk, but the way Nathaniel develops Dan and Joe is done with a gritty northern realism, something we can both relate to.

Linking to the framework

Relating to the overall premise of the book and linking Nathaniel's learning from one community to be a better-performing employee, there are three observations here, one immediate and another where it could take him. Will working through the framework to promote *Greener Grass* make him a better theatre practitioner? Not sure; there are areas that I can see, but that is Nathaniel's path to take. Will working through the framework give the foundations of being a better author? Possibly in the sense that if he taps into current and future readers, the feedback cycle starts and those insights can be acted up on in whatever way he wants.

The third area is where the framework can help Nathaniel to promote his book to a wider audience: the goal is clear, the steps are ready to be taken.

Jake March Jones

David met up with Jake towards the end of writing this book. Jake is an area retail manager by day and by night is an actor (recent roles in *Nell Gwynn* and *Accidental Death of an Anarchist*) and the vocalist for thrash metal band Fall of Edessa who released 'Resilience' in early 2020. He performed at the purist heavy metal festival Bloodstock with a previous band, They Will Rise. Here is a precis of the response Jake gave to the question 'What have you learned from outside of your work that you can apply to make you a better employee?'.

Henri Matisse, 'The Snail'

I have never understood visual art, not the depth or the meaning, or felt something from seeing art. My son, Noah, comes home with a school project, a picture that he is studying of Henri Matisse's 'The Snail'. We laughed at it; basically it looked like a bunch of shapes cut out on a page, like someone at primary school had done it.

It confirmed my view of some of the bonkers bits about art – a pile of books, an unmade bed, I didn't understand it; if I did it, then it would not be art, but they do it and it is art? How is that?

Anyway, Noah comes home and he has to do his own version and replicate it. He did and did a great job and it looks kinda like the original. Anyway we went to London a few months later and went to the Tate Modern and there was Matisse's 'The Snail' there, right there. We screamed, it is massive! We did not realize how big it was, at least a storey high.

Seeing it there helped us understand the story behind 'The Snail'. Seeing it helped us understand why it is art. Matisse was not well but still wanted to carry on doing what he wanted to do, so he got people to help him do this piece of work. When you get right close to the picture you can see the pin marks where he has said, 'No, put that patch here, put it there'. It is so meticulous where he has put the patches. So even when he is in this situation where he is disabled, not very well, he still had the love for art, to be so detailed. It was so poignant and the detail was incredible.

It also meant something to me seeing it, it was a connection; Noah had studied it, we had seen it as a family, and we were shocked at how good it was seeing it up close. We never thought it would be that size. Noah brought home a picture of it on an A4 piece of paper – and wow, how huge it was in contrast. Never thought it would be that size.

It has made me change my opinion on art. It made me feel something. Maybe there is something to certain artists' work – not sure about some of the vulgar elements, but just because I don't get it doesn't mean I dismiss it as 'not art'.

So looking at other things, like Robert Indiana's exhibition at Yorkshire Sculpture Park and Banksy and others at 2021 Scunthorpe, I am seeing through fresh eyes. I learned it is more than what you are actually looking at, it is also the story behind what you are looking at.

Singing and acting

The boundaries of arts, given I sing and act (although I get that thrash metal is not for everyone – I don't get rap, but when you see the written lyrics, it is poetry, really good poetry!), I guess there is no line. Art covers so many forms, it is all about the context. Playing music at Bloodstock, having my music in HMV, to me was something to hold on to, even though I know people don't get it.

What it means for the day job

When you consider performance, performing on stage, that confidence that you exhibit, performing to people you don't know, the concept is strange – you are exposing yourself to people you don't know, being open to criticism by complete strangers. In my work there is a lot of theatre – when you are selling products and when you are offering customer service, that is performing. Demonstrating toys at Hamleys, going into M&M World (or even being a teacher like my wife), it is acting, a performance, it is theatre.

(At this point Jake's wife Beckie says, 'It is like when I am having to pretend to be really cross that a child has done something, but inside I just want to laugh out loud: it is an act.')

It is a bit crass, and this is where context comes in. Do I care about the people who come in enough, urm – some yes, some really no. I have targets to hit; that is where teaching is different – you have to care to do it.

David's review of *Accidental Death of an Anarchist*

Dario Fo's play travels at a really fast pace, really fast. It is full on, almost slapstick in some places. Cast members are throwing themselves at every available prop, including each other and the floor. It is funny, it is poignant, it is political, and it is about relationships, mainly dysfunctional ones! It is based on a real-life 1969 event, one that caused outcry and raised lots of questions at the time.

The pace can make it hard to follow every word, but the flow is one that you can juxtapose lots of 2020s' situations to: what is reality, what is fake, what is covered up, what gets shared? I am really pleased I saw it and the cast were all engaging with their characters. Did I enjoy it? I'm not so sure about that, but then enjoyment is not always the point of art, is it? I was certainly entertained and glad I experienced it. It made me think, I learned some stuff.

Matt Mahoney

Steve met with Matt in August 2022 and interviewed him about how he uses his experience playing as an England touch rugby international in his career as a senior charity leader and volunteer manager. It was striking how much of Matt's approach resonated with the framework and how he consciously seeks out opportunities to learn from, and share to, his adjacent communities. Note also how he takes into his sport his experiences in his career, making it a two-way process of skills and behavioural transfer.

My motivation for playing touch rugby is that I just really enjoy it for a variety of reasons. I love the physical and mental benefits of playing a team sport, especially a ball sport. It's a really fast-paced and inclusive sport with men's, women's and mixed teams at elite level. It's physically and mentally demanding and I love the tactical aspect of high-level touch. I've always enjoyed challenging myself and hitting performance targets, having training goals for a purpose, learning and improving skills, testing myself at the highest level under pressure and being part of a team, having fun, amusing people, motivating and encouraging them.

I was forced through injury and health issues to give up sport, which I loved, for a long time, so playing touch has given me the opportunity to experience that aspect of life again and the challenge of trying to achieve something as part of a team, relying on each other, winning and losing together, meeting new people and making new friends from around the world.

There are a lot of aspects I take into my work as a volunteer manager in a charity. I represent England Men. There are other England teams and we all help and support each other in a collaborative way. This cross-team work is something I do at work too, making myself available to share good practice with other teams for the overall benefit of the organization. I get a lot of satisfaction out of helping people improve. Winning only happens if everyone is as good as they can be – I don't want to withhold knowledge but share it to support everyone to be their best so we succeed together.

Another thing I bring across from playing rugby internationally is leadership practice and experience in a high-performance team. Through rugby I have practised the behaviour of handling pressure, which helps with certain scenarios such as presentations and challenging meetings at work. It means I can focus on the awareness of what else is happening, rather than the situation and thinking of what I'm doing. This gives more mental bandwidth for the work, rather than *thinking* about the work. Also the practice of using other fields to improve my rugby helps me apply that mindset in work. I use techniques of Formula One drivers to increase reaction speed, which helps for rugby. I look at how athletes from other sports train their vestibular system to improve catching and scanning, that's how I train and so on.

I don't do those things in my job, but the behaviour of learning from others I *do* take into work. An interesting example would be when training volunteers how to build rapport quickly. I've shared principles employed by FBI hostage negotiators, which are transferable but also are engaging and challenge people's thinking. I'll look at the context people are working in, the environment and what challenges that brings, not just the fact they are volunteers.

Planning training schedules for rugby has supported skills in project planning for work. Managing injuries helps with resilience and thinking laterally in all of my life. Before a major tournament I had an injury that could have ruled me out because it prevented the training plan, but I adapted my training to give myself the best chance possible of still playing. It worked – rather than see the injury derailing the path to the destination, you just find a different path. That's a useful experience I have applied for work too.

In the elite set-up a lot of the people who work in it are volunteers. My experience at work makes me very aware of this and their world. Also working with people trying to perform a role while under stress. Trying to achieve things as a team while people have a lot of different ways of learning has been a valuable rugby experience too, and understanding the need for time for decompression rather than constant stress and high performance is important. Remote working is also similar to elite training for sport in a team – the time together in-person is limited, so that time has to be maximized for effectiveness. There's a lot that transfers between rugby and work and vice versa.

While I use the learning from touch rugby a lot in work, I most frequently don't refer to it directly. If it's useful to a situation to give an example from rugby then I'll do so if that'll work for the person I'm working with. It could be informal or formal when I introduce it and it could be generic or specific, explicitly referred to or not. I tend to apply it contextually. I'll add or take away as much as will add value to what I'm doing. There's no need to give unnecessary detail. You must understand what people need to hear, not what you want to say. What's the value it gives to that person? What's the point of what I'm doing or saying?

People always receive it positively though. Part of this is again down to behaviours I have learned playing touch rugby and how you help other people to succeed in a way that is generous and motivational.

I want people to come away from me sharing my experiences in rugby thinking it was of value and that they feel engaged, enthused and uplifted. I want people to feel valued as a person and in their contribution. I also want them to feel supported and encouraged and perhaps challenged to do something. All things I want for the team in rugby too.

3.3

Blog responses

We asked the following people to share their stories and shared the framework and the questions within it with them. As you can see, they did not stick to it but rather used it as a starting point for their narratives. These are what we would call blog examples. As you read the blogs from Giorgia, Jilly and Sharon, see if you can spot where they used the framework and the elements within it.

Giorgia Gamba Quilliam

Giorgia is a learning content manager based in the UK. Here she shares her reflections from volunteering and offers some insights as to why training may be designed in a certain way.

From the age of 14 I volunteered in various capacities. I can't say why I felt drawn to it, I just did. At 18, I joined the Red Cross and volunteered for them for the following 30 years in a variety of roles: volunteer manager, trainer, first responder, and I also worked in a refugee camp in Albania for a few weeks. There, I witnessed first hand how entire families had to leave everything behind and live in a shared tent for an indefinite time. And while there was a lot of sadness in that, it also opened my eyes to the resilience of humans and the seemingly infinite ability to start over.

The way the Red Cross trains its volunteers to behave and adhere to its fundamental principles is quite strict and the same the world over – to an extent. At times, that looks rigid, even unjustified. When you are safe, sitting in a training room with other people eager to help, some things seem over the top and difficult to relate to or make sense of. But sure enough, if you stick around, at the right time and in the right place a lot of those things will fall into place and make perfect sense. This is not to say the Red Cross approach is flawless or can't be looked at for iterations and improvement, but that's a story for another book.

Some of the things I learned through my years as a Red Cross volunteer fell into place decades later when I volunteered in another refugee camp, in Calais (France). No big organizations were supporting people in the French camp as it was not officially recognized. Therefore, some smaller, newly formed organizations showed up to help alongside willing individuals with some time to spare. Now, I'm not suggesting any of these organizations or individuals didn't provide much-needed help. However, they occasionally stumbled on issues that could have been avoided or prevented. The story that stuck with me when in Calais was that of a young female volunteer who became close to some of the camp residents and ended up pretty much living there rather than leaving the camp at night. Eventually, her position became unsafe and she had to leave the camp and stop volunteering altogether at the time. Thankfully, there were no serious or permanent consequences in the specific episode. However, it really brought home for me all my previous training on boundaries.

When you volunteer, you can of course be friendly with the people you are supporting but not quite become friends. This seemed harsh and even unfair to some. Some people even thought that this would imply that the volunteers are somehow superior to the people they are helping. This is absolutely not the case, but there can't be true friendship when the playing field is uneven: as a volunteer you are free to stay and help or leave and move on whenever you choose. A lot of the people that volunteers support, and certainly refugees in a camp, don't have such freedom and that creates an imbalance that can't accommodate true friendship. There are, of course, practical implications as well around safety, cultural norms that might not be fully understood, and other ethical considerations that also belong in another book.

So what? I hear you asking. How did that learning serve me in my professional life, which happens to be in... learning!

Well, in so many ways. First, it made me realize that the more you can get people to learn as close to when they need to apply their newly acquired skills, the better. That way, they won't need to wait years until it all falls into place and it will soon make them realize why something needs to be done in a certain way – or suggest improvements based on their experience.

Second, even if it might seem contradictory, it's important to persevere and create space for people to acquire knowledge and skills that they might not need soon or even ever. If I can borrow an example, cabin crew on a plane must know how to react to an emergency landing and keep passengers safe; however, we all hope they'll never need to put that into practice. Motivation here is key. Every learner, adult learners especially, needs to know 'the why'.

Finally, some training might seem too dogmatic but there might be good reasons for it. It's the trainer's gift to share those reasons and bring them to life so that, once again, that motivation becomes clear. But this doesn't detract from the fact that some things just need to be learned the way they are.

So, to finish off, what I have learned as a volunteer that I can apply in my professional life is: make learning contextual, really share the why and trust that the learning will kick in when needed if it has transferred.

Jilly Julien

Jilly is a learning professional based in the UK. Here Jilly shares what she has learned and transferred to her 'day job' from being active in local government.

'So then, Jilly – what on earth possessed you?' is a question that occurs to me quite often. It's also posed to me on a regular basis by others. And you know what? I understand why. Not just getting involved in local politics as a campaigner but standing as a candidate for the local council felt very much like painting a large target upon myself and wearing a neon hat while sticking my head above the parapet. But having spent 20 years supporting people out of their comfort zones, it felt a little hypocritical to be bound by mine.

So what on earth *did* possess me? Frustration, injustice and a profound dislike of the way that voting no longer felt like enough in order to be represented effectively at any level of government. I could shout at the TV all I liked, and rant with like-minded friends in my social media values bubble, but that wasn't going to change a thing. And realizing that gave me two choices – do nothing or do something. I could hear my grandad's voice on my shoulder telling me that if you see something that's wrong, you don't wait for someone else to sort it – you do something. I had to get involved.

For context, you have to understand that I have *never* been particularly comfortable with promoting myself or my work, in any context. So to put myself and my achievements into leaflets that were delivered to thousands of homes made me feel physically sick. My kids came into their own at this point though – aged five and eight, filled with unconditional love and a pride that 'mummy is helping people/the planet/animals/the dinosaurs', they were the dynamo for my self-belief.

The wider support crew I had were incredible, too. For all that politics has been given *such* an awful name, being part of a political party is having a community in which it's a given that common values are held. I won't speculate for all parties, but within my own I can say there's vigorous debate and difference of opinion on lots of subjects, but a real solid core belief that the debate itself is right. (To paraphrase Voltaire, I may disagree with what you're saying, but I'd die for your right to say it. This often holds true for us.) There's real strength to be found in having those people around you who have a shared vision, common values and diverse voices. (I now go out of my way to seek that in every context in life – it's much healthier than an algorithm-approved echo chamber!)

And holding to my values, knowing what's important to me, was everything. Understanding my red lines when campaigning. Exercising my right to say no when someone suggested a campaign line I was uncomfortable with and not being sucked into claim and counter-claim. In fact, amplifying rather than claiming a community success set me apart from the politician stereotype that is all-pervasive. I wore my authenticity like armour, with the knowledge that if nobody voted for me, I was simply not the right representative. That simple premise kept me healthy.

Happily, dear reader, I was elected.

By this stage, my head was well above the parapet mentioned earlier. I felt – and continue to feel – very exposed. But I discovered that for every person who wants to have a go, there are many, many more quietly grateful for what you do. Whether it's increasing road safety, improving the local park or just holding the council to account for doing things the best way for residents, it's doing The Good Work.

And that's been the epiphany that has echoed into my professional life and my personal life – where I've felt the signs of doubt, or going down a rabbit hole, I ask myself the question, 'Who is this in service of?' I find it helps me to distil often complex and highly commercial conundrums back to the real driver/catalyst in the situation. From there I can build my strategy for how to deal with it most efficiently (and efficiency is everything with a day job, a councillor role and two small people to raise and wrangle!).

I also find that question helps me to cut through much of the ego-led effort that's present in both public and private sector life. I'll be leaving that to the career politicians, I think....

What on earth possessed me? Well, the work I'm doing, by standing and now representing my community, certainly scratches that itch to make more of a difference than just shouting my discontent at the screen. And it's definitely emboldened me to take career and life steps that I wouldn't have ever contemplated without that experience.

I'd encourage everyone to explore life outside the silent majority – just like being outside of that comfort zone, it's where great change happens.

And yes, I'll be standing again.

Sharon Fernandes

Sharon works in learning and development in the UK. Here she describes the benefits of her adjacent community in allowing her to pursue her passion and support her wellbeing.

'Thank you for the music, the song I'm singing...' goes the ABBA song and is my description of why I break into song or hum a tune wherever I can. I call it my passion, but my profession it is not. It is, however, the driving force to my volunteer work as the administrator of my organization's employee choir group that meets every term, sings together, records and produces music videos of said singing, and makes us proud to be able to share it widely. A varied group of people, singing abilities and from different departments within the organization, but when learning, singing and recording they produce great melodies.

The choir and its administration work are my testament to adjacent communities and their ongoing benefits. It fuels my passion, allows me to indulge in it during the work week, facilitates meeting new people across the organization and that builds networking with other departments with endless opportunities to further personal and team objectives to start with. The cherry on top is the spotlight it shines on the organization's culture that allows for and champions this benefit for employee wellbeing. Was I trained to carry out the work? No. Did I have transferable skills? Yes.

Some are inherent and some developed through my working life and all transferable for this kind of work. The twist and high point would be the songs chosen and recorded for the term and the process to produce and release them virtually. The group effort in recording individually, blending of voices digitally and the final video, coordinating with producers who again are volunteers in the creative departments, and finally releasing it through the communications department – many steps in the process but efforts of so many freely given. It is so rewarding when requests to mark special occasions with a song recording come in and the release takes place at an org-wide event.

In the name of wellbeing today, organizations have/are striving to offer a lot. The challenge is that it is not always easy to start a new job, in a new environment, and capitalize on the opportunities to explore these avenues from the start. However, they exist and are there for the taking – perhaps as a trial, as it was for me. With a full-time job, kids and family, taking on additional activities during working hours may not sound like something you can cope with. But these communities are not a burden or extra work. The will to engage comes from something that is one's passion and the rest is pure music, as my case was and is. And do not put it off to be explored tomorrow. As you set your routine for work, I recommend having these motivators/wellbeing aids set up side by side, making them go hand in hand. 'So I say thank you for the music, for giving it to me': ABBA.

Over to you

Linking back to our framework, what are your takeaways from the people you have met in this Act and how would you present your story?

ACT 4

The adjacent connections

Setting the scene

What do we mean by adjacent connections? In the corporate learning world the technical element can be seen as things like adult learning theory, the systematic learning cycle, evaluation systems and processes, and how to undertake learning needs analysis as well as human-centred design approaches.

This book clearly does not cover these, nor do we have the space to dive into them in detail. We promised in the overture to highlight some of the inspirational pieces of work we have come across and these are listed in this Act, our adjacent connections.

The final act of a play or film brings together the threads, leaves the viewer with enough information to be able to join the dots. Learning about the technical elements of how people learn and to support what that means in the workplace takes time, energy and effort. People who work in any form of learning need to be role models to the rest of the organization. The intention of this Act is to share with you what we have gained from working out just how to role-model learning ourselves.

Standing on the shoulders of giants

In the research for this book, in fact quite late into the writing process, we came across two books we'd like to mention: *The Medici Effect* by Frans Johansson (2017) and *Expert* by Roger Kneebone (2021). They validate much of what we have covered and the emphasis that one world can learn from another. The books have different approaches, one looking at how breakthrough ideas can come from investigating other fields and the other exploring mastery of craft.

In Johansson's book there are some standout moments and sound advice. 'Hanging out with geniuses' (p166) and 'take Medici visits' (pp215/6) are two that jump out. Both these approaches offer the reader deliberate choice. Essentially, they link to the start of our framework where we ask you to consider your starting point. What is it you are looking to achieve by hanging out with leaders in a field and taking site visits to organizations unrelated to your own, with an intent to explore and be exposed to new ideas and thinking and be curious?

Johansson also offers us an approach to reverse our assumptions. This aligns with our filter stage. He uses the concept of what we know about restaurants and asks us to test our assumptions of what they can be. So for example, a restaurant has menus (assumption) – the reversal will be a restaurant has no menus. He reframes this for the reader to say instead, the chef says, 'This is the food I have bought locally and this is what I will cook', which is not that far removed from the *plat de jour* approach in France. But he does go on to offer deeper alternatives (p56).

Reading Johansson's book connects to an activity to help spark creativity and inspiration. It involved showing a series of pictures, which included bamboo, kittens, leaping salmon, worms and a mole (the animal), an albatross, human lungs, human skulls and a human arm. The challenge was in two parts. First, asking the groups to think what inventions they may have inspired. Some powerful comments usually came back, some correct guesses and some that were inspired links, and a handful of 'I have no idea' responses. The second part of the activity showed 'the answers'. However, the groups had to pair up the images contained on the answer sheet to the first set of pictures. The answer sheet had pictures of a Luxor lamp, cats' eyes on a road, an igloo, conductor pipes, bagpipes, tunnel-boring equipment, a Spitfire aeroplane and a freezer full of food!*

In *Expert*, Kneebone starts off by explaining why he was visiting Derek Frampton, a master taxidermist, at work, setting the context for how if we want to be thought expert in something, we need to explore what it is that experts do, think, act and sacrifice. He argues that we do not see how someone becomes an expert but just the end result. As a doctor, he searches out expertise in a huge number of different fields to establish how to apply it in his world, and he offers insights for others.

Incidentally, there is a wonderful advert for Penguin Books at the end of *Expert*. It starts off with a comment about the founder Allen Lane: 'He just wanted to buy a decent book.' Penguin began with someone having a great idea and following it through... how many great ideas are out there that with the right level of support can be brilliantly executed into action? Without the action, the idea just becomes a passing thought and, perhaps worse, a future regret.

Coming across both of these books took us back to a few other books that have had an impact.

In *Everything We Know Is Wrong*, Magnus Lindkvist (2010) offers the reader opportunities to view the world differently, to explore different perspectives and to look deeper, challenging what we think is happening against the reality. In other words, seeing the unseen! He uses *Back to the Future* (p101), *The Jetsons* (p105/6), *When Harry Met Sally* (p126) the song *Torn* (p131) and numerous references to novels and authors to make his point. In a conference session (Lindkvist, 2011) he used Melodifestivalen, the Swedish heats for the Eurovision Song Contest, to make his point.

In *Funky Business* (2000), Jonas Ridderstråle and Kjell Nordström urge organizations to think differently. They take inspiration from Picasso, John Lennon, The Prodigy and playwright Mark Ravenhill to get their points across and demonstrate how organizations and people within them must embrace new sets of ways of working in order to perform.

Wider L&D resources that have helped us

If you are coming to this book with an L&D background it's possible you have heard of some if not all of these books and authors. If you are coming from a wider HR or people manager background these may be new titles to you. However, as you can see from the very short overview we give, each gives a nod to looking beyond the L&D function to be a better practitioner.

Michelle Parry-Slater, The Learning and Development Handbook (2021)

Michelle uses what she has gained from volunteering with Girlguiding as a source of examples throughout her book and how the knowledge transfer works both ways.

Stella Collins, Neuroscience for Learning and Development, 1st edition (2016)

Stella discusses stories in her book and quotes a haiku poem (p152/3) to emphasize a point to make learning 'sticky', and even uses Abba's *Waterloo* (p205) to drive this point home.

Andy Lancaster, Driving Performance Through Learning (2019)

Andy uses the Tate Modern (p35/6) as a case study on creating a learning philosophy and museums as an example of curation. Andy embodies this thinking too and has taken his team to places like the Tate Modern, the Science Museum and the Design Museum to drive creativity and inspiration as well as for team bonding. In conferences Andy has also talked about what he has learned about communities from observing and researching how bees work together.

Mirjam Neelen and Paul A Kirschner, Evidence-Informed Learning Design (2020)

Mirjam and Paul describe a word credited to comedian Stephen Colbert: *truthliness* (p65). They have a wonderful case study on creativity and music (pp148, 154) to emphasize their point: *is creativity a skill*? They also spend some time comparing two abstract events (p146/7). Within this they say, 'All analogies are ultimately flawed' (p146), which at first read may put a damper on this book. However, they go on to stress that we can only successfully make links with our explicit knowledge and may need nudges to help us see similarities (p147).

Steve Wheeler, Digital Learning in Organizations (2019)

Steve uses a quote from Mark Twain (p7) to start his first chapter and subsequent chapters feature quotes from the arts, including Frank Zappa (p31), George Bernard Shaw (p71), Dr Seuss (183), Bruce Lee (p91) and C S Lewis (p105).

Donald Clark, Artificial Intelligence for Learning (2020)

Donald introduces the concept of AI as starting in 1956 and if L&D professionals need to understand it, they need to 'understand the two-and-a-half-millennia gestation period through *mathematics*' (p7).

Nick Shackleton Jones, How People Learn (2019)

Nick uses a case study based on the fictional characters of Sherlock Holmes and Dr Watson (pp94–96) and uses Wordsworth and Roald Dahl to emphasize a point (p37). And while not solely L&D focused, the book is packed with food for thought and has lots of links to learning.

Naomi Stanford, Organization Design, 3rd edition (2018)

Naomi's mission is to get HR to acknowledge that organization design is *not* the same as altering the organization chart. Her books (and blogs) show her range of experience and credibility. She gives a clear definition of organization design by using a building architecture analogy.

Matthew Syed, in The Greatest (2017) and Blackbox Thinking (2016)

The Greatest is full of what we can learn from the world of sports to be the best we can be. With a background of working with businesses as a consultant, Matthew uses these analogies to guide the research he undertook for *Blackbox Thinking*.

Peter Cheese, in The New World of Work (2021)

Peter offers a few chapters that explicitly discuss learning and uses quotes from Mark Twain, Chekhov, Voltaire and Plato among others to introduce each chapter, again showing how inspiration can be found outside our profession.

WILL BRIMSOM, PARTNERSHIPS, UK

Running has directly benefited Will's resilience and sense of the possible, and he also translates his training for a marathon into other ways of developing in his career

I'm a keen amateur runner. Over the years this has meant building up to running longer distances culminating in running the London Marathon in 2021. There is lots that can be learned from running. I won't go so far as to say that there is some magical meditative benefit or that it has transformed my mindset, but it has built resilience and raised the ceiling of what I believe we can achieve.

To do so we first need to put ourselves in uncomfortable positions. In terms of development and progression I have seen by far the greatest improvements to performance when following the lead of better athletes. In running this means quite literally chasing faster runners around a track, but this can be extended to professional working lives. We need to put ourselves in positions, companies and opportunities that stretch ourselves in order to grow. By challenging ourselves and making ourselves uncomfortable we can raise the ceiling of performance.

> I had to push myself beyond my limits in training for a marathon, a huge commitment in time, energy and focus beyond any amount of training I had done before. As a result a half-marathon that previously was a stretch goal for me had now become a regular weekend activity and so by stretching for an increased goal my overall performance capacity was increased.

Ethical stance

We have explored within this book a range of ideas of how we can be better, learn to transfer learning from one arena into another and perform better as a professional. We have offered ways that those responsible for actively supporting learning in an organization can engage with and help drive individual and organizational performance forward. The stories we have harvested throughout this book all link back into being better at what we do at work.

At an organizational level, is there an ethical issue with encouraging people to bring the benefits of what they do outside of work into their employment? Does an organization have a right to harvest the whole person, not just the bit they have asked for in the job description? In our experience people can often 'become' their job description in the eyes of others, limiting both their work and what they can bring to an organization.

For example, our conversations with people from across professions are littered with anecdotes in which external expertise was brought in, often at great expense, though people inside the organization already had that expertise but outside the remit of their current role. The former hiring manager for a large organization now in an L&D team and not able to support on an L&D project helping line managers be better recruiters, the person doing a master's in UX (user experience) excluded from a project team redesigning a website because their 'day job' was in marketing, not the web team, and so on.

We can be guilty of this in learning too. We spoke with one individual who had attended a training course for managers on mental health awareness. This person not only had professional qualifications in supporting those with mental health challenges but volunteered for the Samaritans and other organizations in their spare time, and they were almost certainly more experienced and better qualified than the person delivering the training. Rather than being excused from the event or even better asked to support the learning, they were instead required to spend four hours as an attendee so a box could be ticked to show that they'd done the mandatory work. Understandably, this person found this both confusing and frustrating.

One message of this book is a reminder to consider that the boundaries of work and out of work are blurred and the rich seam of learning that comes outside of work can play a vital part in organization performance. When we recruit, we often ask 'whole person' questions, such as 'Tell me something about you outside of work'. Recruiters look for evidence of values, behaviours, balance and so on by asking the questions. We'll also often add it as small talk and genuine curiosity in workplace conversations: 'What did you do at the weekend? What have you got planned for your holiday?' And yet we can quickly default to seeing people as their roles immediately the 'formal' activity of work begins.

The increasing challenge faced by many organizations to recruit people into positions highlights the need to consider the whole person, to embrace who they are beyond their job description.

It is a two-way street, thinking about learning beyond work: what are we prepared to encourage within the organization, to recognize, reward and practise in seeing someone bringing their whole self and experience to work, and as an individual how much trust is there that the vulnerability and generosity of bringing that 'whole self' into work will not be frustrating, or exposing, or misinterpreted, or used against someone? What would the motivation be?

There is a danger too for some in making what they do outside of work more formal and so if we encourage and invite people to bring their broader selves and experience, we must also accept that they may not wish to or may do so but then change their mind, and that is their right. Talking to a club runner, he told us he loved the club runs but when he volunteered to be a run leader, it stopped being fun, it started to feel like work – checking the routes, making sure the pace was right for the group, having to be first aid trained, having to report if anyone dropped out. The enjoyment dropped, so he stopped being a run leader and started enjoying running again.

SUE MURKIN, LEARNING MANAGER AND PILATES INSTRUCTOR, UK

Sue explains how being a Pilates instructor has made her think about her career/role

In 2017, at 52 years old, I embarked, for the sheer joy of it, on qualifying to become a Pilates instructor, which meant studying anatomy and physiology and principles of fitness before even beginning to study the Pilates method. I has a vague whim that once I'd qualified, I might teach a class a week but I knew I wasn't going to change my career to teach Pilates full time. Pilates was my hobby, I had done it for years, I did not want it to be the 'thing' that my financial security relied upon.

The journey that lay before me was tough; it took two years of evenings and weekend study, working full time and living through a major renovation of our home, before I qualified. As much as I was motivated to do this to give me another outlet beyond work, ironically it has taught me so much about my approach to work in the 'day job'.

The obvious, that you are never too old to start something new, has helped me embrace new technology and systems at work; as it happens you can teach old dogs new tricks. Hard work pays off; it's not that I did not know this but when you have the point of reference of achieving a 97 per cent pass by understanding the cardiac system, the nervous system, the respiratory system and naming all the major muscles in the body, when two years previously I didn't know my ulna from by radius, well that's some point of reference!

But the lesson that has been the biggest gift is that having something other than the day job to validate who I am (I have always based a lot of my self-validation on my job title) has given me the freedom at work to be more vulnerable in my leadership, let myself off the hook for not being able to solve every problem and not having to know all the answers, and this is a gift that keeps on giving because it has enabled me to build better trust in my team, who do know the answers and have fabulous solutions. By expanding upon who I am beyond my career I feel I have been able to be more honest as a leader in my career.

A word on bias

We have covered a range of examples from different forms of the arts and from our network. However, we recognize that this is only the tip of the iceberg. Our 'inspiration' folder where we captured thoughts for this book has enough to fill a second continuation book and still have more left, and that doesn't include what we have set aside for events and other opportunities we have to talk through our thinking and examples. Further, we recognize our sources have tended to be from the relatively narrow stance of Western popular culture. Going further into the outputs of, say, Bollywood, Russian cinema of the 1920s, Italian arthouse would bring new and different insights. Just within arts, and within arts just looking at cinema, the adjacent learning opportunities will be almost endless.

So we know there is more to learn with adjacent learning. For us this is just the start to make us more effective and to have greater impact in using wider insights from outside of our organization to develop our workplace performance.

MARK HUDSON, IT PROFESSIONAL AND LEAD PARKRUN VOLUNTEER, UK

Mark explains how volunteering has given him skills to transfer to work by providing a 'safe environment' for practice

Volunteering has become a significant part of my life and I love the pleasure it gives me, seeing that my time, skills and even personality give others pleasure, enjoyment and in many cases the downtime they need to improve their mental and physical health. On an average week, I will volunteer about 10 to 15 hours of my time, across a number of roles.

Knowing that my time creates benefits for so many others is a real source of pride and gives me a wonderful sense of fulfilment and achievement. My belief is that volunteers do what they do for free, not because they are worthless but because they are priceless.

In my professional life, the skills I have developed from my volunteering roles have had a huge impact. In a volunteering role, without the pressure to perform or achieve as would be the case in your work life, you build confidence. In a work environment any lack of achievement or failure, no matter how small, costs time and money, which knocks confidence and erodes it. Nurturing people to develop their skills in the voluntary sector allows people to develop without these pressures.

In my experience, learning to talk, organize and manage volunteers develops skills that 'encourage' people, as opposed to a work environment where there can be a tendency to 'tell' or 'demand' people do things. Throughout my career, I have endeavoured to use this encouraging approach and can offer numerous examples of where this has proved more beneficial than instructing people.

A few years ago, when I was an account manager for a technology company, I needed urgent assistance for a client. I approached the support team and I joked, begged and charmed the team, even mentioning they were 'the best team I had ever had the pleasure of working with'! After some banter, they looked at the issue and resolved it quickly for me, much to the delight of the client. Ironically, the very next day, a colleague had a similar issue with one of their clients. He went into the support team's office and told them to look at the issue straight away, as it was their job. They explained that a call would be logged and the problem investigated in due course. My colleague ranted, argued and eventually involved a director to 'make them' do as he wanted.

When you are managing volunteers you need to make them feel valued and appreciate their time, but that does not mean employees should be treated any differently – everyone deserves respect, appreciation and kindness.

Making a living from adjacent learning

We have been lucky to come across a number of people who have been able to transfer what they do and apply it to their role and make a successful business from it. There are also private training companies that link with the arts, for instance actors providing scenario-based learning provision and comedians offering their skills to help individuals and teams be more confident, focused and effective in their communication delivery.

PHIL WILCOX, FOUNDER, EMOTION AT WORK CONSULTING, UK

Phil shares how he was determined to learn from a mistake that ultimately led to him finding his niche within learning

I made a vow that emotions would never get the better of me again. Earlier that week I had got so frustrated during a call with a customer that I had sworn at them down the phone (when I thought I was on mute). I should have been fired but wasn't because I told the truth and was genuinely sorry. The vow took me on a quest to make sure that I knew everything about emotions and how to stop them getting you in trouble.

Around the same time, I found something that I loved to do. Learning was something that I had always enjoyed doing and I found I was quite good at helping others learn as well. I coached a school football team, taught at Sunday school and when I joined the workplace, I found out there was a career in doing what I loved.

Fast forward a decade or two and now I run a business that combines my quest and my love for a career. Emotion at Work is all about harnessing the brilliance and power of all emotion(s) and we do that through helping people, teams and organizations develop and grow. Am I lucky? Every single day. Was it luck that got me here? No, this was me making what I loved and what I needed to know part of my working life.

*Answers to the creativity/inspiration activity:

- bamboo – conductor pipes
- kittens – cats' eyes on a road
- leaping salmon – a freezer full of food

- worms and a mole (the animal) – tunnel boring equipment
- an albatross – a Spitfire aeroplane
- human lungs – bagpipes
- human skulls – an igloo
- human arm – Luxor lamp

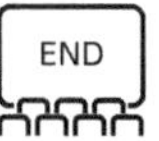

Epilogues

Setting the scene

Frank Hauser and Russell Reich in the paper '12 biggest mistakes directors make' (2003) talk about the dangers of neglecting the audience. They also ask, who is 'the object of the director's attention?'. They argue it is not the audience that is the primary concern for most directors, it is indeed someone the director may idolize, perhaps a significant teacher, a parent, answering critics' feedback. They urge directors to love their audience.

We have put this here deliberately instead of in Act 2 where we explore our audiences. We wanted to consciously think about you, the reader, and why we have written this and the relationship we want to have with you. The editor of any film can be viewed in a number of ways, as slashing content and leaving it 'on the cutting room floor', or as a professional who takes the narrative of the film forward.

FEDERICO GAGGERO, LEARNING DESIGNER, ITALY

Federico shares the journey on his raft, steering his career forward

In my personal and professional life, I am always driven by curiosity and creativity. In fact, professional life and personal passions have always overlapped in my mind, creating a strong bond between what I like and what I do.

My passions for art, design, drawing, cinema conducted me into a long journey – still ongoing – started when I was 19. I was just a kid back then, but deeply fascinated by the world of animation – realizing that a whole professional and artistic world lay behind the frames of the animated movies I love really motivated me and made me want to take action, to try to find my voice as an artist and as a professional. I then moved from Genova, my home town, to Milan to study illustration and animation. I felt a little bit like a sailor on his small raft, although I was leaving a harbour for a city with no sea!

At the university in Milan everything was mysterious, exciting and honestly a bit frightening, but most of all everything was 'new': a new view of the world.

I started draining inspiration from everything around me: even the smallest detail became a source of inspiration that I would then convey in my artworks and the deep study of the technical tools needed to become a good professional. I developed a renewed and deeper connection with music, movies, art and culture, that were not just leisure interests any more.

My love and passion for American pop culture brought me abroad. I left Italy for several years and lived in California, where I studied and worked, and kept absorbing from the surrounding environment to enrich my vision of the world.

My small raft brought me back to Italy and then the UK, where I kept learning and growing. Due to about 15 years of experience, I gained a solid skill set and visual culture that always helps me to (hopefully!) face any professional challenge. I think it is always important to get updated on the new trends and the news in terms of design and art, to try to keep relevant in a very competitive market, and to be able to always deliver good-quality products. The panorama of the new media is exciting, although a bit scary – augmented reality, VR, NFTs, metaverse. It is overwhelming at times and it definitely would be beneficial to deepen my understanding of these new fields that will soon become essential.

The journey is ongoing and I still feel a sailor on my small raft... but I am glad that I can say that I still enjoy the trip! Keeping my curiosity alive is what makes the difference.

Authors' note: Fede created the images used in this book. He can be contacted at federicogaggero.com.

Our virtual cutting room floors have a wide and varied list of things we have learned, and taking advice from our own framework, we filtered out, thinking about you and not making a classic L&D mistake of overfilling with content.

As we began with our stories, we'll close in the same vein.

David's epilogue

April 2017 was a turning point for me in getting this book together. By then the idea had been in my head for about seven years. But it was just an idea, doing nothing other than spinning around in my head. Taking time to reflect on some of the things that have happened since is kinda mind blowing.

Some things have happened by pure chance, by being in the right place at the right time, for instance working with a big four UK supermarket, working in the Middle East and South East Asia and the Cayman Islands, being on and suggesting content for the CIPD podcasts, writing the CIPD L&D factsheets, and perhaps the biggest twist in the tail, being asked to co-author the 4th edition of *Learning and Development Practice in the Workplace* (Beevers et al, 2019). These were never starting goals but happened as a result of talking about my overall plot, my goal – the desire to find my voice and have an impact.

Thinking of the object of the director's attention that Hauser and Reich discuss has helped me muse over just who is the object of *my* attention for writing this book. There are certainly layers of people in it, not all positive: the scars of formal childhood education that run deep, wondering if the person the education authorities let loose on teaching English in the 1970s in a northern school and allowed to call people, including me, 'thick' and 'oiks' was still around to hold this book up to him. And then there are those colleagues in the early days of my career, not the supportive ones mentioned in the Overture but the ones who said, 'You don't want to be wasting your time in training, you want to get out into the real world.'

And then there are family members, close and distant friends old and new, colleagues past and present. In the opening of *Alone on a Wide Wide Sea* (Morpurgo, 2007), Michael Morpurgo's narrator, Arthur Hobhouse, sets out his rationale for writing his story. 'I am a happening,' he says. And so this is a way of being able to say that I, David Hayden, am a happening. A legacy for my children and currently one grandchild, but also a level of feedback to my parents to show what their love, care, nurture, trust and faith have resulted in. Hobhouse's daughter takes the role of the narrator in the second half of the Morpurgo classic. She is so moved by her father's story that she sets off on her own voyage of discovery, recording her movements and ultimately working on her father's life goal. The baton has been passed.

Of course, the relationship with you the reader is important, much more than you will probably ever realize. Feeling confident in my vulnerability to share some of my insights. There was so much more we could have written, so many more people we could have harvested stories from, so many more avenues to follow where great learning happens in one space that can be applied effectively, with impact that drives people, performance and organizations forward.

Learning is our USP; harnessing the power of that learning for good is the legacy I want to leave. Throughout the 20-plus years of this century I have consciously ramped up my learning about learning and there is much left to explore. My aim for you, the reader, is to offer a take, an angle on learning, that has not been explicitly discussed and to encourage you to share wider.

Steve's epilogue

Much has changed in my life since David first gave me the privilege of suggesting we approach this book together. One of the constant threads it has created for me is the greater awareness of how I apply different elements of the framework in my work and my life, and how much I see others taking elements of it by instinct initially but then perhaps not taking them further. Almost as if we are programmed to see specifics as isolated and worthy of attention but constrained rather than as a springboard to more. For me this book is the means to provide that springboard.

One frivolous but apt example that came to mind recently was the *Karate Kid* film. Many who have seen it will know what is meant by 'wax on, wax off'. It's a memorable moment. Daniel spends a day doing chores for Mr Miyagi, waxing his car, polishing his floor, painting his fence and so on, and is frustrated at not learning karate. It's then demonstrated to him how he has in fact spent all day learning karate because the specific moves he's been using for the chores transfer to defensive blocking moves in karate.

How many of us remember that scene? How many of us remember sharing Daniel's delight as he sees the transfer of those moves into practice? How many of us (me included) marvelled at the cleverness of Mr Miyagi but didn't think how there are things we do that can apply in multiple contexts, just like *wax on, wax off*, if only we look beyond the immediate?

There is so much we do that is artificially framed by context, and if as a consequence of reading this book and using the framework people find a way to break those contexts and apply learning and behaviour more broadly, then I'll be delighted.

Actors will sometimes talk of character motivation. So what is my motivation? I know I can, and need to, improve at all I do. I'm driven by a constant drive to be better and the framework, whether as a whole or in parts, is supporting me in doing that all the time. I also believe passionately in creating opportunities for people to explore and develop their potential – learning *can* change lives – and there is something in sharing what works for me which supports that.

I also feel that sometimes we can all unintentionally create a sense of exclusivity around any profession through the language used and through the concepts described. There's a danger that while undoubtedly beneficial, these may also narrow thinking, create barriers to entry, whether real or perceived, and build a groupthink which holds us all back. I'd like to think as a profession learning and development can 'walk the walk' ever more by identifying and bringing in learning from as many different fields as possible for what it is, not necessarily where it came from, and celebrate the value of the transferable expertise people bring from all fields.

Final words from us (or are they?)

It feels a bit strange writing this section. For so long this book to this point has been a part of our lives – for David 12 years, for Steve 4 – and now the relationship changes; it is over to you to write the next chapter. What happens next? Enjoy sharing your adjacent learning.

REFERENCES

How this book works

Rowling JK (2007) *Harry Potter and the Deathly Hallows*, London, Bloomsbury

Overture

Lancaster A (2020) *Driving Performance Through Learning*, London, Kogan Page

Driscoll J (2007) *Practising Clinical Supervision: A reflective approach for healthcare professionals*, Edinburgh, Elsevier

Rolfe G, Freshwater D, Jasper M (2001) *Critical Reflection in Nursing and the Helping Professions: A user's guide*, Basingstoke, Palgrave Macmillan

Brookmyre C (2010) *A Big Boy Did It and Ran Away*, London, Time Warner

Act 1

Sower VE, Duffy JA, Kohers G (2008) Great Ormond Street Hospital for Children: Ferrari's Formula One handovers and handovers from surgery to intensive care, August, https://asq.org/quality-resources/articles/case-studies/great-ormond-street-hospital-for-children-ferraris-formula-one-handovers-and-handovers-from-surgery-to-intensive-care?id=fbc699af11d04980ade06f409a5d6f98 (archived at https://perma.cc/89MH-B5MY)

Act 2

Covey S (1988) *The 7 Habits of Highly Effective Families*, London, Simon & Schuster

Act 2.1

Isaacs J (2019) Kermode and Mayo's Film Review, 20 September [podcast], https://www.bbc.co.uk/programmes/m0008jbz (archived at https://perma.cc/GAW2-GR4X)

Who is Alexandra K. Trenfor? Is this quote accurate? (nd), https://history.stackexchange.com/questions/52280/who-is-alexandra-k-trenfor-did-she-say-the-quote (archived at https://perma.cc/7MRC-68BR)

Boutcher SH (2008) Attentional processes and sport performance. In TS Horn (Ed.), *Advances in Sport Psychology* (pp. 325–338, 467–470), Human Kinetics

Klein S (2012) *Learning: Principles and applications* (6th Ed), SAGE Publications

Hinckley JS (2008) Performance anxiety: Constantin Stanislavski's concept of public solitude, College Music Symposium, vol. 48, pp. 124–130

Nepales RV (2018) Al Pacino on working again with Robert De Niro and Martın Scorsese, 19 March, https://www.thejakartapost.com/life/2018/03/19/al-pacino-on-working-again-with-robert-de-niro-and-martin-scorsese-.html (archived at https://perma.cc/9U6F-PXV8)

Westbrook M (2018) How to stop corpsing on stage [blog] https://actingcoachscotland.co.uk/blog/how-stop-corpsing-stage-or-rehearsal/ (archived at https://perma.cc/9TFC-L3ES)

Konstantin Stanislavski (2022) Wikipedia, https://en.wikipedia.org/wiki/Konstantin_Stanislavski (archived at https://perma.cc/LY4R-U7G5)

Jon Hamm quotes, IMDb, https://m.imdb.com/name/nm0358316/quotes (archived at https://perma.cc/FK4G-494Y)

Kilpatrick D (2019) Tottenham manager Jose Mourinho quotes Nelson Mandela when asked about Man Utd sacking, *The Standard*, 3 December, https://www.standard.co.uk/sport/football/tottenham-manager-jose-mourinho-quotes-nelson-mandela-when-asked-about-man-utd-sacking-a4303326.html (archived at https://perma.cc/2VJG-9J7P)

The Speaking Coach (nd) An innovative, fun and high impact approach to embrace a culture of learning from our mistakes, https://www.thespeakingcoach.co.uk/the-church-of-fail (archived at https://perma.cc/77MB-JT6M)

Bailes SJ (2010) *Performance Theatre and the Poetics of Failure*, Routledge Theatre and Performance, Routledge

Bilmes A (2014) George Clooney: The full interview at home with the world's most affable enigma, 3 January, https://www.esquire.com/uk/culture/news/a5480/the-george-clooney-interview/ (archived at https://perma.cc/W5AA-DGT7)

Farhi P (2012) Bruce Springsteen uses a teleprompter in performances: Does it matter? *The Washington Post*, 30 March, https://www.washingtonpost.com/lifestyle/style/bruce-springsteen-uses-teleprompter-in-performances-does-it-matter/2012/03/30/gIQAQTXGlS_story.html (archived at https://perma.cc/A4VX-6UYA)

Actor Hub (2014) Tips for actors learning lines, http://www.actorhub.co.uk/698/tips-for-actors-learning-lines (archived at https://perma.cc/RUN7-5XZR)

Farmer D (nd) 12 tips for learning lines, Drama Resource, https://dramaresource.com/12-tips-for-learning-lines/ (archived at https://perma.cc/5HUY-K89K)

Murphy Paul A (2012) How actors remember their lines, *Psychology Today*, 22 June, https://www.psychologytoday.com/us/blog/how-be-brilliant/201206/how-actors-remember-their-lines (archived at https://perma.cc/V7NJ-9RAN)

Sobel D (1995) *Longitude*, London, Fourth Estate

Longitude Prize (nd) Origins of Longitude Prize, https://longitudeprize.org/the-history/ (archived at https://perma.cc/F9HK-PAX3)

Kermode M, Mayo S (2013) Kermode and Mayo's film review *About Time* reviewed by Mark Kermode, 6 September, https://www.bbc.co.uk/programmes/p01g8t8x (archived at https://perma.cc/XTF9-SH75)

Kermode M (2015) Kermode and Mayo's film review, Mark Kermode reviews *Harry Potter and the Deathly Hallows pt 2*, 3 February, https://www.bbc.co.uk/programmes/p02j7dcm (archived at https://perma.cc/S9X5-3MX5)

Open Learn (2017) How does JK Rowling use Latin and other classical languages in *Harry Potter*?, 27 July, https://www.open.edu/openlearn/history-the-arts/classical-studies/how-does-jk-rowling-use-latin-and-other-classical-languages-harry-potter (archived at https://perma.cc/9B5G-8HXW)

Bowie-Sell D (2016) The life of an understudy, 25 April, https://www.whatsonstage.com/london-theatre/news/the-life-of-an-understudy_40290.html (archived at https://perma.cc/U23K-P2RM)

Akbar A (2020) David Nicholls: 'I crave to see people touching, kissing and fighting on screen', 19 May, https://www.theguardian.com/stage/2020/may/19/david-nicholls-understudy-radio-play-stephen-fry-drama-after-coronavirus (archived at https://perma.cc/GB2U-YYAP)

Backstage (2022) Swing, Standby, Understudy: What you need to know, 24 March, https://www.backstage.com/magazine/article/swing-standby-understudy-need-know-28/ (archived at https://perma.cc/7ZQV-99Y7)

Nayar V (2010) *Employees First, Customers second?* Harvard Business Press, Boston

Act 2.2

Hopkins C (2022) What Terry Wogan taught us about presenting, https://www.lovepresenting.com/what-terry-wogan-taught-us-about-presenting/ (archived at https://perma.cc/FU33-DXL2)

Markvoić N (2014) Stanislavski and his approach to acting, https://www.academia.edu/12208851/Stanislavski_and_his_Approach_to_Acting (archived at https://perma.cc/3TE7-6FBZ)

Quote Fancy (nd) https://quotefancy.com/quote/812448/George-Bernard-Shaw-The-function-of-the-actor-is-to-make-the-audience-imagine-for-the (archived at https://perma.cc/H8T9-AFWP)

Theatres Trust (nd) How has the design of theatre buildings changed over time? http://www.theatrestrust.org.uk/discover-theatres/theatre-faqs/172-how-has-the-design-of-theatre-buildings-changed-over-time (archived at https://perma.cc/88M3-XE8H)

Nicholson R (2017) 'The journey' has ruined nearly all reality TV – apart from Masterchef, 11 May, https://www.theguardian.com/tv-and-radio/2017/may/11/the-journey-has-ruined-nearly-all-reality-tv-apart-from-masterchef (archived at https://perma.cc/PZD6-XPAQ)

Booker C (2017) *The Seven Basic Plots*, London, Bloomsbury

Nolan C (2017) Kermode and Mayo's film review, *Dunkirk*, 21 July, https://www.bbc.co.uk/programmes/b08xy7x7 (archived at https://perma.cc/VNW7-MCZ5)

George D (2015) The journey of a story, 16 February, https://www.nationalgeographic.com/travel/intelligent-travel/2015/02/16/the-journey-of-a-story/ (archived at https://perma.cc/Z7G4-6YC8)

Werber C (2019) Happiness and grief change depending what language you're speaking, 22 December, https://qz.com/1773683/linguists-found-differences-in-how-we-link-and-experience-emotion/ (archived at https://perma.cc/YGE4-U3AF)

Isaacs J (2019) Kermode and Mayo's Film Review, *Hotel Mumbai*, 20 September [podcast] https://www.bbc.co.uk/programmes/m0008jbz (archived at https://perma.cc/GAW2-GR4X)

Shukla P (2019) Anthony Maras on '*Hotel Mumbai*', https://www.historynet.com/film-recon-interview-anthony-maras-hotel-mumbai/ (archived at https://perma.cc/D58Y-7SP3)

Waller-Bridge P (2014) *Fleabag: The Original Play*, London, Nick Hern Books

Mlotek H (2018) The Almosts and What-ifs of '*Sliding Doors*', 24 April, https://www.theringer.com/movies/2018/4/24/17261506/sliding-doors-20th-anniversary (archived at https://perma.cc/8N5L-B5WT)

Cheded F (2017) The potent poignancy of the '*Atonement*' Dunkirk scene, 8 December [Blog] https://filmschoolrejects.com/10-years-potent-poignancy-atonements-dunkirk-scene/ (archived at https://perma.cc/9JT8-5CR7)

Pauli M (2006) Fact or fiction, https://www.theguardian.com/culture/culturevultureblog/2006/jan/11/factorfiction (archived at https://perma.cc/L8S9-FB2J)

The Psychologist (2016) Heroes and villains, 2 March, https://thepsychologist.bps.org.uk/heroes-and-villains (archived at https://perma.cc/29J9-BHJ2)

Lamar C (2012) The 22 rules of storytelling according to Pixar, 8 June, https://io9.gizmodo.com/the-22-rules-of-storytelling-according-to-pixar-5916970 (archived at https://perma.cc/H2FQ-X9C9)

Clover A (2008) *Dad Rules*, London, Penguin Fig Tree

Curtin C (2007) NASA spent millions on a pen able to write in space, 1 August, https://www.scientificamerican.com/article/nasa-spent-millions-on-a-pen-able-t/ (archived at https://perma.cc/U2JG-HHDA)

Westenberg J (2017) Storytelling is the number one skill you have to improve, 21 May, https://inc42.com/entrepreneurship/storytelling-skill-improve/ (archived at https://perma.cc/NX36-A7QN)

BBC (nd) *The Chris Moyles Show*, https://www.bbc.co.uk/programmes/b006wkqb (archived at https://perma.cc/X35B-YCVC)

Anderson P (2008) Don't get the balance wrong…, 21 November, https://www.theguardian.com/culture/tvandradioblog/2008/nov/21/zoo-radio-chris-moyles (archived at https://perma.cc/3ZAX-3LTY)

BBC (2011) Chris Moyles breaks radio show record for Comic Relief, 18 March, http://www.bbc.co.uk/newsbeat/article/12782536/chris-moyles-breaks-radio-show-record-for-comic-relief (archived at https://perma.cc/JKY5-SU9U)

Act 2.3

Hart J (2018) You cannot design learning, 26 June [Twitter], https://twitter.com/C4LPT/status/1011643314628677639?ref_src=twsrc%5Etfw (archived at https://perma.cc/4Q5C-L9AP)

Stevenson H (2015) Transcending the Drama Triangle, 25 June [Blog], http://www.clevelandconsultinggroup.com/articles/transcending-the-drama-triangle.php (archived at https://perma.cc/FP8W-VXT5)

Sedgman K (2016) Our obsession with theatre etiquette is rooted in the past, 18 August [blog] https://www.thestage.co.uk/features/2016/our-obsession-with-theatre-etiquette-is-rooted-in-the-past/ (archived at https://perma.cc/CMK8-MCK9)

Kermode M (2010) The moviegoers code of conduct, 2 December, https://www.bbc.co.uk/blogs/markkermode/2010/12/the_moviegoers_code_of_conduct.html (archived at https://perma.cc/V8UB-SFXZ)

Pope BR (2019) Character development: How to write great characters, 16 April [blog], https://self-publishingschool.com/character-development/ (archived at https://perma.cc/46LJ-QVSS)

Gold A (2015) The fury over 'hand luggage' plane evacuees, 10 September, https://www.bbc.co.uk/news/magazine-34191035 (archived at https://perma.cc/PC3G-KMBC)

Jones T (2017) Kermode and Mayo's Film Review, *Kaleidoscope*, 17 November [podcast], https://www.bbc.co.uk/programmes/b09czrcy (archived at https://perma.cc/D8ZK-PQ4T)

Warriner K (nd) How to get in the zone and stay there [blog] https://www.headspace.com/blog/2017/04/11/stay-in-the-zone/ (archived at https://perma.cc/9GZZ-R9N9)

Andrews J (2000) Quote to *Milwaukee Journal Sentinel*, February, https://libquotes.com/julie-andrews/quote/lbu4w8a (archived at https://perma.cc/9QS2-GKRE)

Blair R (2015). Notes on empathy, cognitive neuroscience, and theatre/education. p-e-r-f-o-r-m-a-n-c-e , 2 (1–2), 16 November [blog], http://p-e-r-f-o-r-m-a-n-c-e.org/?p=1101 (archived at https://perma.cc/VR8N-Y27Y)

Goldberg W (nd) Quote on *Good Reads*, https://www.goodreads.com/quotes/145142-we-re-here-for-a-reason-i-believe-a-bit-of (archived at https://perma.cc/PP8S-D73Z)

Morong D (2019) How to find inspiration as an actor, 19 June, https://www.backstage.com/magazine/article/find-inspiration-actor-12673/ (archived at https://perma.cc/944Z-CEUN)

Huff Post (2008) Clooney On Darfur: 'If celebrity is a credit card, then I'm using it', 28 March, https://www.huffpost.com/entry/clooney-onLA-darfur-if-cele_n_52758 (archived at https://perma.cc/8WZD-TGZT)

McKinsey Quarterly (2008) Innovation lessons from Pixar: An interview with Oscar-winning director Brad Bird, 1 April, https://www.mckinsey.com/business-functions/strategy-and-corporate-finance/our-insights/innovation-lessons-from-pixar-an-interview-with-oscar-winning-director-brad-bird (archived at https://perma.cc/WDL8-LF4W)

Sinek S (2011) *Start with Why*, New York, Portfolio Penguin

Rogers CR (1961) *On Becoming a Person: A therapist's view of psychotherapy*, Boston, Houghton Mifflin

Hawking T (2014) Eurovision's glorious silliness, 8 May, https://www.nytimes.com/2014/05/09/opinion/eurovisions-glorious-silliness.html (archived at https://perma.cc/6N2X-NHXH)

EBU (nd) Our history, https://www.ebu.ch/about/history (archived at https://perma.cc/26XD-QCN4)

Eurovision.tv (nd) The origins of Eurovision, https://eurovision.tv/history/in-a-nutshell (archived at https://perma.cc/Z9DS-HQ6J)

SongsForEurope.Com (nd) Festival of British popular songs 1956, https://www.songs4europe.com/1956/ (archived at https://perma.cc/LXK9-9H5L)

Spence E (2020) Playing the cards you have, ESC Insight, 8 May [podcast] https://escinsight.com/2020/05/08/eurovision-insight-podcast-playing-cards/ (archived at https://perma.cc/MB8E-56U8)

Hayden D (2020) Here is a question for you [blog] https://talentdelivers.wordpress.com/2020/03/21/here-is-a-question-for-you/ (archived at https://perma.cc/2HDM-YJ9Z)

Cremona P (2020) David Tennant and Michael Sheen explain how their Staged characters were developed, 18 December, https://www.radiotimes.com/tv/david-tennant-michael-sheen-staged-characters/ (archived at https://perma.cc/P4WV-DRUM)

Gansky A (2022) Writing a good first page [blog] https://www.blueridgeconference.com/writing-a-good-first-page/ (archived at https://perma.cc/BN9L-Q6TY)

Act 2.4

IMDb (nd) *Pulp Fiction* (1994) Samuel L Jackson: Jules Winnfield, https://www.imdb.com/title/tt0110912/characters/nm0000168 (archived at https://perma.cc/Y9LF-AFMV)

Scinto J (2014) 5 tips for powerful audience participation, 15 April [blog] https://www.fastcompany.com/3029074/5-tips-for-powerful-audience-participation (archived at https://perma.cc/2KAK-3VGP)

Lannom SC (2020) Breaking the fourth wall: Definitions, meaning and examples, 21 June [Blog] https://www.studiobinder.com/blog/breaking-the-fourth-wall/#why-break-the-fourth-wall (archived at https://perma.cc/DTS8-PJQ5)

Tripney N (2008) When to break the fourth wall, January, https://www.theguardian.com/stage/theatreblog/2008/jan/10/whentobreakthefourthwall (archived at https://perma.cc/L6CR-DJXG)

Goleman D (1995) *Emotional Intelligence*, New York, Bantam Books

Sharma R (2017) The business of business is relationships; the business of life is human connection, https://twitter.com/robinsharma/status/919913339827998720?lang=en-GB (archived at https://perma.cc/K7US-VTFZ)

Peisner D (2020) Concerts aren't back. Livestreams are ubiquitous. Can they do the job?, 21 July, https://www.nytimes.com/2020/07/21/arts/music/concerts-livestreams.html (archived at https://perma.cc/QH8W-6D38)

Shaw I (1969) *Rich Man, Poor Man*, London, NEL

Shaw I (1977) *Beggarman, Thief*, Bungay, BCA

Brinkerhoff RO (2003) The success case method: Find out quickly what's working and what's not, San Francisco, Berrett-Koehler

Michael Chekhov Acting Studio (nd) Philosophy, http://michaelchekhovactingstudio.com/philosophy.html (archived at https://perma.cc/DQ24-3ASP)

Laban's Efforts in Action (nd) Laban's efforts, https://labaneffortsinaction.com/labans-efforts#:~:text=Laban%20named%20these%20Effort%20qualities,of%20Weight%2C%20Time%20and%20Space (archived at https://perma.cc/QR5F-TPTK).

Coleman C (2018) Kermode and Mayo's Film Review, 14 December, https://www.bbc.co.uk/programmes/m0001kk0 (archived at https://perma.cc/QC65-4A7R)

McAvoy J (2021) Movies with Ali Plomb, James McAvoy: Movies that made me, 15 February, https://www.bbc.co.uk/iplayer/episode/p096kpy9/movies-with-ali-plumb-james-mcavoy-movies-that-made-me?xtor=CS8-1000-%5BPromo_Box%5D-%5BNews_Promo%5D-%5BNews_Promo%5D-%5BPS_IPLAYER~N~p096kpy9~P_MoviesWithAliPlumbJamesMcAvoyep%5D (archived at https://perma.cc/6AKY-WH4H)

Act 3

Food and Global Security Network (nd) Soil health: A security threat profile, https://www.foodandsecurity.net/soil-health-report (archived at https://perma.cc/7929-X4XR)

Grindrod C (nd) Delivering regeneration, https://www.foodandsecurity.net/_files/ugd/0f4d79_9925ee60e37243d1a72391e604ae5d54.pdf (archived at https://perma.cc/3C4S-NU55)

Rushe D (2022) Wage gap between CEOs and US workers jumped to 670-to-1 last year, study finds, 7 June, https://www.theguardian.com/us-news/2022/jun/07/us-wage-gap-ceos-workers-institute-for-policy-studies-report (archived at https://perma.cc/6GWQ-ME4F)

Allen M (2019) The real costs of bad management – and what you can do about it, https://gbr.pepperdine.edu/2019/03/the-real-costs-of-bad-management-and-what-you-can-do-about-it/ (archived at https://perma.cc/CRK3-SQTB)

Act 3.2

Redcliffe N (2022) *Greener Grass*, London, Austin Macauley Publishers

Act 4

Johansson F (2017) *The Medici Effect*, Boston, Harvard Business Review Press

Kneebone R (2021) *Expert*, London, Penguin Random House

Lindkvist M (2010) *Everything We Know Is Wrong*, London, Marshall Cavendish
Lindkvist M (2011) Facing the future, CIPD annual conference and exhibition, November Manchester
Ridderstråle J, Nordström K (2000) *Funky Business* (2nd Ed), London, FT Prentice Hall
Parry-Slater M (2021) *The Learning and Development Handbook*, London, Kogan Page
Collins S (2016) *Neuroscience for Learning and Development*, London, Kogan Page
Neelen M and Kirschner PA (2020) *Evidence-Informed Learning Design*, London, Kogan Page
Wheeler S (2019) *Digital Learning in Organizations*, London, Kogan Page
Clark D (2020) *Artificial Intelligence for Learning*, London, Kogan Page
Shackleton Jones N (2019) *How People Learn*, London, Kogan Page
Stanford N (2018) *Organization Design* (3rd Ed), London, Routledge
Syed M (2017) *The Greatest*, London, John Murray
Syed M (2016) *Blackbox Thinking*, London, John Murray
Cheese P (2021) *The New World of Work*, London, Kogan Page

Epilogues

Hauser F, Reich R (2003) 12 biggest mistakes directors make, https://www.academia.edu/36665872/_The_12_Biggest_Mistakes_Directors_Make_by_Frank_Hauser_and_Russell_Reich_co-authors_of_Notes_on_Directing (archived at https://perma.cc/C62S-6PEV)
Beevers K, Hayden D, Rea A (2019) *Learning and Development Practice in the Workplace* (4th Ed), London, Kogan Page
Morpurgo M (2007) *Alone on a Wide Wide Sea*, London, HarperCollins

INDEX

Note: page numbers in *italic* indicate figures or tables

CPSIA information can be obtained
at www.ICGtesting.com
Printed in the USA
BVHW010850160223
658644BV00007B/377

9 781398 608252